Little Maplestead

A Millennium History

*To Judith
with best wishes
from Patricia*

Patricia Fletcher

The Little Maplestead Millennium History Project

First published in 2000 by the
Little Maplestead Millennium History Project,
The Grove, Little Maplestead, Essex CO9 2SN

Copyright © Patricia Fletcher 2000

House photographs copyright
© Judy Gosling and Catherine Nott 2000

ISBN 0-9537656-0-1

In memory of Ann Mayhew

Any profits from the sale of this book will be donated to the Round Church, Little Maplestead

Printed by Jenner (City Print) Limited,
Tower Business Park, Kelvedon Road,
Tiptree, Essex CO5 0LX

CONTENTS

Acknowledgements		5
Foreword		6
I	The Eleventh Century	7
II	The Twelfth Century	25
III	The Thirteenth Century	51
IV	The Fourteenth Century	73
V	The Fifteenth Century	87
VI	The Sixteenth Century	105
VII	The Seventeenth Century	131
VIII	The Eighteenth Century	147
IX	The Nineteenth Century	173
X	The Twentieth Century	199
	Tithe Map, 1841, by permission of Essex Record Office	218
	Glossary	220
	Little Maplestead field names	222
	Index	223

Photography	Judy Gosling
	Catherine Nott
Village maps	Debora Dench
House floor plan page 93	Iain Nott
Index and glossary, research	Geoffrey Love
Census transcriptions	Nadine Scurr
	Karen Sunnucks
Trade directory transcriptions	Margaret Crudgington
Interviews	Lyn Westby
Cover	Radius Colour Photocopying
Editing, proof reading	Gail Baker-Bates

The Little Maplestead Millennium History Project team

Paul Allison, Gail Baker-Bates (secretary), Margaret Crudgington, Debora Dench, Patricia Fletcher, Ernie Garner, Judy Gosling, Geoffrey Love, Catherine Nott, Nadine Scurr (treasurer), Karen and Andrew Sunnucks, Lyn Westby

ACKNOWLEDGEMENTS

The Little Maplestead Millennium History Project thanks everyone who has helped us financially with the production of this book. In particular we are grateful to the following who have given so generously towards the costs:
Dr Donald Adamson JP; Miss Yvonne J. Albon; Stewart Ashurst; R.P. and G. E. Baker-Bates; Div Supt David Bouchard OStJ; Lord Braybrooke; John H. Burrow; Sir Richard and Lady Butler; Sir John Carter; Lt Col R.W.L. Charlton OBE, DL; Cheshire St John Council; Glenn and Heather Cooper; Rod Cooper, RC Engineering Ltd, Woodburner & Flue Specialist; Crown Roofing (Essex) Limited; Ann Goodman, Cambridgeshire; Chris and Judy Gosling; Iris Haslam DStJ; Little Maplestead Parish Council; James Mackaness on behalf of St John Ambulance, Northamptonshire; the Maplesteads 'It's a Knockout' Fund-Raising Team; Maplestead Kennels; Christine and Ernest Marshall CStJ; Colonel Geoffrey Morgan; Mrs M. Joyce Muir; Mrs Malcolm Nolan; Mr and Mrs N.M. Nott; Mr and Mrs John O'Reilly-Cicconi; Dennis Parker; Dr Norman Paros; the Lord Petre; June Pollard; Rural Community Council of Essex; St John Ambulance – Northumbria; St John Ambulance – Warwickshire; St John the Baptist Church, Little Maplestead; St John Fellowship – Nor'Easterly Branch, London; Colin and Nadine Scurr; Frank Smith & Sons, Outfitters, serving the Halstead area since 1895; Charles Sparrow; Tessa and Jim Sunnucks; Peter and Betty Train; Les Webb MBE, KStJ, Former Commissioner St John Ambulance Eastern Area London; Dr M.A. Weller OBE, KStJ; Woodview Nursery; Alan Wright Consulting Engineers Ltd, Little Maplestead, and also those donors who prefer to remain anonymous

Many people have given the project team advice, information or documents. We would like to record our thanks to the following for their help:
Mr Merrick Baker-Bates; Miss Helen Blomfield; the late Mrs Carrie Coe; the late Mr Cecil Cook; Mr Peter Cook; County Librarian (Records & Archives) Colchester County Library; Reverend Peter Dakin; Essex Record Office; Mrs Francis; Mr Chris Gosling; Mrs Jean Grice; Halstead Library; the late Miss Winnie Mayes; the late Mrs Evelyn Newton; Mr and Mrs D. O'Connell; the late Mr M.R. Orchard; Mrs O'Reilly-Cicconi; Major Bruce Rust; the Order of St John, Clerkenwell; Mrs Tokeley; Mrs F. Vickers; Mr Alan Whyte; Mr Alan Wiseman

FOREWORD

Readers of this book may be interested to know how it came to be written. In response to an invitation by the parish council to all villagers to submit suggestions on how best to celebrate the millennium here in Little Maplestead, I put forward the idea that we might produce a written history of the village. As I am a house historian I thought that this might best be done through the history of its houses. The idea was accepted and with the encouragement of the chairman of our parish council, Gail Baker-Bates, and Nadine Scurr, we circulated a questionnaire to each house so that we had some facts and figures to start with. I soon had an enthusiastic team of volunteers without whose hard work and support I could not have managed this project. The entire cost of production was covered by donations kindly given and detailed acknowledgement of these is accorded.

The result is this book, *Little Maplestead, A Millennium History*. Above all, it is an amateur production. I am only a humble archivist not a social historian and I have had to rely heavily on outside help. In particular, I owe a huge debt to Lord Asa Briggs's excellent *A Social History of England* which has guided me throughout.

Whilst I have done my utmost to ensure the accuracy of all the information given here, I hope the reader will forgive any mistakes which may have crept in; in particular it is not always possible to be strictly accurate over census entries - few houses were named and the order in which they were listed depended upon the route that the enumerator took round the village; nevertheless, I have done my best to get my facts right. Further, the 1841 census is notoriously casual about age, often rounding up or down at random, and all historical records contain a certain flexibility of spelling; any apparent discrepancies are not mistakes.

Finally, I am sorry that not every house in the village could be mentioned in the book - the reasons for this are either that the house has not always been in the parish or, that try as I might, I have been unable to find any relevant historical records. I am also sorry that not every house in the village has a photograph - we were limited in what we could do by cost. But I sincerely hope that everyone will feel that this book is a fitting gift to celebrate one thousand years of village history and that they will enjoy reading it as much as I have enjoyed writing it.

Patricia Fletcher
December 1999

CHAPTER I

THE ELEVENTH CENTURY

After this the king had much thought and very intense discussion with his witan about this country, how it was occupied and with what kind of men. Then he sent his men all over England into every shire.[1]

THE ORIGIN OF THE NAME OF LITTLE MAPLESTEAD

THE NAME Maplestead first appears in writing in 1065, one year before the Norman Conquest and twenty-one years before the production of the Domesday Book. The reference is to *Mapulderstede* in a Saxon charter roll[2] but it is not clear whether it refers to Little or Great Maplestead. As far as we know, the full name of Little Maplestead was not recorded before 1186 when there exists a reference to *parva Mapeltrestede*[3] in the collection of legal documents known as the Cartulary of the Knights Hospitallers of St John of Jerusalem. From the same source we find what is probably the first reference to Great Maplestead, *Mapultrestede magna*[4] in 1220. In this context the word 'little' would have meant that, of the two settlements, Little Maplestead was the smaller, as indeed it still is today.

The meaning of the main part of the name, Maplestead, is clear. It derives from two elements, the maple tree and a second element *stede* which means a place, site or building[5]. However, when a tree name is combined with the element *stede* in a place name it usually means a group or grove of such trees. As the maple tree would have been the field maple, *Acer campestre*, the only maple native to Britain and a common hedgerow tree first recorded in 770[6], it is very likely that the name would have indicated a distinct copse of maple trees, something at least to form some sort of landmark. Thus the name of Little Maplestead originally meant the smaller settlement by the copse or grove of maple trees.

The site of this settlement, which eventually developed into the village of Little Maplestead, was probably chosen for several reasons: the land around is fertile and gently undulating, suitable for both arable and pastoral farming; it is close to the River Colne and its bridging point at Halstead; there is easy access to water in the form of streams flowing through the settlement site towards the river, and there is plentiful well water.

LITTLE MAPLESTEAD in

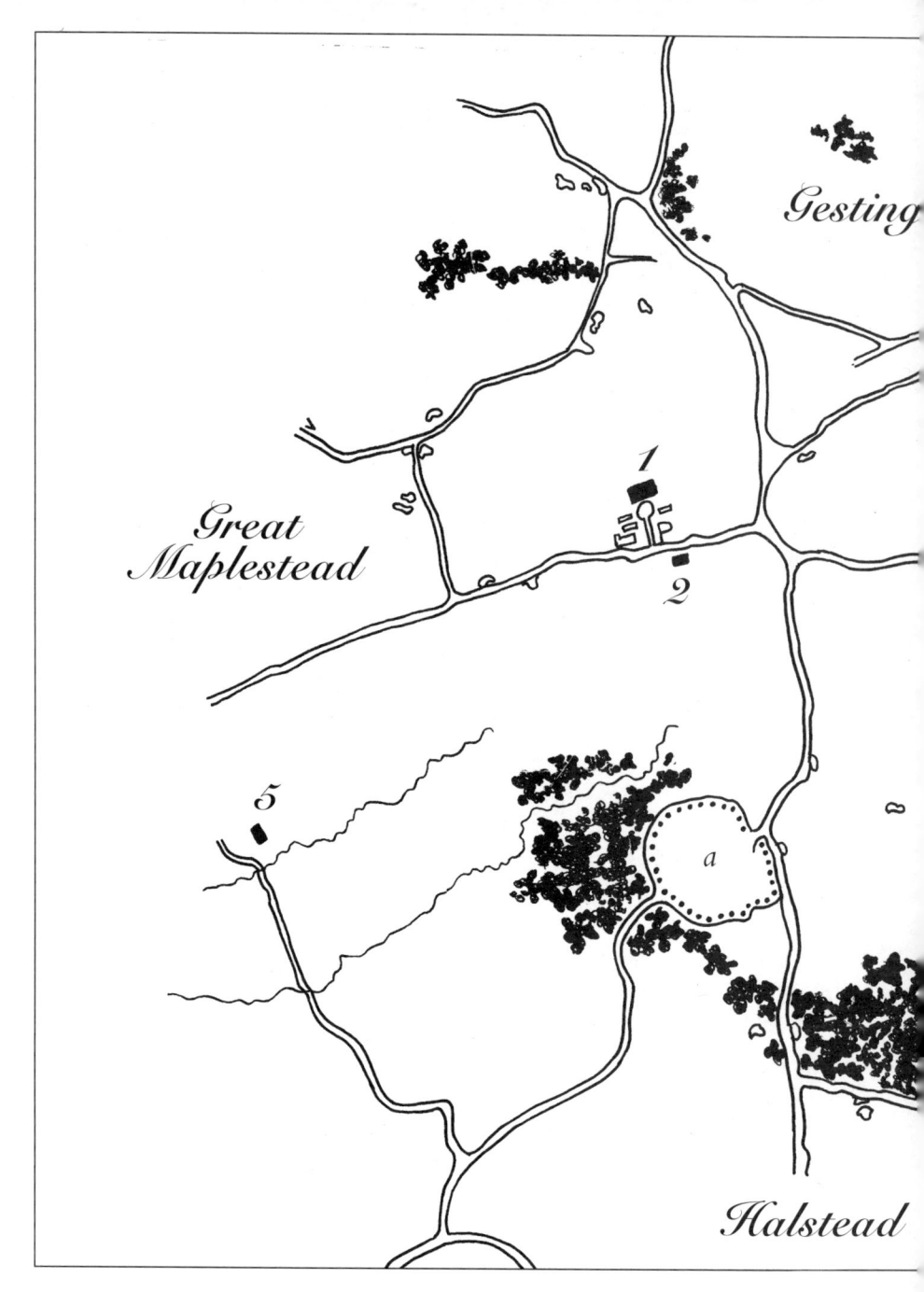

the ELEVENTH CENTURY

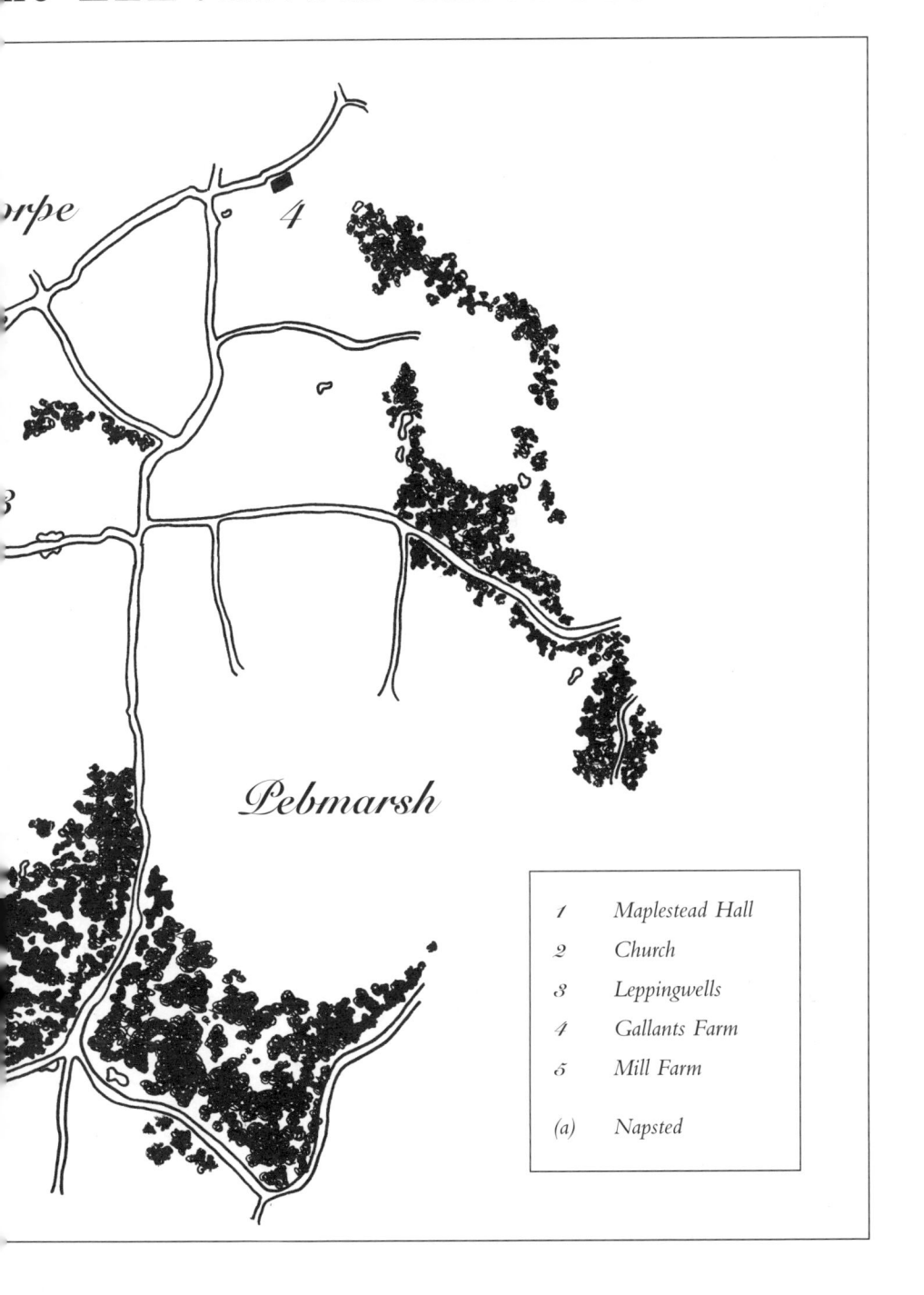

Pebmarsh

1	Maplestead Hall
2	Church
3	Leppingwells
4	Gallants Farm
5	Mill Farm
(a)	Napsted

LITTLE MAPLESTEAD BEFORE THE NORMAN CONQUEST

IN THE early eleventh century, the tiny community of Little Maplestead existed against the background of a country that was slowly evolving into the England that we would recognize today. At this time England was divided into two regions - Wessex, the south and west, still under Saxon rule and Mercia and East Anglia, the north and east, which had been invaded and settled by waves of Scandinavians. But by the tenth century society had become well structured. England was already divided into shires, later to become the counties that we are familiar with today. Each shire had a court which met twice a year and was presided over by the king's representative, the shire reeve or sheriff. The shires were divided into units called hundreds and Little Maplestead was, and still is, in the Hinckford Hundred (*Hidinga-forda*[7]).

By this time, Little Maplestead, like all other parishes, would have had well established parish boundaries and manors; there were at least two manors in this parish, the manor of Little Maplestead which corresponded roughly with the parish boundaries and the manor of Napsted (see page 16).

At this time, in many respects, the pre-Norman regional culture of North Essex still reflected that of the ancient kingdom of East Anglia from which it had evolved. It had its own distinct agrarian and social pattern and, with its fertile soil, the suitability of some of its land for sheep farming and its proximity to European trade, it was one of the most prosperous areas in the country.

Furthermore, the inhabitants of Little Maplestead would have been subject to the region's law, the Danelaw, which had been shaped by the Danish settlers. Importantly for the villagers, the hundreds had their own courts for use by the rural population. In the case of Hinckford Hundred these courts were held at Crouch Green in Castle Hedingham. Later on the Danelaw was to influence the whole of the development of English law.

Before the Norman Conquest every man's place in his community was determined by law, by custom and by title. This social structure, which was a feudal system, had at its top the king's companions, the *eorls* and *thegns*, who were often warriors and were social parallels to the Norman barons and knights who were to replace them. These lords were highly privileged but with this privilege came a responsibility for the well-being of their community or manor. The lords were served by their peasant bondmen, and the very word bondman is an important clue to the relationship between these men and their landlord. This relationship was based upon a personal bond of loyalty between the lord and the economically dependent peasants who served him.

Of these peasants, those at the very base of the feudal system were completely bound men and women, in effect they were slaves. They were *ceorfs* with no land of their own. The *ceorfs* were often descendants of pre-Saxon people, the original ancient British. Above them in the social structure were peasants called villeins who, besides owing a duty to their lord, had some land of their own to till so that they had some small measure of independence. Above the villeins were the cottagers who were legally free men, although they were obligated to their lord and were bound to perform certain labour services and to make regular payments in stock, seeds, crops and money. But East Anglia had an additional class of small farmers called *sokemen*, unique to the region, who were virtually independent of any landlord, and although they had to pay some rent or perform light services they were freer than any of the other peasants.

LITTLE MAPLESTEAD AT DOMESDAY

WE CAN gain a detailed picture of what the village of Little Maplestead would have been like twenty years after the Norman Conquest by examining one of the six Domesday Book entries relevant to the village. In 1086, William I sent out teams of surveyors to list every item of every settlement in the land so that he would have a complete over-view of his newly acquired realm. Later this would enable him to impose new and higher taxes to augment his coffers.

In the Domesday Book, under the heading of Maplestead, William's surveyors recorded the following:

> Osmund holds Little Maplestead from John which Grim, a free man, held before 1066 as a manor for ½ hide. Then 2 ploughs in lordship, later none, now 1. Then 2 smallholders, later 1, now 5 and 1 priest; always 2 slaves. Woodland, then 60 pigs, later and now 16; meadow, 3 acres; then 1 mill, which William of Warenne now holds as a pledge. Then he acquired nothing; now 2 cows, 14 pigs and 57 sheep. Value then 40s; later and now 30s.

From this Domesday entry we learn that Osmund, a Norman, is now in possession of the feudal lordship of the manor of Little Maplestead. Earlier, in 1066, Grim had been lord. It is likely that Grim was a Dane probably usurped by Osmund shortly after the Conquest and the inhabitants of Little Maplestead would have found themselves at the mercy of an alien French lord who did not speak their language. Osmund's manor was taxed at the rate of half a hide. A hide was originally a quantity of land, enough to support one family for a year, and was estimated at about 120 acres and so Osmund's manor of Little Maplestead probably only consisted of about 60 acres. Only one plough-team of eight oxen was now kept to till this land, although earlier, at the time of the Conquest, there had been two. Recently the manor had increased in population because now, instead of one or two small-holders, the manor supported five cottagers or half-free men and two slaves, or *ceorfs*, who had no land of their own. There was enough woodland on the manor to provide acorns and other fodder for sixteen pigs but this had recently diminished as in 1066 there had been enough woodland to support sixty pigs. The disappearance of woodland was probably due to an increased felling of trees for building. Apart from the arable land there were three acres of meadow and a mill, which would have been a water-mill, and which at this time had been acquired by the Norman baron, William de Warenne (later to become Earl of Surrey) who held it as a pledge, probably as security for a loan. This water-mill was probably on the site of Mill Farm through which a stream still runs.

MILL FARM

IT IS BELIEVED that the name Toldishall, an area near to Mill Farm, derives from the fact that a toll was charged on each sack of grain to be ground. It is thought that some sort of tollbooth may have been set up where the present-day Toldishall is and a payment exacted from those on their way to the mill. This toll may have been paid to the miller but it is more likely that it was to some other person over whose land villagers had to pass.

In a survey done of the village in 1817[8], Osgood Gee was the landowner of Mill Farm and John Freeborn was his tenant. Only part of Mill Farm is included in the survey, as the rest of the property at that time was in the parish of Great Maplestead, the parish boundary in fact ran through the house. Now the entire farm is in Great Maplestead.

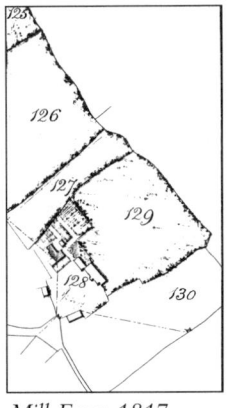

127 part of Hoppett

128 part of House and homestead

129 Back pasture

130 part of The Ley

5 acres in extent

Osgood Gee also owned:

part of Tolldish Hall, tenant John Freeborn

125, 126 part of Tolldish Hall field

Mill Farm 1817

By the 1841 tithe award Mary Gee was now the landowner and Theophilus Harrington was the tenant:

117 field arable

118 Backpasture hops

119 Hoppett grass

120 Homestall

121 part of The Ley arable

121(a) part of field arable

5 acres [see tithe map pages 218-219]

THE EARLY CHURCH

SIGNIFICANTLY the Domesday entry for 1086 also records the existence of one priest in Little Maplestead; at this time it was usual for the priest also to have been a household servant of the lord of the manor. The fact that there was a priest supports the theory that by this time, twenty years after the Conquest, there was an established church on the manor. This early church would have been a simple rectangular building, perhaps with an newly apsed end, most likely standing on the same site as the present church; we have no evidence that it was elsewhere.

The font

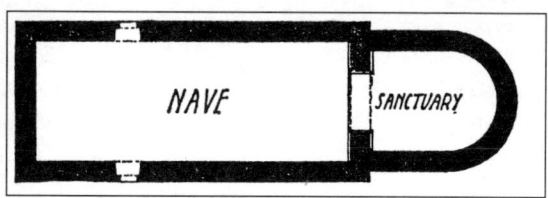

Plan of early church

This early church was probably built by the first Norman lord of the manor, for the good of his community, but it is quite likely that it replaced an even older Saxon church. We know from later documents that the first church in Little Maplestead was dedicated to All Saints[9] and its early Norman font still exists and can be seen in the Round Church. It is a massive limestone bowl, originally square but made roughly octagonal, probably during the sixteenth century, by the chamfering of the four corners. The four main sides are decorated in crudely carved low relief, two sides with round-headed arches, one with scrolled spirals and one with the St Andrew's cross of archaic pattern. Legend has it that St Andrew was the first bishop of Byzantium (Constantinople) and this link with the Crusades, which were already underway at this time, is a possible explanation of the presence of his cross on the font. The bowl is also large enough to be used for baptism by immersion in the Norman style.

WITH ALL THE information gathered so far, it is not difficult to build up a picture of how the manor of Little Maplestead would have looked at the time of the Norman Conquest. The surrounding land was more densely wooded than it is today and the manor would have been linked by rough tracks through the trees to neighbouring settlements such as Great Maplestead, Gestingthorpe and Pebmarsh with other more widely used tracks to the major communities such as Halstead or Sudbury. The layout of routes through the village would have been recognizable today. There would have been some thirty to forty inhabitants on the manor of Little Maplestead living in a handful of dwellings amid the cleared agricultural land of some sixty acres. The lord's house, on the site of Maplestead Hall, would have contrasted with the simple cottages with their gardens and orchards and the even poorer dwellings lived in by the slaves. The manor was of course totally self-sufficient and everyone would have been occupied in some form of agriculture whether growing crops or raising stock, particularly pigs, or grazing sheep in the drier hilly fields near the mill. The small-holders may have had strips of land in a communal arable field (see Gallants Farm, pages 17-19) but they may also have farmed in the East Anglian manner in separate and irregular holdings, getting together only to watch any sheep in shared sheep pens. All the peasants would have owed varying amounts of duty to the lord mainly in the form of agricultural work. And while he, for his part, had built them a church to tend to their spiritual needs, life for the peasant would have been physically very hard. The tenth-century monk, Aelfric, gave a vivid description of the work of a ploughman like those on the manor of Little Maplestead[10]:

> I work very hard. I go out at dawn and I drive the oxen in the field and yoke them to the plough. However stark the winter is I dare not stay at home for fear of my lord. I have to yoke the oxen and fasten the share and coulter to the plough and every day I have to plough a full acre or more. I have a boy who drives the oxen with a goad and even now he is hoarse from cold and shouting. I fill the ox-bins with hay and water and I clear out the dung.

LITTLE MAPLESTEAD IN NORMAN ENGLAND

THERE IS no doubt that the Norman Conquest would have had an impact upon the tiny village of Little Maplestead. Although William the Conqueror had expressed a desire that there should be continuity in his new kingdom, the Conquest did have social, political and cultural implications for the country which would have trickled down to be felt by even the smallest community. To begin with, the peasants would have discovered that there was now a language barrier between them and their new landowner and probably their priest too. All around them, they would have been aware that the old thegnhood was losing all its land and the new tough Norman aristocracy was taking its place. The peasants of the manor of Little Maplestead, now under the Norman Osmund's rule, would also have known that Ulwine, the Saxon thane at [Castle] Hedingham, had lost everything when William took his lands and gave them to one of his best soldiers and most important knights, Aubrey de Vere.

Countrywide, although the Normans kept the shire organization and the local courts remained, there was one essential difference; English society was now being geared to equip a powerful fighting force. Some two hundred Norman lords shared out the land immediately after the Conquest. This alien aristocracy was organized for war and its purpose was to provide mounted knights for the king's army. For the first time, certain tenants owed their landlords a duty of military service besides the usual agricultural and financial dues. Normans now held key positions in government. Norman sheriffs controlled the shires, Norman clerks presided over the English chancery, Norman bishops filled the English sees, and a council of Normans advised England's king. There was a new ruling class and a new culture. Officially Latin and French replaced English, French manners were adopted at court, and new buildings were influenced by French architectural styles. William and his Normans began to rule England as no Anglo-Saxon king had done before. The greatest impact felt was that of the character of the new king. Energy, drive, ruthlessness and determination transformed the character of English government and William ruled with absolute authority. The Domesday survey enabled the king to tax his subjects more harshly than ever before and he re-imposed old taxes and introduced new ones. These taxes were theoretically only payable by landowners but in effect they were paid by the peasants. Such peasants were no longer allowed access to the justice of the local court in matters affecting their status. Furthermore the peasant and his family could now be bought and sold and treated without any consideration, so that he would be given no warning when he would be required to work for his lord which made the cultivation of his own patch extremely difficult. The Norman yoke was real and weighty. It supported a feudal system based on land-holding and authority rather than a reciprocal bond of personal loyalty. There was no land without the lord and all land belonged ultimately to the king. But in spite of the changes which had so quickly overturned the English ruling class, and with it the ecclesiastical hierarchy, the rebellious uprisings against the invasion of the Normans died out by 1075 and the new Norman ruling class became slowly accepted and assimilated. The result was not a sharply divided society but all three cultural threads running through it, English, French and Scandinavian, contributed to the future of England, its law, its language, its politics, its government, its religion, its art and ultimately its strength.

THE MANOR OF NAPSTED

THE MANOR of Little Maplestead was not the only manor in the village. A neighbouring manor called Napsted was also recorded in the Domesday Book and, although no such place exists today and there are few records to point us to its original site[11], there are clues which suggest that it was probably situated in Little Maplestead. The entry in the Domesday Book is as follows:

> *Aubrey's wife holds Napsted from the Bishop which 8 freemen held before 1066 for 22 ½ acres. Always one plough. Woodland, 20 pigs; meadow, 6 acres. Value always 30s.*

This entry mentions a woman who is the wife of Aubrey; this was the wife of Aubrey de Vere who had been given Ulwine's lands at [Castle] Hedingham and other lordships in Essex. Aubrey's wife was called Beatrice and she was the half-sister of William I, a woman of independent means and, obviously, of considerable influence. Her small manor supported eight freemen and was probably near Hedingham. The name Napsted gives us a clue to where it might have been sited. This clue comes from the ancient name of a house in Little Maplestead, Hampers, which derives from the name *Hanaper*. This house is situated in an island of land in the middle of Little Maplestead which until relatively recently was part of the parish of Great Maplestead. All this points to the possibility that *Nap*sted may have derived its name from

Ha*na*pers and that the manor corresponded with the island of about thirty acres of land surrounded by Little Maplestead.

There is another reference to Aubrey de Vere's wife in the Domesday Book, this time regarding her additional possession of five freemen and 1¼ acres in Little Maplestead and in the neighbouring village of Pebmarsh.

GALLANTS FARM

THE DOMESDAY BOOK records the possessions of Robert Gernon who held land in forty-three Essex parishes including Great Maplestead and Pebmarsh. According to P. Reaney[12], Robert Gernon gave his name to the house in Little Maplestead called Gallants and it is possible that this was one of the five small-holdings of the manor of Little Maplestead referred to in the Domesday Book. Reaney suggests that the surname Gernon/Garnon became corrupted to Garland and from thence to Gallant. It is known that a Ralph Garnon owned a tenement and land in Little Maplestead in about 1240[13] and it is also known that in 1258 Benedict Gernon held a tenement in Pebmarsh. However, the same source[14] reveals that Roberto Galaunt held land in Twinstead during this time and more recently, in the nineteenth century, a John Gallant lived in the village.

Gallants, as it exists today, dates from the sixteenth century, or perhaps even earlier; it is timber-framed, with later alterations and additions[15], but it seems likely that the house has eleventh-century origins. After the eleventh-century, Gallants disappears from the written records although, on a primitive map of part of the village dated 1600 we see a tiny Gallants with ancient strip fields nearby, one of which can still be seen in the map of the 1817 survey as Long field.

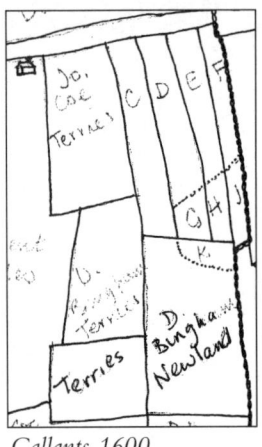

Gallants has evidence of its past in its seventeenth-century flooring and eighteenth-century doors and finishings but the house does not reappear in the written records until we find Gallants Farm included in the private survey of Little Maplestead drawn up in 1817. By this time it was no longer part of the manor of Little Maplestead but was owned by George Firmin and the farm consisted of:

Gallants 1600

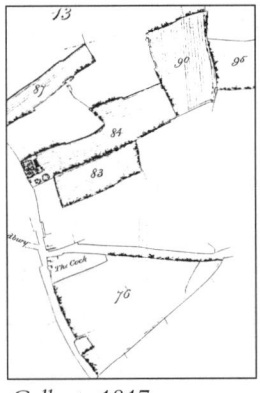

76	Burnthouse
83	Barn field
84	Upper field
85	The house or homestead
87	Long field
90	Lower field
95	Wood field

In extent about 36 acres

Gallants 1817

George Firmin still owned the land in 1841 at the tithe award and we discover that James Chatters was his tenant.

The farm had shrunk in size a little and it now consisted of:

73	Burnthouse Field
80	Barn Field
81	Upper Field
82	Homestall
83	field
87	Lower Field
90	Wood Field

In all 23 acres [see tithe map pages 218-219]

- 18 -

The 1841 census reveals that James Chatters had sub-let his property to Edward Willsmore, a dealer, who lived in the farm with his wife Mary and their sons Edward, 19, Samuel, 15, William, 13, and George, 7, who were all agricultural labourers. The farm was not named but from Kelly's Directory we know that from 1855 to 1859 it was called Garlands and was farmed by Edward Willsmore until 1863 during which year the name Gallants was used. The census for 1861 listed the farm as Gallants; Edward Willsmore, now a farmer of forty acres (employing two men and one boy) still lived there with his wife. By 1866 Mary Willsmore was a widow but she still farmed Gallants. In the 1871 census the farm was referred to as Garlands again and Mary Willsmore, now 78, was still farming twenty-eight acres, employing two men and one boy. Occupying Garlands with her was Eliza Willsmore, her grand-daughter, who was a 'straw-plaiter'. The cottage industry of straw-plaiting will be discussed on page 168. By 1878 the Willsmores had left and the farm was occupied by Mr Frederick Fairbank who was described in the 1881 census as a Congregational minister living in Gallants with his wife, Hannah, and daughters Caroline and Amelia. By 1891 Gallants Farm was occupied by Abraham Cox, who was a farmer and machinist, his wife, Jane, and a large family - five sons, Felix, Algernon, Jesse, Percy and Basil, and daughters Ethel and Agnes.

After 1891 there is a gap in the history of Gallants until the second half of the twentieth century when the land that once belonged to the small farm of Gallants was lost to other larger farms and the house became a private residence. But, before this final and inevitable change, throughout its history, from probably as long ago as Domesday, Gallants had always been a small farm or small-holding, a testimony to the unchanging nature of life in Little Maplestead.

LEPPINGWELLS

TOGETHER WITH Maplestead Hall (see page 33) and Mill Farm, the tiny cottage of Leppingwells also has the distinction of a specific entry in the Domesday Book. The approximate date of the building which exists today is about 1600[16] but its history goes back some 500 years before this. Under the heading '1 freeman's annexation' we find the entry:

> In *Liffildeuuella* 1 freeman held and has always held 30 acres. Value 6s 8d.

The name Leppingwells comes directly from the name *Liffildeuuella*, which probably means the spring or stream of a woman called Leofhild[17]. The stream cannot be exactly located but it may have been the name of the brook flowing from Spoons Hall which passes near Levits Corner in Pebmarsh; the word Levit may be a further corruption of the name Leofhild. However another explanation of the name Liffildeuuella may simply be 'the field well'. Whatever the derivation, we know that Leppingwells was once part of the ancient manor of Pooley in Pebmarsh and the possessions of this manor extended from Pebmarsh to Little Maplestead, Gestingthorpe and Bulmer.

We can follow the name of Leppingwells down through the centuries, first as Lefledewelle in 1210[18], when William, son of Alured de Wicham [Wickham] granted to Colne Priory annual rent from his land of Lefledewelle. Other early references include Leffeldewell in 1235[19] and Leffeleswell in 1258[20], where we have mention of Hugh Spon, Benedict Gernon and Avicia Leffeleswell as having a tenement which was in either Pebmarsh or Gestingthorpe. It is interesting that these three names reflect the names of Spoons Hall and Gallants as well as of Leppingwells. In 1285 when Henry FitzHugh and Alice his wife complain that Nicholas de Cruce (from Crouch House, Gestingthorpe) encroaches on their tenement we have a record of Leffedewell[21]. The prior of Colne owned land in Little Maplestead and Pebmarsh in 1291[22] and this included land called Lefheldewelle. We also know that William de Lefheldewell from the Hinckford Hundred was a juror at the Forest Court at Chelmsford in 1291 and he and others of the family in the early fourteenth century were mentioned in connection with the Knights Hospitallers.

Leppingwells

Between 1302 and 1344 there are records of the family of Robert de Leffeldewelle[23], who lived in Little Maplestead but was vicar of Gestingthorpe in 1344; his land was said to be 'held of the manor of Byham Hall'.

In a Pebmarsh rental of 1508 we find mention again of a William Leffingwell and Alice Leppingwell and of land once belonging to 'Simon Leffingwell in Maplested parva, between the King's highway from Sudbury to Halstead and the land of William Bery once Gedges [Gages] called Macres and land called Mellemont Lande abutting on Redinge'.

From a survey of the Honour of Clare in 1561[24] Leffingwelles in Little Maplestead included fields called Blackes and Quene acre and was held by Thomas Sexten. Symon Leffingwell had held a messuage near the 'woode of the hospital called the Hoo' and land 'now in the hands of Deane [Hall]' and we also learn that Roger Leffingwell from Pebmarsh had held a garden and two crofts of land in Little Maplestead. By 1578 Leppingwells was held by the widow and daughter of Thomas Sexten.

In 1619 Robert Gardener leased Leppingwells to Richard Ashby and in 1627 the field Longcroft, and one other croft, in all six acres, are leased again to William Botts; the remainder of the property is described as 'all that messuage or tenement called Leffingwells with the Barn etc and a close of land containing four acres in Little Maplestead on the backside of the Barn abutting on the wood of George Gould'.

In 1629 Leffingwells belonged to Thomas Harrington who willed his land in 1652 to William his grandson. In this document we find mention of copyhold land called Lammes Croft 'abutting on the highway from Maplestead to Halstead and on Asseesfield[25]'. There is also reference to Seagers and Hilliards Grove, all ancient field names. By 1668 Leppingwells was leased to Jos Cooke and John Morley. In 1673 there is a reference to two fields, Spit Croft, a four-acre field and The Pent, ten acres. These fields belonged to Leppingwells. The name Spit Croft is of ancient origin, there is a reference to *Spitelcroft* in 1240[26].

In the Court Book for the manor of Little Maplestead dated 1693 there is an entry:

> *Freehold of John Cooke and now John Cooke his son for certain lands called Leppingwells (3s). Freehold of the same for a parcel of land called Hillards (Hill Yards) late William Harrington's (6d).*

In 1700 John Cooke died leaving Sarah his widow and in 1704 their daughter Mary inherited Leppingwells. By 1742 Mary Cooke had married Abraham de Horne Vaizey and in 1774 George de Horne Vaizey owned Leppingwells. A collection of leases and mortgages from 1789[27] shows ownership by George de Horne Vaizey who gave it to his son John. In 1805 Leppingwells was leased to Mr Samuel Amiss, farmer, by John de Horne Vaizey. John Sewell had held the lease before him.

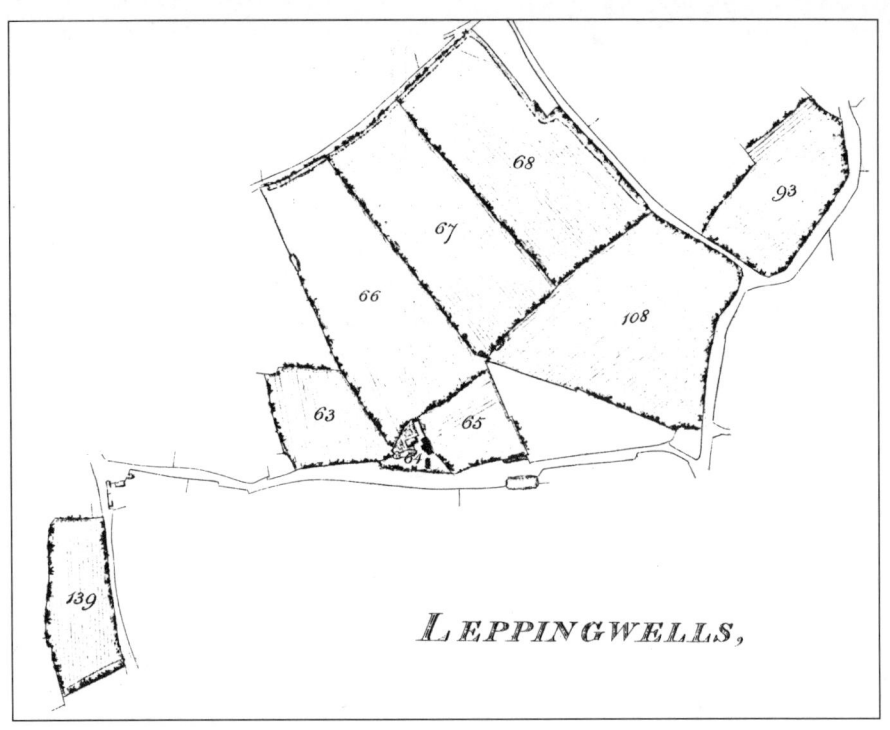

Leppingwells 1817

In the 1817 survey of the village Leppingwells was owned by George de Horne Vaizey, and John Vaizey was named as tenant; it consisted of forty-two acres:

63	Leppingwells
64	Homestall
65	Barn Field
66	Long Croft
67	Wood Field
68	Hill Yard
93	Spit Croft
108	Singoes Field
139	Collins

Leppingwells remained unchanged at the 1841 tithe award but from the 1841 census we know that William Porter, an agricultural labourer, lived in Leppingwells with his wife Ann and young son George. William Porter still occupied Leppingwells ten years later. He was then a farm bailiff employed by John Vaizey.

In 1873 Leppingwells was named as part of the Vaizey estate and in 1877 the farm was leased to Mr Henry Ray Shave of Bentalls Farm for nine years. At this date Leppingwells had forty-one acres and consisted of: Leppingwells Pasture, Homestall, Barn Field, Long Croft and one arable field made from Wood Field, Ingoes Field, Hill Field and Pages Croft. All this was held freehold except for eight acres which were leasehold for a term of one thousand years from 11 November 1651 at a peppercorn rent. An 'inconsiderable slip by the roadside' was held copyhold from the lord of the manor.

It was important for the lord of the manor to keep a record of all the lands he owned and rented out to other farmers. Some of the land was held freehold and some was held copyhold. Freehold land was held from the lord of the manor with no duty of service attached (although there might be a duty of knight's or military service which could be commuted to a rent) and the land could be passed down through the family by inheritance. Copyhold land was held of the manor for a duty of service to the lord or rent and any change of ownership had to be referred to the manor court. The lord of the manor had a greater control over the land.

By 1881 Leppingwells was lived in by relatives of the Willsmores of Gallants, William Willsmore, a farm bailiff, his wife Mary and daughter Eliza, a straw-plaiter. Later, in 1891 William Willsmore who was now a widower, was no longer a farm bailiff but worked as an agricultural labourer looked after by his unmarried daughter, Eliza.

Leppingwells was by now a tied farm cottage; in 1919 it belonged to Wilfred Wright of Gages Farm and in that year the late Cecil Cook, whose father worked at Gages, was born at Leppingwells. He lived there until 1936 and remembered his boyhood in the cottage well. In an extract from his *Memories* he writes:

> The barn at Leppingwells used to be filled with sheaves. When the time came for threshing the corn I have seen three horses on the drum struggling to pull the thresher through the mud. A portable steam engine was used to drive the drum and elevator. As the barn got empty the sheaves would be heaving up - this was the rats underneath, us boys killed many with sticks and dogs. In the mid-twenties sugar beet was grown here for the first time, a factory being built at Felsted and Mr Wright grew eight acres on the field behind Leppingwells ... Bill Turp the tramp used to sleep in a manger in Leppingwells barn. Rats ran over him at night biting his face. He also used to live in Bill Simmond's 'garage' at The Cottage which was his little house, until he was turned out. He used to go off to the workhouse periodically to be cleaned up.

By the 1970s Leppingwells had been sold away from the farm and since then it has been a private house. Between the house called Leppingwells today and the house called Liffildeuuella in 1086 there are more than nine hundred years of history. And it is the same with Mill Farm, Toldishall and Gallants Farm, names we are all familiar with today in our village and names that are a remarkable testimony to the continuity of history, spanning nearly one thousand years, linking the present-day village with the village at the time of the Norman Conquest.

Notes to Chapter I

[1] *The Anglo-Saxon Chronicle:* a revised translation, ed. D. Whitelock (1962)
[2] Charter Roll in the Public Record Office (PRO)
[3] *The Cartulary of the Knights of St John of Jerusalem,* ed. M Gervers (OUP, 1982), document no. 91
[4] Cartulary document, no.170
[5] *The Concise Oxford Dictionary of Place-names,* 2nd edition (Oxford,1940)
[6] From a Saxon chronicle quoted by Oxford English Dictionary (London, 1971)
[7] *The Domesday Book;* The Concise Oxford Dictionary of English Place-names
[8] From a book of the survey held by the late Mrs E. Newton of Great Maplestead, Essex
[9] Cartulary documents, nos. 91-94
[10] Quote from Asa Briggs, *A Social History of England* (London, 1983)
[11] Cartulary document, no. 170
[12] P.H.Reaney, *The Place-names of Essex* (CUP, 1969)
[13] Cartulary document, no. 160
[14] Cartulary document, no. 752
[15] Essex County Council Department of Planning, Listed Building Register
[16] Essex County Council Department of Planning, Listed Building Register
[17] P.H.Reaney, *The Place-names of Essex*
[18] From a document in the Bodleian library
[19] From an Assize Roll in PRO
[20] From the *Feet of Fines* for Essex (1899-1928)
[21] From an Assize Roll in PRO
[22] From the *Pleas of the Forest,* roll in PRO
[23] Cartulary documents, nos. 848, 849, 880
[24] From an Elizabethan Rental
[25] First mentioned in Cartulary, document no. 155
[26] Cartulary document no.108
[27] Document in Essex Record Office, D/DVz 366

ELEVENTH-CENTURY EVENTS

1066   *Edward the Confessor dies: Harold elected king. William of Normandy invades England and Harold is killed at Hastings*

1075   *The Turks conquer Jerusalem and the Holy Places*

1086   *The Domesday Book, a survey of England, completed*

1095   *Pope Urban II summons Christian nations to the First Crusade*

1098   *Crusaders attack and take Antioch*

1099   *Crusaders attack and take Jerusalem*

- 24 -

CHAPTER II

THE TWELFTH CENTURY

A knight there was, and that a worthy man
That from the time that he first began
To ride abroad, he loved chivalry
Truth and honour, freedom and courtesy.[1]

EXACTLY one hundred years after the production of the Domesday Book an event took place in Little Maplestead that would change its history and give the tiny village an importance its inhabitants could never have imagined.

During those hundred years the people of Little Maplestead had become adjusted to Norman rule and the Anglo-Norman way of life, with all that entailed. But the country as a whole had endured a great deal of strife, including baronial rebellions and a civil war, so when Henry Plantagenet, who had both Anglo-Saxon and Norman blood in his veins, came to the throne in 1154 as Henry II, England at last hoped for the strong rule its people longed for. Henry embodied the Anglo-Saxon conception of king as keeper of the peace and guardian of the people and a measure of unity was re-established in the country.

At a local level, East Anglia and Essex did not experience the devastation that some areas suffered during the civil strife and the region had already begun to show the influence of its Norman masters in its architecture as new castles, churches and domestic buildings were constructed. The inhabitants of Little Maplestead would no doubt have known that their king, Henry II, had built himself a magnificent castle not so very far away on the coast at Orford. A cathedral was begun at Norwich and nearer to home the villagers of Little Maplestead would have witnessed the spectacle of the building of the vast Norman castle at Hedingham.

This castle was built at the command of the great crusading knight, Aubrey de Vere II, the son of Aubrey I and Beatrice. It was built to impress (it had the largest Norman arch in Europe) but also to defend against siege in what were uncertain times. The erection of the great stone keep, started in 1140, must have been the source of much interest and amazement to those whose dwellings had walls of mud and clay with roofs of simple thatch. The villagers would have been conscious of the increased activity and employment in the neighbourhood at this time. For instance, the facing stone for the entire castle was transported to Hedingham from

LITTLE MAPLESTEAD i

Gesting

Great Maplestead

1

2

5

a

Halstead

The TWELFTH CENTURY

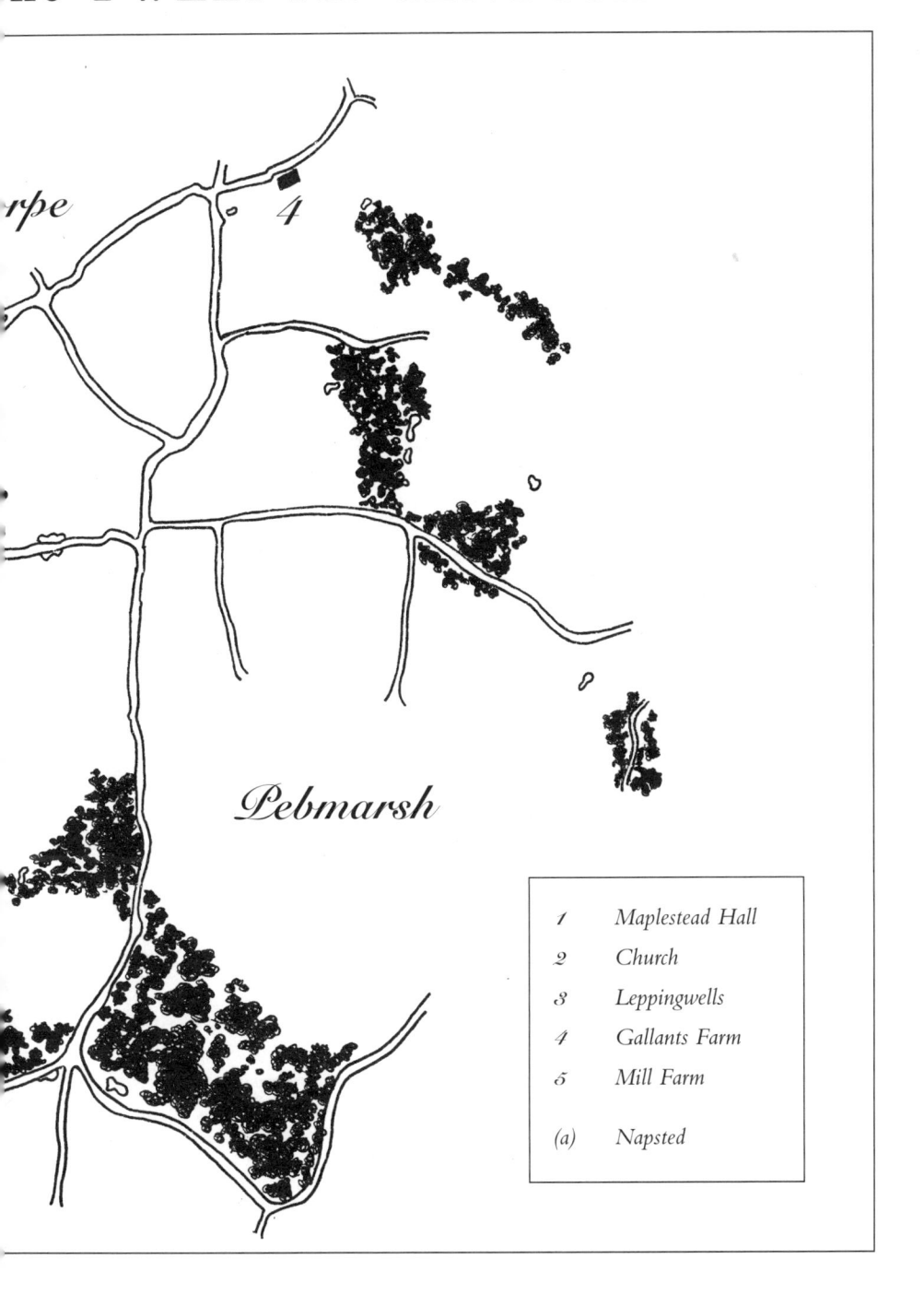

Pebmarsh

1	*Maplestead Hall*
2	*Church*
3	*Leppingwells*
4	*Gallants Farm*
5	*Mill Farm*
(a)	*Napsted*

the quarries of Barnack in Northamptonshire and local flints were gathered and used to fill in the castle walls; this must have provided welcome extra employment for those of the Little Maplestead community free to do such work.

But against this background the villagers of Little Maplestead would have continued to carry on their day-to-day struggle for survival. At the beginning of the twelfth century nine out of ten people still lived in rural communities and country rhythms dictated the pace of life which continued to be harsh. The urban population at this time was relatively small and, apart from London, the nearest large urban centre to Little Maplestead would have been Norwich which had five thousand inhabitants and was one of the largest towns in the country.

The Normans had brought no real changes to farming - except for the cultivation of some vineyards - and agriculture was left to continue in much the same way as it had done in pre-Conquest days. However many Norman lords of the manor now rented out their lands to sub-tenants and ceased to manage them directly; even the old enforced labour services were giving way to wage labour as villeins commuted their labour dues by paying money to the lord instead. This money rent would have been earned by the villein in a number of ways, often by selling his own agricultural produce, bread or beer, perhaps by labouring or perhaps by a craft - masons, potters, weavers and tanners all existed within the rural community.

Overall, at the end of the eleventh century, the lords of the manor had cultivated between 33% and 40% of the arable land in use; of the remaining land, villeins (41% of the community) held 45% of land; cottagers or small householders (32% of the community) held 5% of the land; free men (14% of the community) held 20% of the land; and serfs (10% of the community) held no land[2]. But during the twelfth century there was a striking growth in the population of England, to more than four million, which was at its most pronounced in Norfolk and Suffolk. This led to an eventual scarcity of good land to cultivate and was the beginning of a forced expansion of cultivation into woodland and poorer land such as marshland.

Importantly, in Norman England, all land, of whatever kind, ultimately belonged to the crown and all the great land-holders, such as Aubrey de Vere, were the king's tenants-in-chief. Such men held their land at the king's gift and in return for services to the crown. There were no absolute freeholds, secular or ecclesiastical, and when the tenants-in-chief parcelled out their land they required knightly service from their tenants who included both the great and the small. These knights were expected to fulfil the Norman French code of honour of loyalty, chivalry and courage, an ideal which was virtually impossible to fulfil and which was tested most harshly in the barbarous wars of the Crusades.

THE CRUSADES

THE CRUSADES were a series of wars fought to 'reconquer and redeem' from the Arab world parts of the Holy Land, the heart of which was Jerusalem. The hazardous journey to Palestine was also regarded as a pilgrimage, the crusaders combining secular and religious motives, inspired both by devotion and the desire for conquests in the East. By 1095 the Seljuk Turks were pressing hard on the Byzantine Empire in Asia Minor, harassing pilgrims from Europe as they travelled through Syria to the Holy Land and desecrating the holy places in Jerusalem. The Christian emperor appealed for help from the West, and on 15 August 1096 the First Crusade set off to come to his aid, followed by another wave of crusading knights in 1147-8 and yet another in 1190-92.

A crusading knight

Christian pilgrims had been visiting the holy places in Jerusalem for centuries, they saw it as the ultimate way to seek indulgences and pardon from sin. These pilgrims, often exhausted and weak after a journey which would have lasted many months, were extremely vulnerable to the effects of a different climate, strange food and foreign illnesses. Frequently they were debilitated and in need of care and attention and hospices, or rest houses, were set up to look after them. One such hospice was established in the mid-eleventh century by merchants from Amalfi, a small republic on the south coast of the kingdom of Naples. They were permitted to purchase a site in Jerusalem and there they built a new hospice together with a Christian church which was run by a group of monks. The eight-pointed white cross, associated with the republic of Amalfi, was adopted by these monks as their religious symbol and later became known as the Maltese cross.

When the first crusaders captured Jerusalem in 1099 they found the merchants' hospice intact and working, busy looking after the sick and wounded from both sides. The warden there was called Gerard; he came from Provence and his assistants were Benedictine monks. At this time most people's attitude to illness was that of fear, the sick were shunned and the duties of caring for them were normally undertaken by the lowest social classes. The crusaders were impressed by the care shown to all the sick and wounded by Gerard and his brethren and some of the knights joined the monks to help with their good work. Others endowed the hospice, now more like a hospital, with donations of money and even gifts of land back in their own countries from which the monks could receive rent.

The Maltese Cross

With such support the monastic brethren were able to reorganize and expand. They acquired the monastery of St John the Baptist in Jerusalem and adopted him as their patron saint, thus becoming known and recognized as the Order of the Hospital of St John of Jerusalem. The symbol of the eight-pointed cross, the Maltese cross, has been used by the Order of St John of Jerusalem ever since.

Following the establishment of this monastic hospital, the order also took up arms to defend the Christian states which had been set up by the crusaders in the Holy Land and they became a wealthy, powerful and warlike force but the Hospitallers themselves, often of noble birth, always displayed a gentle Christ-like approach to treating the sick and the poor of any country or creed. This attitude was unique at the time and perhaps was their greatest contribution to medicine.

THE MANOR OF LITTLE MAPLESTEAD

IN 1186 the manor of Little Maplestead was held by a woman, Lady Juliana, the daughter of a Norman, Robert Doisnel[3]. Lady Juliana was married to King Henry II's steward, William Audelin. Shortly before this date, Henry had been approached by the Patriach of Jerusalem, Heraclius, and Roger de Moulins, the Grand Master of the Hospitallers of the Order of St John of Jerusalem, who had come to seek more military aid for the ongoing struggle in the Holy Land[4]. For political reasons Henry was advised by his barons not to provide high-profile leadership but rather to support the cause in more subtle ways. To this end Lady Juliana made a gift of her entire manor and church at Little Maplestead to the Hospitallers for the purpose of establishing a preceptory there. This preceptory was intended to treat those crusading knights who had returned home sick and diseased and also to act as an administrative and recruiting centre for the order.

We do not know whether Henry put pressure on his steward to have this particular gift made, or whether William Audelin, seeking to gain favour from the king, made the offer on behalf of his wife or indeed whether Lady Juliana herself decided to make the offer. Certainly there were important spiritual benefits to be gained by such a gift. Whatever the truth, a grant by William Audelin and Lady Juliana to the Hospitallers of the church at Little Maplestead with its lands, tithes, offerings and advowson together with the entire 'vill' of Little Maplestead was made on 17 March 1186[5]. And so, one hundred years after its entry as a manor in the Domesday Book, the manor and village of Little Maplestead were on the brink of great changes.

Soon after William and Juliana's grant was made, the inhabitants of Little Maplestead witnessed the coming of the Knights Hospitaller to the simple manor house which was on the site of the present-day Maplestead Hall opposite the church. These knights were often from wealthy families but as members of the Order of St John of Jerusalem they had sworn an oath to observe poverty, chastity and obedience and wore 'poor garments' always with the eight-pointed cross on their breasts[6]. There in the manor house by the church, they began to establish their preceptory. Soon to be known as L'Hospital[7], it was run by a small community of the brethren, of probably no more than fifteen members. These Knights Hospitaller, who could still be liable for service abroad, were overseen by a master and his servants. The master took the place of the lord of the manor and administered the manorial tenancies which now belonged to the order. From the poor manorial tenant he accepted the usual feudal dues (and may have employed such tenants as servants) but money rents were now collected from tenants wherever possible, and these helped to fund the order. Before long the preceptory also began to receive donations of land, many given by local landowners anxious to support the Crusades and to enjoy some of the benefits of the order, often requesting that prayers be said for themselves and their families by the knights. Among the donors were Robert de Vere, Earl of Oxford at Hedingham Castle, John Dyn and Margaret his wife from Dynes Hall in Great Maplestead, Hugh Hoding from Great Maplestead, William Joye from Little Maplestead and Sir Simon de Odewell, who had given them a considerable estate at Odewell and elsewhere in Gestingthorpe[8]. One can also imagine the poorer inhabitants of Little Maplestead striving to give what they could - perhaps humble gifts of produce according to the season - in order that they too should gain some small spiritual benefit from the order and be looked upon kindly by the brethren. In all, over one hundred land grants were made and the rents from this land soon began to swell the coffers of the foundation which rapidly increased in wealth and importance, enabling the knights to set about expanding their premises.

From contemporary documents we know that the preceptory would have included several domestic buildings such as a refectory, a brewhouse, a bakehouse, kitchens and dormitories (both for the brethren and for the sick) and a chapter-house plus other subsidiary buildings, all probably grouped round a courtyard in the style of the monasteries of the time. No traces of the preceptory can be seen today but Maplestead Hall still possesses some fine ancient timbers which could have been present in the Hospitallers' manor house[9]. The remains of the knights' stew-ponds, essential to the order for a supply of fresh fish, can also be seen today in the small lake in front of the house. We also know that there were vineyards at Little Maplestead in the thirteenth century[10] and there is little doubt that these too would have been at L' Hospital.

A summary of day-to-day expenses[11] for L'Hospital included wheat for baking bread, malt for brewing ale; flesh, fish and other necessaries for the kitchen; robes, mantles and other items for the brothers; the stipend of two chaplains, the fee of the steward administering the business of the house, the stipends of four clerks collecting the *fraeria* or rents, the stipends of a bailiff, a cook, a baker and a porter, a palfreyman and a page for the stable. Consideration of this list brings to life the daily activities of the members of the order which the villagers of Little Maplestead must have observed. Living out their own simple lives, they must have watched with wonder the comings and goings of those at L'Hospital. The village must have benefited greatly from the arrival of the knights; with such a wealthy community at its centre, there must have been opportunities for all types of casual work and trade hitherto unimagined. It is also very likely that the Hospitallers would have treated all those sick villagers who came to them for help so that the fortunate inhabitants of Little Maplestead also had access to what would have been at that time unparalleled medical expertise. Furthermore, the villagers must have absorbed much from the new situation in which they found themselves; they must have become quite worldly and well-informed, their horizons broadened by stories, rumour and gossip of the knights' experiences in the Holy Land, of the bloody Crusades and of life abroad in general. We have evidence of how sophisticated their culinary taste had become when we find rents part paid in spices, for example, in cumin, cloves and ginger[12] brought back from the Holy Land.

THE CHURCH

DESPITE THE SPATE of secular building and the expansion of the preceptory, Little Maplestead church was left structurally untouched. In form it was probably still a simple apsidal Norman building with a rectangular nave. We know from the records that this church, dedicated to All Saints, was still being used in 1240; but at the time of the establishment of the preceptory the knights of the order, to whom it now belonged, needed to worship there. We know that Ivo the clerk, who was rector in 1186, resigned when the knights arrived[13] but we do not know how the villagers of Little Maplestead reacted to this and to the fact that their parish church now no longer existed solely for their own use.

The parish church was a familiar feature of the landscape and of fundamental importance to the community. The rites of the church encompassed all the main events in the life of the individual, birth, marriage and death. All learning came through the church at local level and the priest was the intermediary between the villager and his maker. The boundaries between the religious and the secular were blurred and the teaching, which had been adapted to the needs of everyday life, was still mingled with old beliefs. Such teaching was often more by eye than ear and the interior walls of most churches were decorated with vivid wall-paintings; there is no reason to suppose that this was not so in the church in Little Maplestead at this time.

Eventually the problem of accommodating both knights and parishioners was solved, a compromise was reached and a solid wooden rood screen was erected, completely dividing the church into two[14]. The chancel, now made quite private and with a separate entrance, was used by the Knights and the rest of the church could continue to be used by the villagers as before. This solid rood screen remained in place up until the eighteenth century when it was removed.

MAPLESTEAD HALL

AS WE HAVE SEEN, the villagers of twelfth-century Little Maplestead had witnessed the establishment of L'Hospital, the preceptory of the Knights Hospitaller of St John of Jerusalem, in the centre of their community. It stood where the original manor house of Little Maplestead had been built, on a slight rise in the land close to the church, and its buildings extended over what are now the grounds of Maplestead Hall. The present-day house stands on the site of the first manor house and probably on its foundations. We know that the house is of fourteenth-century origins and was a hall house with many of the original timbers incorporated into a later rebuild[15]. One of these timbers has recently been revealed in the roof while repairs were being carried out; it is a massive carved beam with incised trefoils along it which was very likely part of the ancient L'Hospital.

For nearly three hundred years L'Hospital continued its work treating the sick, recruiting members, and administering its land and tenancies. It was at the height of its importance during the fourteenth century but by 1463 we know that the Hospitallers had ceased to reside there, instead the 'hospital of St John of Little Mapulstede' was farmed by a layman, John Syday[16]. The order had decided that it was more economic to let the property out to provide an income and by then it was administered by the order's headquarters at Clerkenwell in London. However, the order continued to provide a chaplain to conduct services in the church and arrangements were made to collect the rents which were also probably received there.

Maplestead Hall

The Knights Hospitaller continued in possession of the manor of Little Maplestead until the dissolution of the order by Henry VIII in 1540. In 1541 Henry granted the manor and farm to George Harper, Esq[17]. The manor then passed through a series of owners – the Wisemans[18], the Guyons, the Bullocks[19] – and during this time the house was rebuilt and converted back into a domestic dwelling[20].

One of the Wiseman family who inherited the lordship of the manor of Little Maplestead in 1602 is worth a special mention. This is Edmund Wiseman who was a soldier and follower of Robert Devereux, Earl of Essex and one time favourite of Queen Elizabeth I. Robert Devereux's untimely beheading in London was partly due to negligence on the part of Edmund, who failed (by oversleeping) to deliver a letter to the Queen which might have saved Devereux. Edmund could never forgive himself for this and, swearing never to sleep comfortably again, had a bed and bolster carved in one piece out of the trunk of a large oak and slept on this for the rest of his life.

In the earliest of the rental books for the manor of Little Maplestead[21] dated 1693, entitled *Acetiam de Maplestead Parva: Anno Dui 1693, Edrus Bullock, Armiger Dus,* a list of all the properties existing as part of the manor is included. These comprised the following properties many of which can easily be identified, and are discussed in the book. The words in square brackets were pencilled in on the document at a later date.

- 34 -

Copyhold tenement and yard in Gestingthorpe abutting onto Byham Hall land

Copyhold cottage abutting onto land called Aldricks, Little Maplestead

Freehold for lands called Leppingwells

Freehold parcel of land in Little Maplestead late Parkes

Freehold land called Hillards in Little Maplestead

Copyhold land called Scurborks Little Maplestead

Freehold tenement and croft near Hillards wood [near the road leading to the Cock and Joys Wood]

Freehold Land at High Wood

Freehold Barne Croft, Little Maplestead

Freehold Wood called Hillards

Freehold tenement called Dranes, and land called Little Brokholls [in the green lane leading from the Cock to Little Maplestead Church]

Freehold tenement lately burnt down and croft called Barres in Little Maplestead [on Hurrells Green]

Copyhold land called Braggs, Goodins Wood and Meadow in Gestingthorpe, Bushy and Joys Wood

Copyhold parcels of land called Aldricks and Smiths in Gestingthorpe

Copyhold land in High Field [where the windmill stood] in Little Maplestead

Freehold land called High field near Link Hills in Great and Little Maplestead

Freehold marsh ground by Link Hills in Great and Little Maplestead

Freehold land called Bakers [on the road to Pebmarsh]

Freehold land in Little Maplestead near Braggs farm [Gestingthorpe boundary]

Freehold lands belonging to College of Sudbury in Great and Little Maplestead

The list also included some properties in the village which cannot be linked to any known site.

> Copyhold tenement and croft in Little Maplestead called Merryman
>
> Copyhold Willsons, land and tenement in Little Maplestead
>
> Freehold croft of land in Little Maplestead called Stonards
>
> Freehold Cox Croft in Little Maplestead
>
> Freehold Land called Harwoods in Little Maplestead
>
> Copyhold Turpitts in Great and Little Maplestead

The rental also listed other properties which existed outside Little Maplestead; these were in Gestingthorpe, Halstead, Sible Hedingham and Belchamp Walter and these were remnants of the lands once owned by the Hospitallers.

In 1705, Mr Joseph Davis, a member of a church of Sabbatarian Dissenters which worshipped in East London, where it also owned property, purchased the manor of Little Maplestead from Edward Bullock[22]. He set up a trust to receive rents from the manor for the purposes of benefiting his church. When his son died in 1731 without issue the estates passed to the church trustees in lieu of an annuity. Maplestead Hall was now blended with the other East London properties owned by the trust under the common title of the Davis Charity.

The original deed of trust of the Davis Charity estates provided that the meeting house in East London should always be used for dissenting Protestants, and that the income from its properties, which included Maplestead Hall, should be used to pay all repair bills, rent, and taxes with an annual fee being paid to the perpetual curate of Little Maplestead. In the late 1700s the Dissenters' church attendance dwindled and the number of trustees was reduced but Maplestead Hall continued to be administered by the Davis Charity.

JOHN SEWELL

IN THE EARLY 1800s, Maplestead Hall was occupied by a tenant called John Sewell, under whom the estate became a very successful and profitable enterprise. It consisted of the manor of Little Maplestead which included Hall Farm, its gardens and lands which amounted to about 315 acres and also Bricks Farm which was about sixty-eight acres and a farm called Falshams which exists today only in the name of a field. The trust was lucky to have John Sewell as a tenant; he was a dedicated and progressive farmer. He regularly reported his new techniques and experiments in the *Annals of Agriculture*, the leading farmers' journal edited by Arthur Young[23]. He was particularly interested in seed-growing and in improving agricultural implements.

Apart from the usual cereal crops, two of the crops he grew were something of a speciality to the Maplesteads, these were coriander and caraway which were sent up to London to be used for drug-making and for flavouring. He also grew teazels for the cloth industry in Halstead. John Sewell supplied the land for these crops and prepared it by ploughing, then he offered out the contract to tend and harvest the crops. Thus many women in Little Maplestead found work hoeing and then, later on at harvest, cutting and sorting the teazels. Hops were also being grown at Maplestead Hall. The high rate of wages at the time, eight shillings a week, indicates some measure of local prosperity[24].

The 1817 survey of the village lists the following information about 'Little Maplestead Hall' and its farm (see map pages 38-39):

Mr Joseph Slater, trustee

John Sewell, tenant

21	Lower Smithers
31	Rosy field
35	Upper Smithers
36	Malting piece
37	House, homestead, gardens
37a	The pound and a cartlodge
38	The Pightle
39	Steeple field
116	Potash Office
119	Church Hook
121	Pound Field
122	Little Mill Field
123	Long Meadow
124	The Chaldron
131	Pope's Meadow
132	Starch House, hop ground
133	Madges Hill
134	Ozier Ground
135	Great Mill field
136	Down Wood meadow

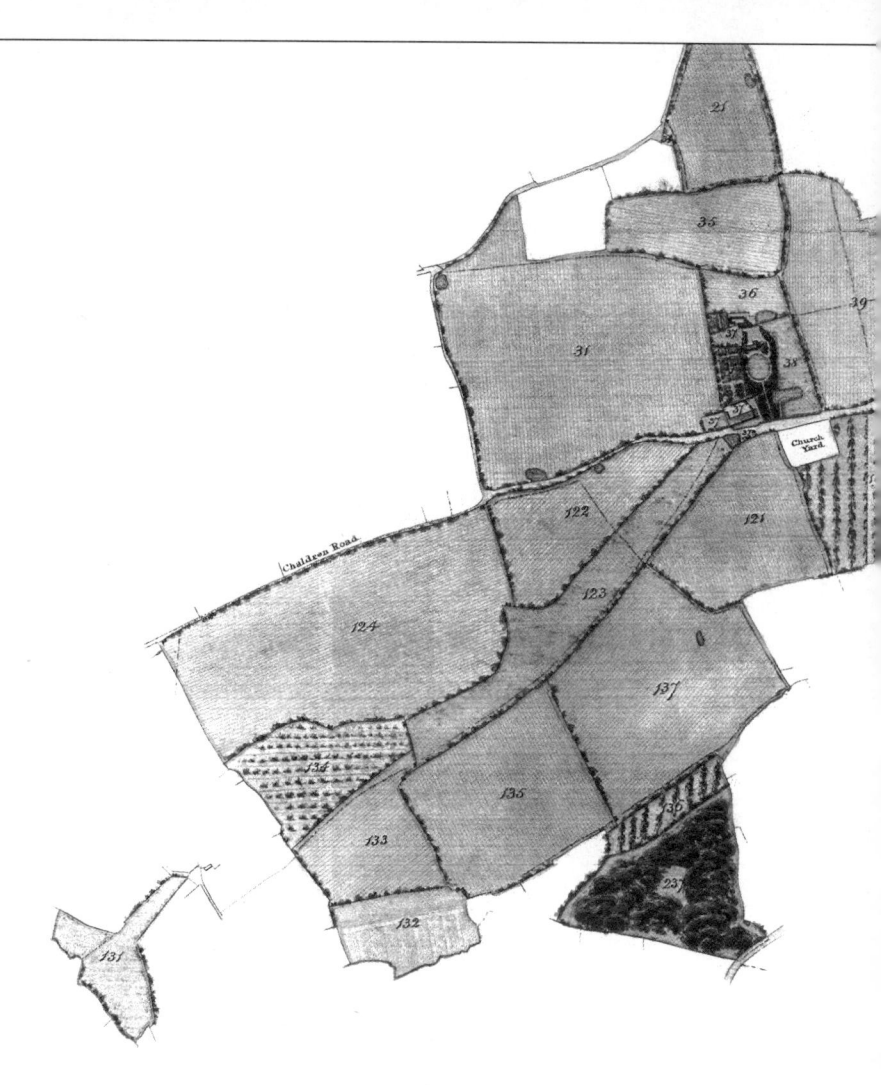

LITTLE MAPLESTEAD HALL.

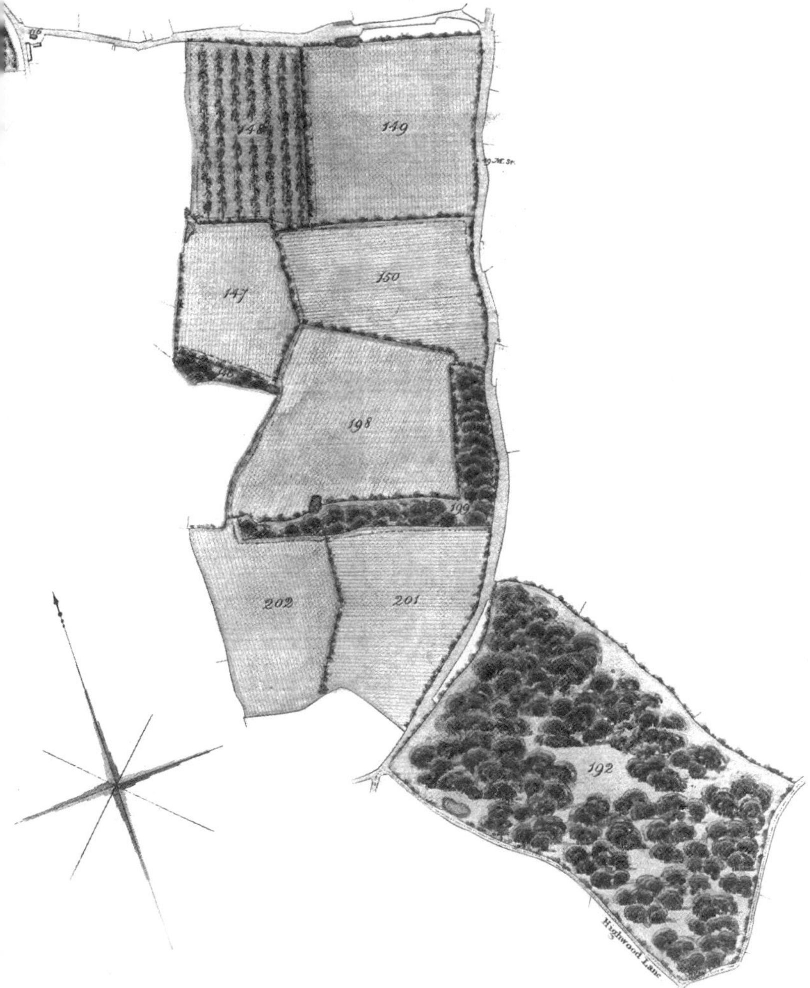

148
149
19 M. St.
147
150
146
198
199
202
201
192
Highwood Lane

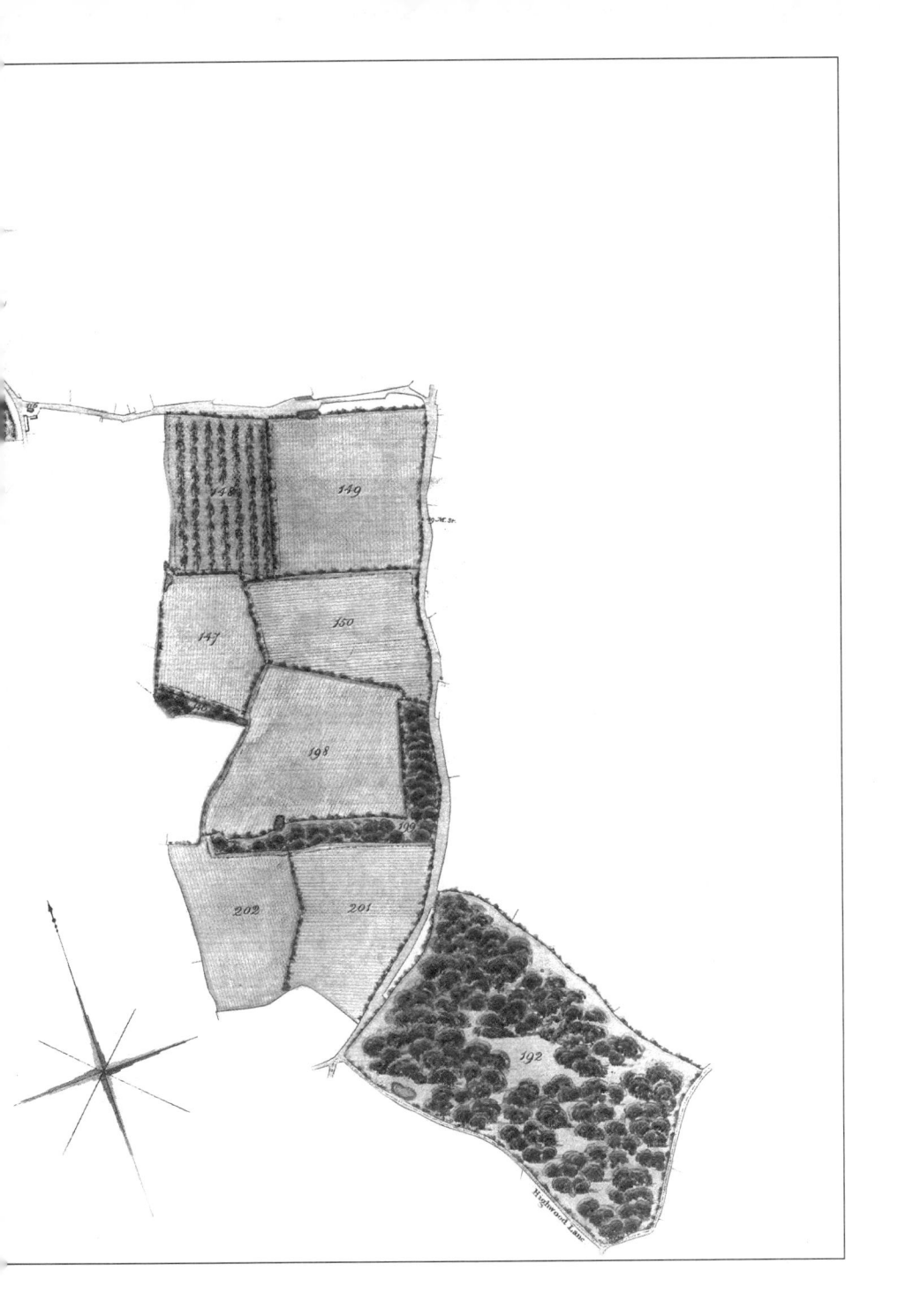

137	Great Mill field
146	The Grove
147	Hurrells Went
148	Little Easty field
149	The Ley
150	Bell field
192	High Wood
198	Great Easty Wood
199	Oxley Wood
201	Great Oxley
202	Little Oxley
237	Down Wood
34	encroachment on the waste

Following the appointment of new trustees in 1823, an extensive survey and valuation of the Maplestead Hall estate was carried out on behalf of the Davis Charity estates. John Sewell was described as a 'desirable' tenant on a lease which was due to expire at Michaelmas 1828[25].

In this survey, Maplestead Hall was recorded as consisting of:

> 314 acres 3 rods 11 poles of arable, pasture, hop ground, gardens, osier grounds and woodland with a respectable Farm House suitable and well situated for occupation.

There was also a large double barn, stables, cowhouse, hopkiln, granary and other useful agricultural buildings. The Hall Farm was described as being in a creditable state of cultivation.

But despite the fact that the trustees had thought John Sewell a desirable tenant and a successful and progressive farmer, five years later, at the end of 1828, he did not renew his tenancy. The survey of the estate had revealed that, due to a lack of care on the part of the trustees over the last few years, all the buildings had become neglected and run down. This had also caused the state of cultivation to deteriorate. The proposed repairs and rebuilding were inevitably going to result in an increase in rent and it was this and the lack of support from the trustees which caused Sewell to quit.

THE BREWSTERS

JOHN SEWELL'S place was taken by James Brewster, from White Notley Hall, in 1829 and for the next four years major repairs and improvements were planned and undertaken at both Maplestead Hall and on the farm. While these upheavals were in progress the state of cultivation on the farm inevitably suffered and the whole period was fraught with financial argument[26].

The major repairs which had to be done to the house were described in a report to the trustees:

> *The house has undergone a thorough repair which has proved more extensive than was anticipated as when stripped the Timbers were in part decayed from the Sill to the top of the Roof.....the brick foundation was required to be taken out and made new all round the old foundations being only of three and four Bricks deep ....the error ... had caused the House to settle in various parts and the floors had risen throughout.... when the projecting roof was proposed by Mr Rayner the Builder I approved the same having seen the effect of the water beating upon the old front by the decayed state of the lath and plaster which considering the time the House had been built ought to have been perfectly sound if protected. The Portico is as plain as can be imagined ..the staircase is decidedly an alteration and improvement to add to the comfort of the Tenant....*

The trustees continued to be reluctant to finance the repairs to the Maplestead estate and a lively correspondence regarding further repairs continued. In April 1832 the following list was made of 'works proposed to be done'; this contains some interesting information about Maplestead Hall, its buildings and grounds:

> *Floor in the Parlour at the west end of the House to be laid and the Walls plastered. Scurtain board in the back Chamber. Hopkiln - Tiling to be repaired and pointed, the sides drawn in, the Beams secured by dogs and a post at each end. A small plate at each side of the Beams to take the bearing of the floor joists and a similar wall plate at each end next the kiln with a post in the centre. The floor to be cased with french deal - the boards laid in a contrary direction to the present floor boards. Doors and Windows to be repaired. New doors to the Chaise House. Fence from the Wall to the corner of the Cart lodge. Gates to the Yard next the small stable. Fence in front of the House and from the North West corner of the House to the stile - to enclose the back yard. Gates by the Road and some in the fields. Brewhouse to be repaired. Well to be sunk and Pump for the same.*
>
> *Mr Rayner states that the old chimney in the left side of the Hall was in so bad a state that it must be taken down if rebuilt in the same place*

> as the lower part had settled from the Beams that he could put his arm through - notwithstanding the weight of the upper part which hung upon the beams has pressed them down much out of a level - the new chimney was built at less expense than if the old had been restored - the old chimney had been at some former period much cut away below.

On 24 October 1834 the trustees at last approved the estimates and the final repairs went ahead. In a list headed 'Observations on the several Bills at Maplestead Hall' the following tradesmen are mentioned:

> E Allen for lime bricks, tiles and slates, H Hawkins for Smith's Work 'the most exorbitant Smith's Bill I have seen lately', H Drane for Smith's Work, R S Wilson - Plumber, Glazier and Painter, J Raynes - Bill for Clinkers, John Possel - Bill for Copper Troughs and Pipes, G Lufkin for Stone work, J Hilton for Bricks, Abraham Rayner for day's work Sawing, John Lewsey's Bricklayers Bill, John Butcher's Bill for Thatching.

With financial disputes out of the way James Brewster began to settle in to Maplestead Hall and concentrate on the business of running his estate.

In the countrywide survey and valuation known as the tithe apportionment, we find the following information for Maplestead Hall estate in 1841:

> Landowners: Joseph Clover, John Joseph Slater, Trustees of Davis Charity.
>
> Occupier: James Brewster
>
> 20   Smythies Field, arable, 14a 27p
>
> 31   Rosy Field, arable, 26a 3r 28p
>
> 35   Malting Piece, grass, 1a 2r 16p
>
> 36   Homestall, grass, 1a 3r 32p
>
> 37   Lawn and Pightle, grass, 3a 21p
>
> 38   Steeple Field, arable, 13a 1r 14p
>
> 88   Fallshams, arable, 6a 2r 33p
>
> 91   Pulleylands, arable, 16a 1r 5p
>
> 92   Hither lands, arable, 21a 1r 13p
>
> 108 Church Hook, arable, 8a 3r 13p
>
> 109 Church Yard, grass, 1a 3p
>
> 110 Pound Field, arable, 9a 32p

112 Little Mill Field, grass, 7a 3r 14p

113 Long Meadow, grass, 9a 3r 10p

114 Hither Chaldron, arable, 13a 1r 10p

115 Further Chaldron, arable, 12a 1r 28p

122 Part of Popes Mead, grass, 3a 1r 19p

123 Madges Hill, arable, 10a 3r 6p

124 Ozier Ground Piece, arable, 6a 1r 14p

125 Little Mill Field, arable, 13a 39p

126 Downwood Mead, arable, 2a 25p

127 Great Mill Field, arable, 16a 3r 5p

133 Hurrells Pent, arable, 8a 1r 19p

134 Little Easty, arable, 10a 2r 9p

135 The Ley, arable, 15a 2r 25p

136 Bell Field, arable, 11a 1r 18p

140 Lower Bricks Field, arable, 3a 2r 13p

141 Homestall, arable, 1a 11p

142 Bricks Pasture, grass, 3a 3r 1p

164 Bays Land Wood, wood, 1a 1r 18p

165 Bays Land Field, arable, 13a 2r 23p

177 Highwood Wood, wood, 39a 2r 25p

184 Great Easty Field, arable, 21a 1r 35p

185 Little Oxley, arable, 10a 3r 8p

186 Great Oxley, arable, 11a 3r 5p

214 Downwood Field, arable, 9a 35p

Total acreage: 382 acres 3 rods 12 poles. [see tithe map pages 218-219]

James Brewster was also listed as a landowner of:

54 occupied by William Bush and others, tenements

53 occupied by Samuel Bush, garden

111   occupied by John French, cottage

187   occupied by Ann Hart, cottage

116   occupied by James Brewster, part of Toldishall Field

He was also listed as the occupier of land belonging to Deans Hall.

James Brewster kept a series of account books for his farms. In the 'Accounts of Little Maplestead Farm 1841-2' there is a memorandum inside the front cover which shows his concern for the stomachs of his farm workers and tenants:

September 17 1841

The men had their harvest supper on the above day when I had cooked for them a large round of Beef and a large shoulder of Veal and some boiled Pork which proved just about sufficient for their being in number about 27 or 28 men and boys

October 18 1841

Gave my cottage Tenants their supper about 21 of them and cooked a large round of Beef, a small knuckle of Veal and some pork besides pudding but it was not sufficient without putting on some cold veal, must cook more another year.

Under the heading 'Particulars of Servants' we find the 'Workmen's Time Account' for the week ending 9 October 1841. This gives us an insight into the number and names of men employed and the variety of tasks being carried out on the farm at this time:

Wm Bush	*jobbing, brewing, 1 week's work, 12s*
Sam Bush	*carting manure, gardening, filling tumbrell in Chaldron, spreading in Chaldron, cutting bushes, jobbing, 5¾ day, 9s 7d*
Henry Nice	*as above and ploughing in Chaldron, 3 days, 6s 3¾d*
James Lot	*driving away Tumbrell out of Home Yard, carting and spreading manure, ploughing, driving away drill, 1 week, 10s 6d*
David Howard	*as above but also turning over dung in Pound Field, 1 week, 9s*
[ ] Davey	*as above but drilling for Willsmore, 4 days, 6s 8d*
[ ] Dixey	*Willsmore, ploughing, jobbing and spreading, 1 week, 10s*

Burkett	ploughing and spreading etc, 1 week, 8s
Curtis and Boy Moss	Hauling, carting, beating wood, shared, 14s 2d
Sam Willsmore	Harrowing, jobbing, driving Tumbrell to Yeldham, 4¼ days, 4s 11d
[ ] Patrick	filling Tumbrel in yard, hauming, turning over dung in Pound Field, 18s 2d
Joe Cockerton	howing turnips (did 8 acres) 15s
John Stuck senr	Thrashing wheat at Bricks, 18s 9d
John Stuck jun	Thrashing wheat at Deans Hall, 10s
Jabis Bishop	began to thrash wheat at Hall with his boys Tom, Ben, Jeff, £1 9d
George Bishop	hops, spreading, driving away drill, 2s 8d
Henry Cockerton	Thrashing wheat at Lodge, 8s.

By the time of the census for 1851, the farm at Maplestead Hall had expanded to employ some forty-three men and twelve boys and Brewster had taken on two farming pupils. However, by 1861 the number of employees had dropped dramatically:

John Dixey	hedging Steeple Field, ploughing Further Chaldron, sizing up 4 acres of Further Chaldron, 1 week's wages, 6s
James Saumons	strike furrows in Mill Field & as above, 10s 6d
William Howlett	ploughing, 5½ days, 8s 3d
John Mays	ploughing Hurrells Farm, Further Chaldron, 1 week, 8s
William Coe	Steaming, Hoeing turnips, 1¼ days, 2s 7½d
John French	Steaming, turning manure, 1¼ days, 2s 7½d
Sam. Bishop	Steaming at Hampers, hoeing, 2s 7½d
Mark Patrick	jobbing, hoeing mangolds, 1s 3d
[ ] Curtis	jobbing, steaming, 1s 3d
James Watkinson	ploughing, carting chaff, 1 week, 6s
Thomas Dixey	steaming, 1 week minding stock, 9s.

In Pigot's Directory for 1870 the trustees of the Davis Charity are listed as lords of the manor together with James Brewster Esq JP and are the principal landowners in Little Maplestead. But by 1871 James Brewster, now in his early sixties, had left Maplestead Hall and had moved to Ashford Lodge, on the Halstead road[27]. His son, Charles, had taken over the farm of 380 acres employing ten men and five boys[28]. At this time Charles Brewster was unmarried and sufficiently wealthy to be able to live on his own, looked after by two domestic servants, a married couple, together with their two sons.

In Charles Brewster's account book for 1871-72, the nine farm labourers working on the estate in September 1871 are listed, together with their weekly wages:

Dixey John	11s 6d for a week's work
Mays John	10s
Patrick Mark	7s 6d
Coe Alfred	11s 6d
French John	10s
Richer Isaac	10s
Cockerton Saml	10s
Fairbank Edw	10s
Curtis John	7s 6d

By the 1881 census, Charles Brewster was married with three sons and the acreage of the farm had increased slightly to 415 acres employing fifteen men and three boys. Ten years later, by the 1891 census, we see that Charles Brewster's family had increased. His three sons were not now living at home, they were most likely at boarding school, but he now had five daughters and besides his housemaid and cook he also had need of two nursemaids and a governess. It was probably around this date that Hall Cottages were built to house the farm foreman and the head cowman.

Charles Brewster continued to farm at Maplestead Hall for the next twenty-eight years. A memorial plate in the Round Church records the fact that there were Brewsters in the Hall from 1829 until 1919.

And so, with Charles Brewster, clearly a farmer who so whole-heartedly threw himself into every aspect of his work, an era drew to a close. When he died, the ancient and historic manor of Little Maplestead in the form of the Maplestead Hall estate was broken up into its constituent farms and copyhold properties. The charity that Joseph Davis had set up some two hundred years earlier had come to an end, its original religious and benevolent concept outdated and no longer viable. The separate village properties which consisted of a variety of farms, land, houses and cottages were all purchased from the Trustees of the Davis Charity and sold off independently.

Hall Cottages

THE BLOMFIELDS

ALFRED BLOMFIELD, who had been born in 1858 at Blamsters Farm in Halstead, purchased Maplestead Hall and its farm and moved in. The year was 1919. Alfred Blomfield, who had previously been living at Orange Hall, Gosfield, and had been agent to the Gosfield Hall Estate, farmed at Maplestead Hall until 1933, when his son Joseph Blomfield took over from him.

Joseph Blomfield and his wife Laura lived at Maplestead Hall for some fifty years. In his Memories Cecil Cook gives us glimpses of life at Hall Farm during the 1930s. He remembers how, before Mr Joe Blomfield bought a tractor, four sets of horses might be seen ploughing one field, taking a week to plough twenty acres; how sowing was done with horse-drawn seed drills and weeding was done with hoes and thistle hooks; how binders were used to harvest the corn which was then arranged in 'shocks' in the field before being carted off to be stored before threshing, done with the help of a portable steam engine. He also remembers Mr Blomfield's large herd of Friesian cows and how all the hedges round the pasture fields on Hall Farm had to be made cattle proof by 'laying' in the winter with special hand tools to make them thick and dense. The head cowman was Bill Simmonds, with three under-cowmen, Frank Simmonds, Claud Nichol, and Jim Wiseman, who had to milk by hand three times a day. The milk was bottled in the dairy and sold by means of two milk roundsmen, George Felton and Reg Simmonds, who went round Halstead and a third, George Page, who went round Sudbury. Milk was also sold to the local schools. After 1937 when electricity came to Little Maplestead, milking machines relieved the cowmen of some of the hard work and milk vans replaced the horse and cart.

Joseph Blomfield's sister, Helen, also has memories of Maplestead Hall during the Second World War when evacuees were taken in. These were twenty small children from a London nursery school with their matron and three helpers. They had been taken at very short notice and the first night they had no beds but had to sleep on hay-filled sacks. Next day Bill Simmonds drove up to London to get all the beds and then, in a real community effort, everyone took part in a rota to help care for the children who stayed for nine months.

Throughout the years Maplestead Hall, still very much the manor house of the village, regularly opened its doors to villagers. The annual Sunday school treat was always held there and parties were given there on national days of celebration. Cecil Cook remembers going there on the day of the 'King and Queen's Jubilee' in 1935 and in 1977 the present Queen's Silver Jubilee was marked in the same way with both occasions being hosted by Mr and Mrs Joseph Blomfield.

In 1982 Mr and Mrs Blomfield moved out of Maplestead Hall to live at Woodertons Farm, and Nigel Nott, Laura's nephew, and his wife Cathie came to live there with their two young sons, Iain and Andrew.

Notes to Chapter II

[1] Geoffrey Chaucer, *The Knight's Tale*
[2] Statistics from Asa Briggs, A *Social History of England* (London, 1983).
[3] Cartulary document no. 93
[4] *The Cartulary of the Knights of St John of Jerusalem*, ed. M Gervers (OUP, 1982) p xxvii, note 19
[5] Cartulary document no. 93
[6] William Wallen, *The History and Antiquities of The Round Church* (London, 1836)
[7] *Transactions of the Essex Archaelogical Society*, vol iii
[8] Information from various cartulary documents
[9] Essex County Council Department of Planning, Listed Building Register
[10] *The East Anglian, Notes and Queries*, vol 11, p157
[11] *Report of the possessions of the Hospital in England* made by Prior Philip de Thame to the Grand Master, 1338
[12] Cartulary document no. 243
[13] Cartulary document no. 92
[14] William Wallen, *The History and Antiquities of The Round Church*
[15] Essex County Council Department of Planning, Listed Building Register
[16] De Banco, Mich. 3 Edw. IV, 362
[17] Stow's *Annals*, p 579
[18] Document in Essex Record Office, D/DU 463/5
[19] Reverend Philip Morant, *History and Antiquities of the County of Essex* (reprinted 1978, Wakefield)
[20] Essex County Council Department of Planning, Listed Building Register
[21] Document in ERO, D/DDd M6
[22] Reverend Philip Morant, *History and Antiquities of the County of Essex*
[23] *The Annals of Agriculture*, 1804-1808
[24] *The Maplesteads*, WEA booklet, 1986
[25] Document in ERO, D/DOp B6/5
[26] Document in ERO, D/DOp B6/1
[27] Information from census, ERO
[28] Information from census, ERO

TWELFTH-CENTURY EVENTS

1100 Henry I becomes king

1135 Stephen becomes king, period of civil war

1147 Second Crusade sets out, ends in failure

1154 Henry II becomes king

1167 Oxford University founded

1170 Thomas à Becket, Archbishop of Canterbury, murdered

1174 Saladin launches a Holy War of all Muslims against Christians

1187 Saladin recaptures Jerusalem

1189 Richard I becomes king

1190 Third Crusade begins led by Richard I, the Lionheart, and Philip of France

1191 Crusaders take Acre

1192 Richard concludes armistice with Saladin

1199 John becomes king

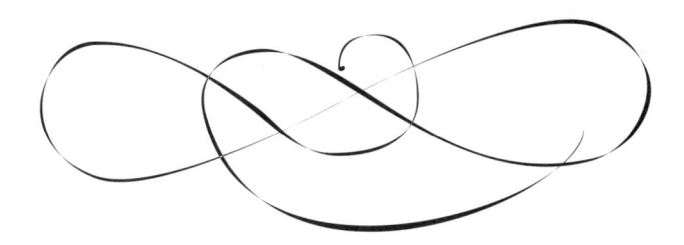

Inside the Round Church, 1807, before Victorian renovations

CHAPTER III

THE THIRTEENTH CENTURY

*After these things
the abbot caused an inquiry to be
made throughout each manor, concerning the annual
quit rents from the freemen,
and the names of the labourers and their tenements
and the services due from each:
and he put all this in writing.*[1]

IN 1215 King John set seal to the Magna Carta, the most famous document in English history. Civil war and unrest in the land, in a large part due to ever-increasing taxation, had led to a meeting between king and barons at Runnymede. There the king was forced to agree to a detailed programme of government reform which took the form of a charter of liberties which eventually became a potent symbol of men's struggle for freedom and human rights. The charter embodied, for the first time, the principle that the king was subject to the law and it also established that liberties were held in common by all men: anyone who had been unjustly deprived of lands, castles, liberties or rights was to have them restored, anyone fined unjustly was to be compensated and no man was to be imprisoned, deprived of his lands, outlawed or exiled except by due process of the law.

ROBERT DE VERE

ONE OF THE barons responsible for confronting the king with Magna Carta was Robert de Vere, third Earl of Oxford, whose castle at Hedingham was close to Little Maplestead. Besides being the local tenant-in-chief who held land in the village, the earl had taken part in the Crusades and was probably well-known to the villagers of Little Maplestead as he journeyed to and from his castle perhaps making occasional visits to the Knights of St John of Jerusalem at L'Hospital to whom he had made generous grants of land and rent.

However, Robert de Vere paid dearly for the humiliation of King John; along with many others, he was excommunicated. This rebellious group of barons then retaliated by offering the crown to Louis, the French dauphin, whose troops came to

LITTLE MAPLESTEAD in

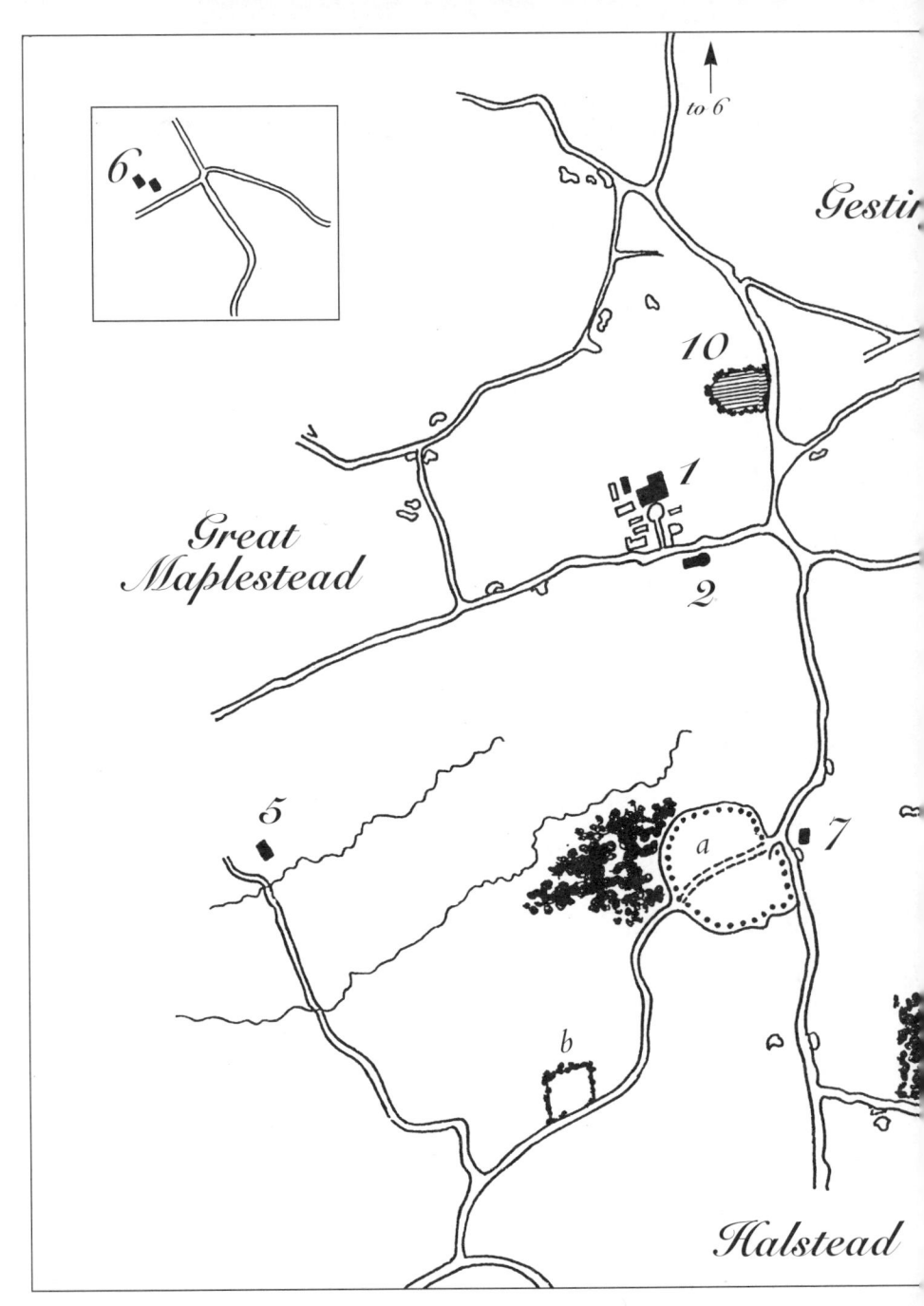

- 52 -

THIRTEENTH CENTURY

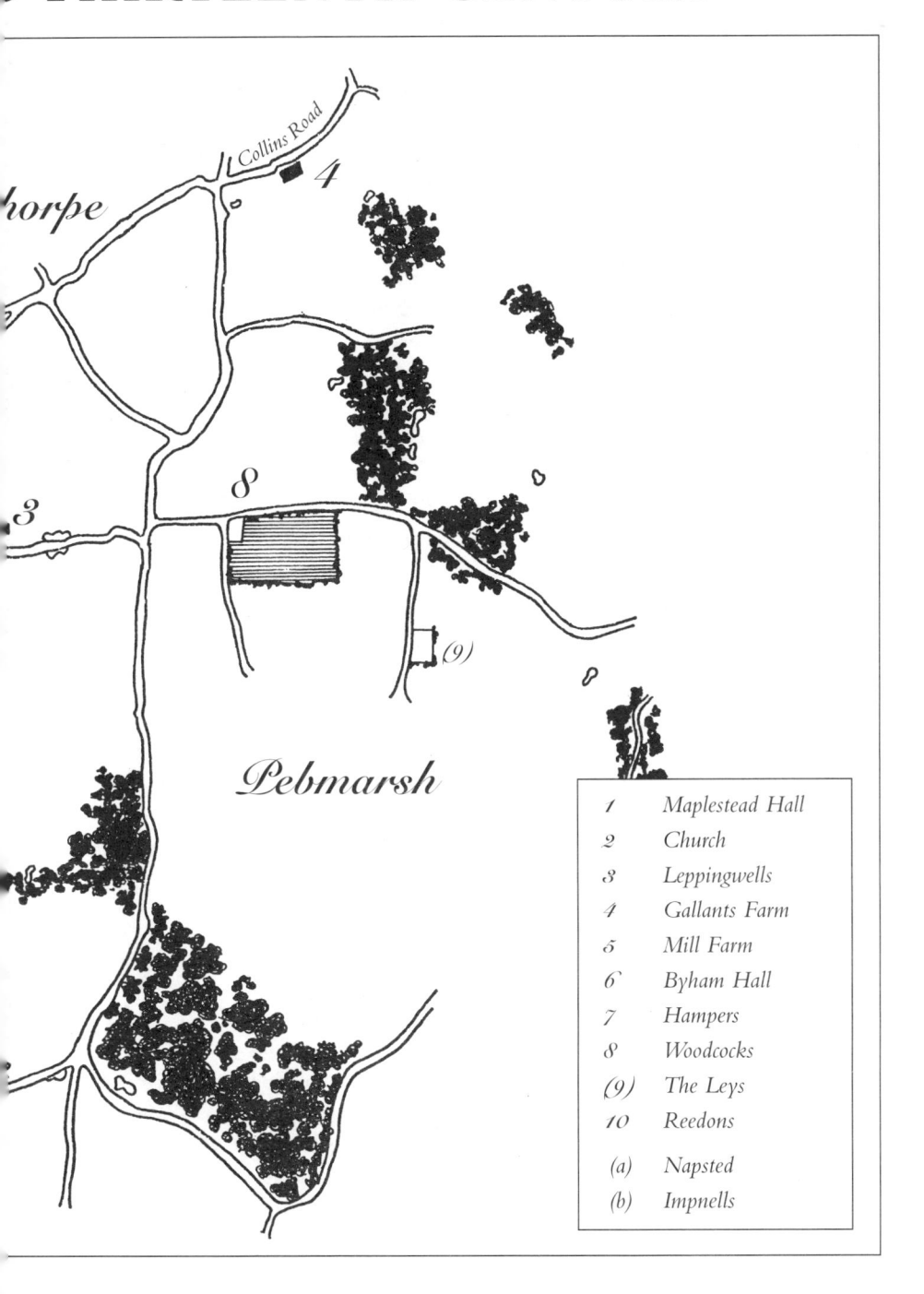

Pebmarsh

1	Maplestead Hall
2	Church
3	Leppingwells
4	Gallants Farm
5	Mill Farm
6	Byham Hall
7	Hampers
8	Woodcocks
(9)	The Leys
10	Reedons
(a)	Napsted
(b)	Impnells

England and, encouraged by the rebel noblemen, occupied Colchester Castle as a first step to seizing power. But King John besieged the castle and the French surrendered. The king then turned his wrath on Robert de Vere and set siege to his castle at Hedingham which, after a long and fierce resistance, eventually fell. The earl then suffered the confiscation of all his lands. A year later, in 1216, the French retaliated and besieged Hedingham Castle, retaking it for Robert de Vere after a desperate struggle. Fortunately for the earl, a few months later King John died and the new king, Henry III, restored all the earl's lands to him.

Whilst the villagers of Little Maplestead may not have felt any obvious and immediate benefit from the signing of the Magna Carta, the fact that their local tenant-in-chief was so implicated in its enforcement must have affected them. Suddenly the stability of their particular feudal system was shaken and they must have been afraid of the upheaval which was going on all around them; they would have been horrified when the fighting came to their very doorstep with the besieging of the earl's castle in Hedingham by the king's troops. All, whether peasants or lords, were ultimately servants of the great tenant-in-chief Robert de Vere who had vast influence and control over their lives. The villagers must have been afraid that they too would suffer at the hands of the king's army but they were fortunate that their lord of the manor was the master of L'Hospital, someone who would not readily be usurped. When King John died, in October 1216, it must have been to the great relief of all the villagers that Robert de Vere had all his lands returned to him by Henry III and the *status quo* was restored. Part of the earl's lands were those of Byham Hall.

BYHAM HALL

BYHAM HALL has an ancient history stretching back at least to the beginning of the thirteenth century. Always a farm, the house, partly rebuilt in the sixteenth century incorporates part of a fifteenth-century building. However this fifteenth-century building[2] was most probably built on the site of an even older house. There is a well which may be of medieval origin. The name Byham is Anglo-Saxon and means 'Beage's Farm'[3] or 'the land of Beage or Beaga', a woman's name, short for Beagmund[4]. The land belonging to Byham has always been shared between the three parishes of Little and Great Maplestead and Gestingthorpe.

The earliest reference to the name Byham in the Cartulary of the Knights of St John is dated around 1214-21[5]. Robert de Vere, Earl of Oxford, was the owner of *'terra de Beyham in parochia de parva Mapeltrestede'* (the land belonging to Byham in the parish of Little Maplestead). Robert Hildehard was a sub-tenant who owned all or part of Byham's land and the earl granted his rent of two shillings to the Hospitallers.

> *Grant in free alms[6] by Earl Robert de Vere to the Hospitallers of the 2s rent which Robert son of Richard Hildehard[7] owed for the land of Byham in Little Maplestead.*

There is however an even earlier reference to Byham dated 1203 in the property list called the *Feet of Fines*. Here Walter de Crepping, the owner of the demesne or home farm, had sub-let 'one messuage and two acres of land' to his tenant William FitzSabin. Later, around 1220, we have reference to a grove held by Wulfmaer of Byham[8] and again around 1240, to Wulmerus de Hehham holding *'terre de Behham'*. It is probable that Wulfmaer was another sub-tenant.

Byham Hall

Then in 1245 we have the first mention of 'Basilie de Beyham' [Basilia of Byham] concerning two-and-a-quarter acres of land which she had bought from Robert Hawenild[9]. Basilia is also named in a grant by her father, William Joy of Little Maplestead, to the Hospitallers of:

> *...all his lands with rents in Gestingthorpe, Halstead and Little Maplestead ...in Little Maplestead the fields of Alfledesfield, Cherleye and Storiesfield, Gosemere croft, 1 dole on Kuckelawe, 1 on Middlefield and 7 acres called Basiliesland [Basilia's land]. In addition the annual rent of 6d from Basilia of Byham, 10d from Hugh son of Goddard, 6d from Gunnilda Howe, 1d from Andrew of Orsett, 1d from Basilia, William's sister, 8d from Walter the butler, 5d from Walter the baker, and $^1/_2$ lb of cumin from Robert Hawenild and his wife[10]...*

Basilia was now a sub-tenant farming the land of Byham and she is not the only thirteenth-century woman landowner we shall come across.

In 1255[11] Basilia de Begham is again mentioned in connection with a wood - *in bosco de Begham*. In this legal document the Hospitallers received the right to raise a ditch in Byham Wood in Great Maplestead to separate the land granted to them by Basilia of Byham from her own land. Like a number of other Hospitallers' orders, extra income was derived from the keeping of sheep[12] and the Maplestead Order of Hospitallers had its own livestock. This proposed ditch was to prevent livestock straying.

By 1275 Byham had grown to become a hamlet, *hameletto qui vocatur Bestham*[13] and at this time there is a record of a meadow called *Pole medwe* which name may be reflected in the present-day meadow Pale Close.

In 1339 Robert Pierpont, chaplain to Richard of Othulvesho[14] from Gestingthorpe, is described as lord of Byham manor, *manerii de Bethham*, in a legal document concerning an eighteen-foot-broad way which ran between Joy's Pightle and Odewell lane and crossed the land of Byham manor. An agreement was reached in which the Hospitallers had a right of way across Byham land via this track. In 1383[15], not for the first time, this right of way was under dispute. At this date the lords of the manor of Byham were Robert of Muskham and Thomas Sewale. Another agreement was drawn up whereby the prior of the Hospitallers was given right of way for livestock and carriage between his manors of Little Maplestead and Odewell across the land of Byham manor. It would seem that both Robert and Thomas held a share of Byham's land; we know that Thomas Sewale held his part from William de Ufford, Earl of Suffolk, who already held land in Gestingthorpe and at this date most of Byham's land was considered to be in Gestingthorpe.

By 1418 Robert Sexton of Lavenham held part of the manor of Byham and it continued to be held by his family until 1594 when it was bought by George Coe of Gestingthorpe. Coe died in 1625 'possessed of a capital messuage and farm called Byham-hall held of the manor of Overhall in Gestingthorpe'. It passed down through the Coe family until in 1751 Byham Hall was in the hands of the Robinson family from Earls Colne and by 1761 rented to a relative, David Rist.

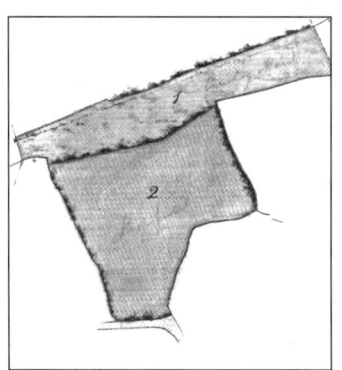

Byham Hall 1817

By the time of the survey of the village in 1817 Osgood Gee Esq owned Byham Hall and Charles Townsend was the tenant farmer. The farm owned two fields in Little Maplestead (numbers 1 and 2).

- 56 -

By 1841 at the tithe apportionment, Mary Gee had succeeded Osgood Gee and the land was farmed by Robert Townsend. The fields in Great Maplestead were listed on the tithe map as follows:

    312 Buckland

    313 East Lodge Field

    315 Homestall and chase

    316 Orchard

    317 Pale Close

    337 Church field

    338 Little Sudbury

    341 7 acre ley

    342 8 acre field

    343 Byham Hall field

In the 1841 census Robert Townsend, aged 30, is listed along with his wife, Eliza, young children Frederick, Clara and Emily and a servant-girl, Hannah Smith. Twenty years later, at the 1861 census, Henry Myhill, 45, was farming 243 acres at Byham Hall, employing fourteen labourers and three boys; his wife was Eliza and he had three young children. Henry Myhill also employed a governess, Lavinia Fitch, a nursemaid, Mary Ann Wright and a house servant, Ann Moore. By 1871 Thomas Beddall, 30, was farming the 243 acres at Byham Hall employing ten men and three boys; his wife was Sarah and they were living with her sister Eliza Jennings. In 1882 the owner of Byham Hall was local farmer Arthur Bentall Collis who also farmed Odewells where he had been living and farming for more than ten years. In 1881 Collis was decribed as a corn and seed merchant and farmer of 700 acres employing forty labourers and nine boys and in the 1881 census Byham Hall was occupied by Jonathan Pawsey, who was one of Collis's agricultural labourers. In 1888 after the death of her husband Sarah Collis sold the estate of Byham Hall to the Brewsters at Maplestead Hall. There was a reference to Byham's ancient history in the sale catalogue where it was described as the 'reputed manor'. By 1891 another farm labourer was occupying Byham Hall, this was George Whiting who lived there with his wife Elizabeth.

At about this date the records show that Byham Hall, Deans Hall and Maplestead Hall formed harvesting companies each year. Their harvesting books show that they co-ordinated their harvesting and kept detailed records of their daily progress and the weather. In the account books for Deans Hall, Byham Hall is included and incorporates School Farm[16].

In 1919, along with many other village properties, the estate of 223 acres with its 'ample and substantially built farm premises' was sold off privately by the Brewsters.

THIRTEENTH-CENTURY VILLAGERS

AT THE BEGINNING of the thirteenth century the population of England stood at about four million. This represented an amazing increase of almost four-fold since Domesday, a period of less than 150 years. This population explosion had a far reaching and profound effect on the lives of all - whether lords or peasants - but it was the peasant farmer who was most affected as he strove to exist by tilling his small plot of land. An increase in poverty was inevitable and, as the village settlements began to become overpopulated, so the people were forced to bring into cultivation poorer quality 'waste' land such as marshes and water-logged areas, so that they could continue to try to support their families.

However the villagers of Little Maplestead seem to have been protected against the worst effects of the population increase by the wealth of the community of knights in their midst. Indeed the picture gained from records of the village at this time is one of considerable wealth and affluence as L'Hospital continued to receive more and more local land, mainly by gift. The wealth of the foundation inevitably spread out into the community at large and the villagers benefited from increased opportunities for employment and trade. From the cartulary we have records of Rose the laundress, Roger the butcher, William the cook, Walter the baker, Walter the butler and two smiths, Laurence and William. Surprisingly perhaps, some of these individuals are recorded as making grants of land or property to the Hospitallers or, as in the case of Rose the laundress, the rent from a simple tenement in the village:

> Grant in free alms ... by Rose of Little Maplestead, laundress, to the Hospitallers, of all right in the tenement she held in that vill.

It is unlikely that such individuals could normally have afforded to give away their property, even for the promise of eternal life, and it is probable that they were encouraged to do so by the offer of free board at L'Hospital in return for their service. Rose's services, of course, would have been essential to L'Hospital.

Local freemen farmers also strove to make gifts of land to the knights:

> Grant by John of Harlow and Avice his wife to the Hospitallers of the small meadow in Little Maplestead called Hokholt.[17]

Grants could also include spices which were at that time precious commodities brought back by the Knights from the Holy Land:

> Grant in free alms by Ralph, son of Hugh of Hosden, to the Hospitallers of the 1lb of cumin or 1d rent which the Order used to pay him for the land formerly held by Fabian, son of Warin Long of Little Maplestead.

REEDONS

ANOTHER GRANT to the Hospitallers concerned a piece of land called Riedpihitell[18] - or Reed Pightle[19]. And in 1230 Walter of Little Maplestead made a grant to William the cook of Riedpihitell croft in Little Maplestead. This means that for all of its history of nearly 1000 years there has been a pightle, croft or field called Reedons in Little Maplestead. It was once part of Hurrells Farm and it is clearly named in the 1817 survey of the village when it was owned by George Firmin who used it to grow hops.

In April 1997, for the first time on Reedons, the building of a house was begun by the owners of the field, Mr and Mrs Rees. They have a honey farm, the latest use for the ancient site.

THE EVOLUTION OF THE VILLAGE COMMUNITY

AS THE THIRTEENTH CENTURY progressed the demands put on the land by the rapid increase in population inevitably resulted in the soil becoming exhausted and agricultural yields gradually began to fall. Monasteries often led the way in good agricultural management and it is likely that L'Hospital was no exception. Landowners and farmers switched from a two-field to a three-field crop rotation; this accommodated all new land brought into cultivation and reduced the amount of fallow needed. Changes in cropping were also carried out and fertilizing increased; farmers realized it was better to use fresh seed corn every year and that it benefited the soil to grow more peas, beans and vetches. As farming practices developed, some lords began to employ a hayward - an active overseer whose job it was to check woods, crops and meadows to make sure they were being farmed properly. We know from contemporary documents that the knights employed both a bailiff and a steward to oversee the numerous tenants and ensure the smooth running of the estate and the manor of Little Maplestead was very likely in the forefront of good agricultural practice.

At this time the village of Little Maplestead, with perhaps a four-fold increase in population, would have consisted of half-a-dozen substantial small-holdings farmed by freemen and an increasing number of rough and ready peasant cottage dwellings, built of mud and clay with thatched roofs, sparsely furnished but with patches of garden and fruit trees. These humble dwellings would most probably have been scattered along what are now Gestingthorpe, Oak and School Roads and would have been in stark contrast to L' Hospital, which together with its barns and outbuildings would have been built of superior materials with better roofing. As we have seen, the villagers were subordinated to this religious community, just as they would have been to an individual lord, and we know that they paid a voluntary contribution to L'Hospital. Despite Magna Carta there were still many constraints on the individual - status remained fundamental, there was no protection for the villein against eviction, no damages against the lord. But things were changing, over the period as a whole labour dues were, bit by bit, being commuted to wages, grants of freedom were on the increase and with this came the ability to trade.

WILLIAM JOY

ONE OF THE villagers at this time, a freeman who was an exceptional individual, was William Joy II. He was the son of William Joy and had a wife Elizabeth, daughters Basilia (of Byham) and Evelyn, a son William III and a godson Luke, a clerk. His mother was a Spanish woman, Gila, whose nationality may account for the field in the village called Spanish field. It is possible that Gila was brought to the village from Spain by William Joy I.

William Joy II was responsible for many land transactions, for instance:

> Grant by William Joy of Little Maplestead to Luke the clerk, his godson, of 4 acres with ditches and hedges in Little Maplestead called Wallcroft and Spitelcroft, rendering homage and service, 20d annually and 50s sterling as gersum (10s of which is for William's wife, Elizabeth). Witness Roberto de Panimere.[20]

However the most interesting fact about William Joy is revealed in his grant dated 1245[21] in free alms to

> the Hospitallers of 2d rent to light the chapel of St John the Baptist in Little Maplestead which 2d rent his daughter Evelyn owed him for the $1/2$ acre of land he gave her before going on pilgrimage to Jerusalem.

William Joy, a wealthy village freeholding farmer, had decided to make the long and arduous pilgrimage to Jerusalem, possibly accompanying a group of knights from L'Hospital. On his safe return he had granted to the Hospitallers a sum of money which had accrued while he was away to buy candles to light what was described as the knights' chapel of St John the Baptist. As we know, the early church, built on land originally given by Walter Poulain[22], was dedicated to All Saints and from the records we know that this same church was still being used in 1240. However, by 1245 it had been rebuilt or altered to the round form, re-dedicated and was referred to as *capella sancti Johannis Baptiste*[23] a dedication retained to the present day.

It is quite possible that the rare form of the Round Church may have resulted from William Joy's pilgrimage to Jerusalem when the spiritual goal of his journey would have been the Anastasis rotunda of the church of the Holy Sepulchre. On his return William Joy may have encouraged the alteration of the existing church to incorporate a new rotunda, perhaps even financing part of the building to give thanks for his safe return, and his granting of two pence to light the chapel may have been to celebrate the dedication of the new structure. At this date, two pence would have been approximately a day's wages for a labourer.

WOODCOCKS

THE OLD NAME of this house, now re-named Plum House, may reflect the name of a thirteenth-century villager mentioned in the cartulary. He was William Woodcock and he was listed as a witness to one of the many grants. There are no early records for Woodcocks but at the 1817 survey of the village it was owned by John Sewell and occupied by Daniel Roberts and Joseph Bryant.

At the 1841 tithe award the cottage was owned by George de Horne Vaizey and was occupied by James Wicker. In 1871 James Watkinson, 39, a carpenter, lived there with his wife Rebecca, eldest son James, 18, who was a groom, four younger sons and a daughter. The cottage was shared with the Bartholomew family, Charles, an agricultural labourer, his wife Mary Ann, son George, also an agricultural worker, younger son William, and daughter Louisa, a silk weaver. By 1881 the Watkinsons were still at Woodcocks with a family of five sons and three daughters, the eldest son at home was Arthur, a farm labourer. A second family shared the cottage, Walter Downs, a farm labourer, his wife Emma and their two young children. Ten years later, in 1891, we still find James and Rebecca Watkinson, with only two children now remaining at home, Nathaniel, 18, who was a weaver and a daughter Jessie, 14. Walter and Emma Downs were also still at Woodcocks with daughter Ellen, 13, and son Joshua, 11.

COLLINS ROAD

THIS ROAD probably owes its name to another thirteenth-century villager, John Colyn, who is mentioned in the cartulary in 1230. His name is also remembered in a deed made in 1667 between John Parke, from Parks Farm, and John Cooke concerning a messuage or tenement called Collens. There are further references to fields called Great Collens and Little Collens; and we know that later, in 1873, Collins Field was occupied by Edward Willsmore who rented it to Frederick Mayes, a yearly tenant with no written agreement.

THE WOOL TRADE

BY THE END of the thirteenth century England was producing the best wool in Europe and even the most ordinary arable farm had sheep in abundance. We know that the Hospitallers kept flocks but it was not just the lords of the manor and smaller farmers who dealt in wool; the peasant farmers too began to keep a few sheep. As the thirteenth century came to a close the home production of cloth from the wool was beginning to take place and this was later to become an increasingly important part of village life. As more cloth was produced at home by peasant spinners and weavers there would be less need to export the raw wool overseas and import cloth: a period of substantial economic activity was just dawning for certain parts of the country, especially East Anglia, as wool was spun and woven by villagers, sent to local fulling-mills for thickening and then dyed before selling. We know that the villagers of Little Maplestead were part of the emergence of this new trade and there is an early record of a dyer in the village.

IMPNELLS

IN 1275 a grant was made by Richard son of Roger of Impnells, dyer, of two acres of land at Impnells[24]. Impnells is one of the 'lost' houses of Little Maplestead but we know its likely site. In the 1693 manor book for Maplestead Hall there is an entry for 'a certain field called Impnells, 5 acres, near the Starch-house gate'. Starch-house is another lost house but we know where it was and we can therefore place Impnells near Starch-house in the manor of Napsted. To date there is no satisfactory interpretation of the name, Impnells.

HAMPERS

ANOTHER HOUSE anciently sited in the lost manor of Napsted is Hampers and it was possibly the original manor house.

Hampers was built late in the fifteenth century, with later alterations and additions[25]. However, its site may be that of an even older house which could have been built for a special purpose.

Hampers was probably named after an occupant bearing the name of le Hanaper. The name derives from *hanapier*[26] which is Old French for a maker of two-handled goblets. These had to be kept in special crates called *hanapiers* which gave rise to a second meaning, 'hanaper or container especially for documents or money', and it is this meaning that is reflected in the present-day name. Hamper was a widely used contraction of *hanaper*.

The earliest reference to such an occupant is found in 1291 where we have John le Hanaper as a witness to an agreement concerning the Hospitallers[27]. Later, in the lay subsidy levied in 1327[28], we find Joan la Hanyper, who could have been the widow of John.

In the king's court there was a department of chancery called the Hanaper. It was responsible for handling the fees due for the sealing and enrolment of charters and for storing them and it was so called because the documents were kept in the special *hanapier* baskets already described. It is highly likely that John le Hanaper was in fact a clerk who fulfilled a similar roll, taking fees and storing documents on behalf of the Hospitallers. They certainly must have had need of such a person; there are at least 951 Hospitaller documents in the cartulary, most of them grants of land. The fact that these are still in existance bears witness to the care with which they were all kept. Hanaper's, commonly contracted to Hampers, must have been the house where all the documents would have been safely stored.

As we have seen Hampers was probably situated in the lost manor of Napsted. In fact the records show that in 1220 there was a way leading from Little Maplestead church to Napsted, *chemin ... ecclesia de Parva Mapultrestede versus Napsted*[29] and it is tempting to believe that this is marked today by the footpath which runs from directly from Hampers across the fields to the church. This also lends weight to the theory that the house was closely associated with the Hospitallers.

Later, the records show Hampers, now a small farm, passing freehold down through the centuries[30]. Its owners included:

> *John Hale owning One tenement and certain lands thereto belonging called Hempers, 19 May 16 Eliz. [1574].*
>
> *Thomas Hale owning One messuage called Hempers and Diverse lands thereto belonging, 23 April 1661 and again in 12 October 1669.*
>
> *John Hale owning One tenement called Hempers and Diverse lands, 9 October 1677.*
>
> *Mary, wife of John Leake owning One tenement called Hempers and Diverse lands thereto belonging. On the death of previous owner John ffrench. 16 January 1687.*
>
> *John Tyler owning A messuage and lands called Hempers. Alienation: John Leake. 22 December 1701.*
>
> *Isaac Tyler owning a A farm called Hampers late of John Leake. Death: John Tyler. 20 October 1739.*
>
> *John Cock owning A messuage or tenement called Hempers and Diverse lands thereto belonging. Alienation: Jemima Tyler. 13 June 1767.*

The use of the spelling 'Hempers' probably reflects the pronuncication of the time. A reference[31] to Thomas Hale in 1661 reveals the following incident:

> *5 August 1661. James Bowles of Great Maplestead, labourer, on 26 December, 12 Chas II, there about 3 am broke into the house of Thomas*

Hale and stole a 'woman's headdressing' worth 6d, four linen caps worth 12d, 'one greene say apron' worth 12d, two linen aprons worth 2s, three shirts worth 12s, two smocks worth 4s, and two petticoats worth 15s.

In the 1817 survey of Little Maplestead we find the part of Hempers Farm in the village owned by the landlord John Turner with fields:

    145   James field

    218   Foots

    219   p/o Moses Ley

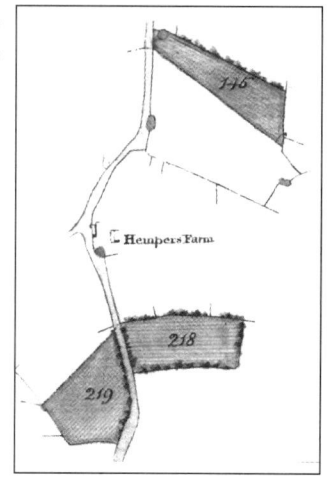

In the 1841 tithe award for Great Maplestead the house, the farm and its land were owned by Hannah Turner and were occupied by John Hart. By this time the holding was a small arable farm of some fifty-six acres.

    392   Bryants Field
    395   Barn Yard
    397   Barn Field
    398   Kiln Field
    400   Moss Ley
    401   Front Field
    402   Little Field
    403   The Homestall
    404   The Orchard
    405   Upper Malling Field
    406   Lower Malling Field
    407   Newmans Pightle
    408   James Field
    411   Gooseberry Field[32]
    412   Woody Field
    413   Hilly Field

Hampers 1817

The occupants of Hampers Farm according to the 1841 census were John Hart, aged 40, a farmer, Mary, his wife, aged 35, and Mary Chifnell, aged 15, a female servant. By 1861 Hampers Farm was occupied by Samuel Bush, aged 43, an agricultural labourer, Sarah, his wife, aged 52, a straw-plaiter, their three sons of 19, 17 and 12 who were all agricultural labourers and their daughter Hannah who was 15 years old and a straw-plaiter like her mother.

In 1871 the house was clearly home to two families: the Bushes had been joined by Charles and Mary Patrick, aged 26 and 20, an agricultural labourer and a silk factory hand-weaver. Mary probably worked at the silk factory in Halstead. Samuel Bush was listed as an (farm) engine driver, and his two elder sons seem to have left home. However Hannah and his youngest son John, still working on the land, were living with their parents; Hannah and her mother were still listed as straw-plaiters.

A note in the margin of the 1881 census tells us that in 1885 Hampers was to be transferred to the parish of Little Maplestead. At this time the house was occupied by James Pearman, 44, a farm engine driver, his wife and their three small sons. Ten years later the occupants of the house were William Cant, a widower aged 89, his daughter Emma, 44, an unmarried laundress, and his two grandsons, Arthur Coe, 16, a baker's assistant, and Walter Cant, aged 12.

In the sale catalogue of 1919 when Hampers, with many other properties in the village, was put up for sale it was described as an old fashioned gabled brick, timber, plaster and tiled farm house 'now used as two cottages'. The farm premises included poultry houses, a two-bayed thatched barn, a granary, a loose box, stabling for four horses, a chaff house, a horse shed and horse yard, a drill shed, a wagon shed, an implement shed, a carpenter's shop, a timber shed and a concrete sheep-dipping and washing bath in the adjoining paddock.

THE LEYS FARM

YET ANOTHER house now lost to the village was The Leys farmhouse. Its name probably derives from La Leghe or La Leys, a field name mentioned in a thirteenth-century grant.[33]

The early history of The Leys is unknown but by the 1817 survey of the village the proprietor was Thomas Sewell and the tenant farmer was Samuel Hart.

Not all fields were named and only those that were are listed here:

110	Pages Croft
152	Bell Meadow
153	Bell field
159	Woodcocks
170	Three Acres
171	House and homestead

172	The Chase
173	The Malting Place
174	p/o Five Acres
188	Perry field
190	Seven Acre Ley
191	Four Acre Ley

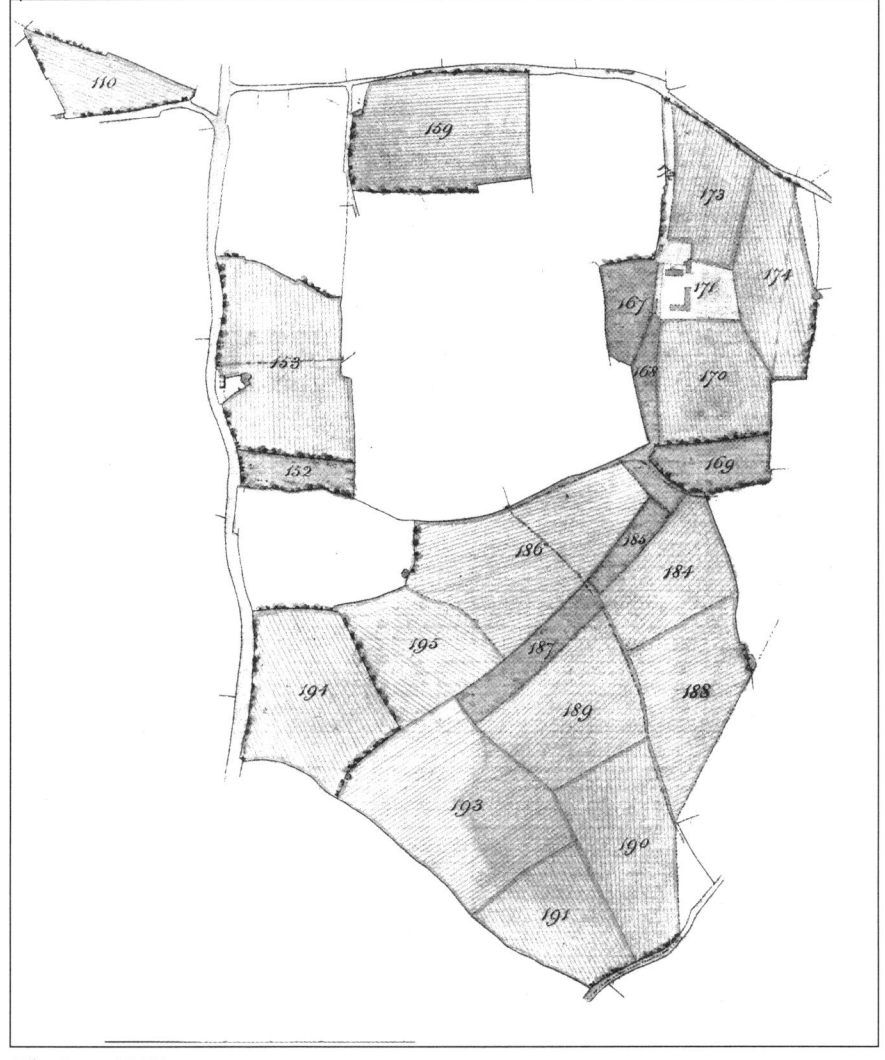

The Leys 1817

At the 1841 tithe award, (see map pages 218-219) Thomas Sewell was named as the proprietor and Thomas Richbell was the tenant farmer:

100	Pages Cross
138	Bell Meadow
139	Bell Field
144	Woodcock Field
154	pasture
155	Chase Pasture
156	Three Acre field
157	Homestall
158	Chase
159	Malting Piece
160	part of Five Acres
167	field
169	field
170	field
171	field
172	field
173	field
174	field
175	part of Seven Acre Field
176	Four Acre Ley
178	field
179	field
180	field

99 acres

At the 1841 census Samuel Richbell, 45, a farmer, was recorded as living alone at The Leys.

In a sale catalogue[34] of the 'freehold valuable estate called The Lyes' dated 24 June 1845 we find the following description:

> *Timber and tiled messuage, parlour, keeping room, kitchen, dairy, 4 bedrooms, attics, cellar, coal place, detached bake office. Timber and tiled 2 floor malting, now granary. 2 timber and thatched barns, stable, cow house, calf pens, piggeries, cistern, gardens, orchards, 106 acres, excellent arable, rich old pasture. Surrounded by turnpike and other good roads. Abutts on to lands of George de Horne Vaizey and James Brewster. This valuable property has been for many years in the occupation of Mr Thomas Richbell, a highly respected tenant who has 8 years unexpired lease.*

The property was purchased at the sale by George de Horne Vaizey for £3360.

In a deed dated 1870 The Lyes, as it was sometimes spelled, was rented to John Ray Shave of Bures for a term of sixteen years. The fields listed were:

> *Perry field, Lyes meadow, Pond meadow, Pond bottom, the Chase and the Homestead, Parlour meadow and the orchard, London field, Four acres, Three acres, Upper orchard, Malthouse, Stebbing field and part of Claypits.*

At the 1871 census John Ray Shave farmed the sixty-four acres and lived at The Leys with his wife, Sarah, and three daughters. Ten years on Sarah was a widow and had taken over the farm with the help of her daughter, Ellen, who was described as a farm labourer. In 1891 Sarah Shave, now 80 years old, was still described as a farmer and still had the help of her unmarried daughter Ellen.

In Cecil Cook's *Memories* he writes that in 1923 his aunts and uncles lived at The Leys farm. One of his uncles was head horseman. He remembers the 'large house with attics above the bedrooms, large cellar and large barn for six cart-horses.' The house was pulled down in the late 1950s.

THE FOUNDING OF PARLIAMENT

AS WE HAVE SEEN, the thirteenth century started with the Magna Carta. The signing of this document in 1215 gave rise, towards the end of the century, to the founding of the true English parliament where, besides great lords, bishops and abbots, the 'commons' began to be summoned. These were the knights and townsmen who had begun to demonstrate their power and growing consequence in the local community. This broader cross-section of people in parliament was to result in a greater control over the king and taxation and ultimately the development of a more complex society with a richer culture in which significantly, English dialects began to climb back up the social scale. For the first time in their history, the simple peasants of Little Maplestead were on the brink of having their voices heard.

Thirteenth-century inhabitants of Little Maplestead taken from the Hospitallers' cartulary

- Agnes daughter of Laurence the smith
- Alfreda wife of Walter Loveday
- Avice wife of Laurence the smith
- Basilia daughter of William Joy II
- Beatrice mother of Simon of Narford
- Catherine of Panimere, wife of John Helewise
- Christine Prudhomme daughter of William the smith, wife of Stephen Prudhomme
- Elizabeth wife of William Joy II
- Evelyn daughter of William Joy II
- Fabian son of Warin Long
- Hugh, brother, chaplain
- Hugh Joy I
- Joan wife of Richard Wood
- John the chaplain, priest
- John Colyn
- John I, son of Hugh Joy
- Laurence the smith
- Matilda, wife of Robert of Harlow, freeman
- Richard Friar the chaplain
- Richard Wood
- Richard de Wolfhale, brother, preceptor
- Robert of Harlow, freeman, brother of Sarah
- Rose the laundress
- Sarah, sister of Robert of Harlow
- Simon of Narford, son of Beatrice
- Thomas atte Portweye
- Thomas son of John the chaplain
- Walter the parson
- William the cook
- William Hakin

William of Panimere

William Prudhomme the smith

Notes to Chapter III

1. *The Chronicles of Jocelin of Brakelond,* ed. H. E. Butler
2. Essex County Council Department of Planning, Listed Building Register
3. P.H.Reaney, *The Place-names of Essex,* (CUP, 1969)
4. *The Concise Oxford Dictionary of Place-names,* 2nd edition (Oxford, 1940)
5. Cartulary document no. 95
6. See Glossary (page 220)
7. See Field names (Page 222)
8. Cartulary document no. 689
9. Cartulary document no. 189
10. Cartulary document no. 112
11. Cartulary document no. 540
12. Trevor Rowley, *The High Middle Ages* (Glasgow, 1988), p309
13. Cartulary document no. 901
14. A Gestingthorpe family who farmed much of the Hospitallers' land
15. Cartulary document no. 211
16. Document in Essex Record Office, D/DU 1558/8
17. See Field names (Page 222)
18. See Field names (Page 222)
19. See Glossary (page 220)
20. Cartulary document no. 108; see also Field names page 222
21. Cartulary document no. 107
22. Cartulary document nos. 155-159
23. Cartulary document no. 107
24. Cartulary document no. 673
25. Essex County Council Department of Planning, Listed Building Register
26. P.H. Reaney, *The Origin of English Surnames*
27. Cartulary documents, nos. 641-2
28. *The Lay Subsidy of 1327,* ed. Jennifer Ward, Essex Historical Documents, 1 (1983)
29. Cartulary document no. 170
30. Document in ERO, D/DGd M5
31. Document in ERO, Ass 35/102/1/29
32. See Field names (page 222)
33. Cartulary document, no. 124
34. Document in ERO, D/DU1473/17

THIRTEENTH-CENTURY EVENTS

1201 Fourth Crusade sets out

1215 King John forced to accept Magna Carta at Runnymede

1216 Henry III becomes king

1218 Start of Fifth Crusade

1229 Sixth Crusade recovers Jerusalem

1263 Start of two-year civil war between king and barons, led by Simon de Montfort

1265 Simon de Montfort summons first Parliament

1272 Edward I becomes king

1291 Acre, last Christian stronghold in Syria, is lost

The Round Church, 1820, showing the sizeable porch

CHAPTER IV

THE FOURTEENTH CENTURY

God is deaf now-a-days and deigneth not to hear us
And prayers have no power the Plague to stay.[1]

THE DAWNING of the fourteenth century was not auspicious for the villagers of Little Maplestead. The population in the country as a whole had increased explosively to nearly five million. Food production even from an improving but still feudal agricultural system was unable to cope with the demands of such a sudden increase in numbers with the inevitable consequence that a large proportion of the people were badly undernourished. As we have seen, the villagers of Little Maplestead were protected to a certain extent by the flourishing and wealthy community of the Knights Hospitallers of St John of Jerusalem in their midst, the master of which was their lord of the manor. Due in part to high quality land management practised by the order, which would have been imposed upon its tenant farmers, and also to the ready availability of other employment arising from the presence of L'Hospital, the villagers were probably spared the worst effects of this population increase - but they could not avoid what was to come.

AN ACT OF GOD?

THE FOURTEENTH CENTURY began with what came to be called the Little Ice Age - ten or more years of bitterly cold weather - followed by three years of torrential rainfall which caused the Great Floods. At the same time, and possibly as a result of the bad weather, from 1313 to 1319 there were epidemics of sheep and cattle plagues so bad that horses, which were immune, had to be substituted for oxen at the plough. Countrywide, the prices of grain and livestock doubled between 1305 and 1310 and the poor were reduced to scavenging for food. It is unlikely that the villagers of Little Maplestead escaped the consequences of these natural catastrophes and both the community of knights at L'Hospital and the ordinary villagers must have suffered to some extent although they were probably buffered against the worst effects. However it is possible that even L'Hospital had to reduce its help to those in need as charity dried up all round and even the gifts of land and livestock to the order dwindled. We have a 'snap-shot' of the village at this time - a list of the better-off villagers who were liable to pay a tax on their personal property. This list, of course, does not include the poorer inhabitants of Little Maplestead who had no personal property of any value at all.

LITTLE MAPLESTEAD in t

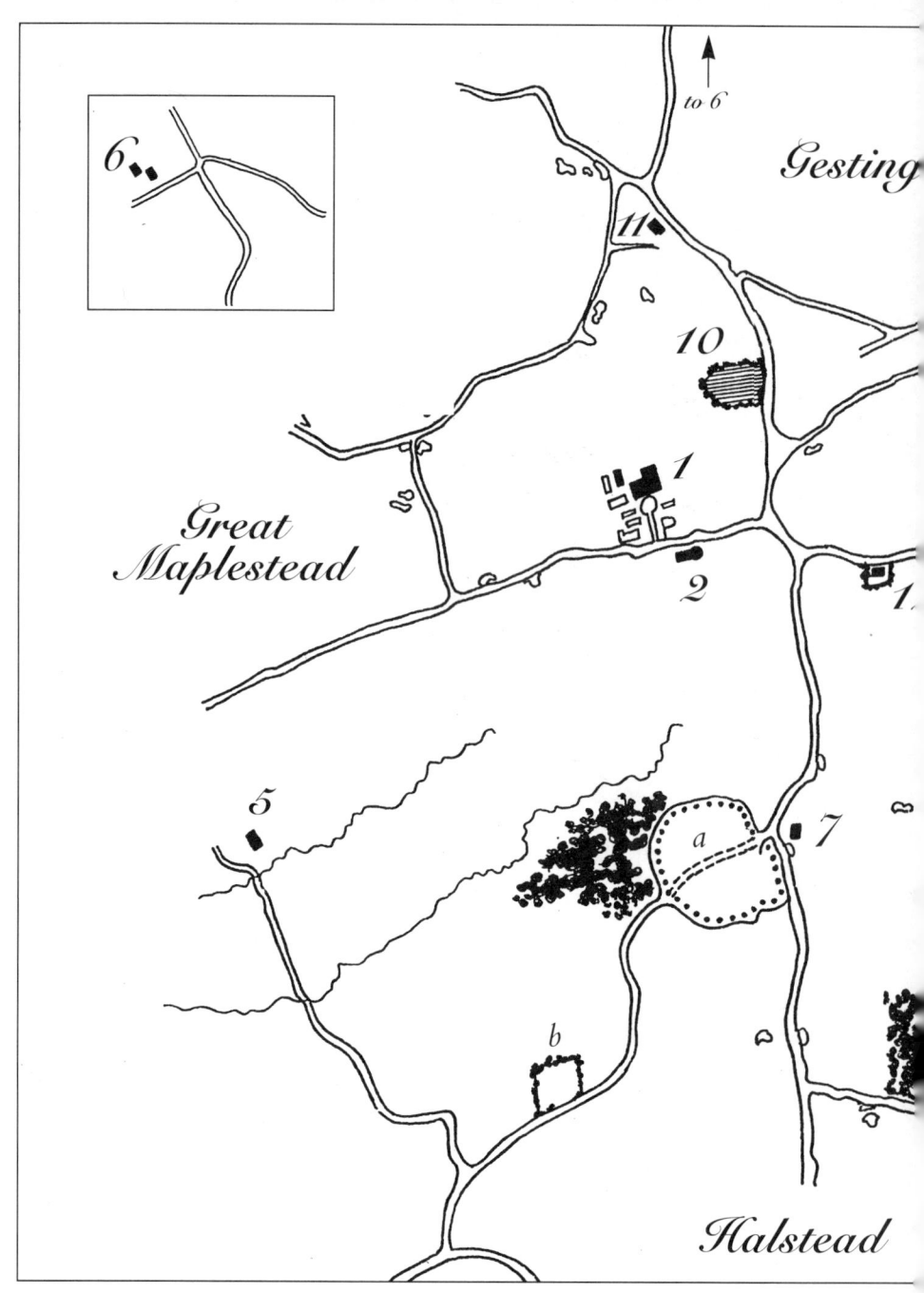

FOURTEENTH CENTURY

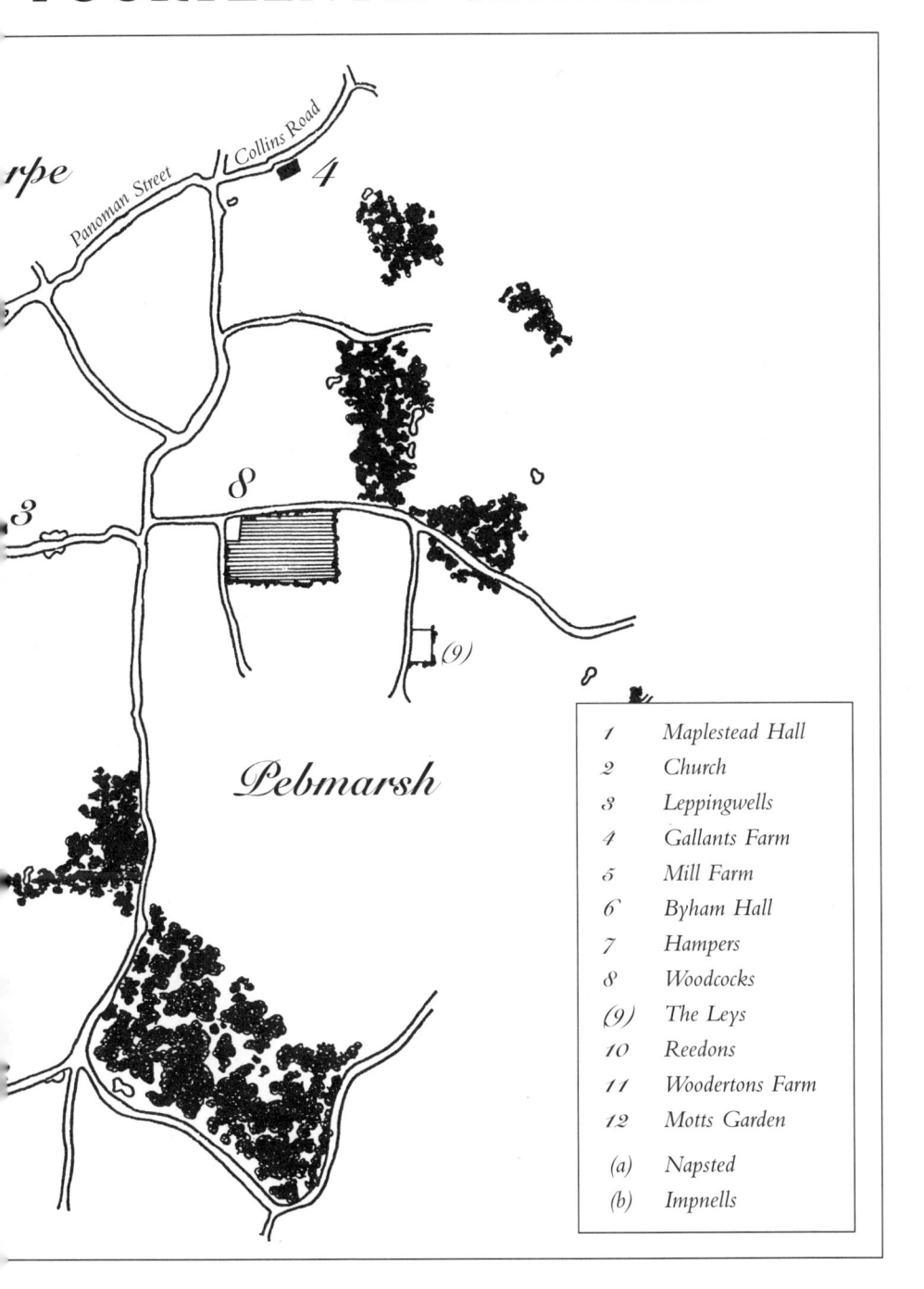

Pebmarsh

1	Maplestead Hall
2	Church
3	Leppingwells
4	Gallants Farm
5	Mill Farm
6	Byham Hall
7	Hampers
8	Woodcocks
(9)	The Leys
10	Reedons
11	Woodertons Farm
12	Motts Garden
(a)	Napsted
(b)	Impnells

The tax payers for the 'township of Little Maplestead' in the 1319 lay subsidy[2] include the master of the L'Hospital, Laurence de Panymer, John Mere, William Saxi, William Carpenter, John Hereward, William the Smith, John le Cartere, Philip Panymere, Robert le Blake and two surnames only, Colyn and Harlow.

PANOMAN STREET

THE NAMES of Laurence Panymer and Philip Panymere are of particular interest. The Panimere family name crops up several times in the thirteenth century[3] and the fourteenth century. Later we find early references to the name Panoman Street or Panymerstrete in 1429[4] and Panymers in a 1592 rental. On the Chapman and André Map of 1777, the upper part of Cock Road, nearest to the Sudbury Road, is named Parmers Street and in the 1861 census the Cock Inn is located near Panoman Street. In the tithe award of 1841 there are two fields named Panamas which belonged to the now lost Starch-house Farm. The name Panamas is clearly derived from the same name and the family must have been important landowners in the village.

Life in the fourteenth century was not only harsh economically, the country was also in a bad state politically. A period of civil strife followed the murder in 1327 of Edward II during whose unhappy reign the feudal system had begun to disintegrate. The feudal obligation of military service was often no longer demanded and little by little other ties were being broken. But the peasants still suffered and saw all around them great contrasts of poverty and wealth. To their eyes the greatest wealth was concentrated in the church, the monasteries and the abbeys. This eventually led to much unrest particularly in Hertfordshire, Cambridgeshire, Norfolk and Suffolk including, in 1327, an uprising by the poverty-stricken townspeople of Bury St Edmunds. Our villagers in Little Maplestead would no doubt have been aware of the battle between the church and peasants in a town so close by but very probably they had no reason to confront the knights at L'Hospital in the same way - the benefits of L'Hospital to the villagers were too valuable to risk losing and at least their religious foundation was set up to carry out an obvious practical and charitable purpose, that of looking after the sick. Again, from the tax records[5] we have a list of the better-off villagers for this year. They are the master of L' Hospital, Roberto Blake, Roberto de Grotene, Johanne Colyn, Willelmo le Smyth, Johanne Hereward, Rogero le Wrighte, Johanne atte Mere, Nicholao Joye, Cristina de Paumere and Willelmo Saxsy.

L'HOSPITAL IN 1338

IN 1337 what was to become known as the Hundred Years' War with France began, accompanied by a substantial and unpopular rise in taxation to pay for it. For the peasants this was the final straw and it was to have lasting repercussions.

We have a full account of the community at Little Maplestead at this time, given in the *Report of the possessions of the Hospital in England* made by Prior Philip de Thame to the grand master in 1338[6]. This report was made in an effort to review the overall financial stability of the Hospitallers in England.

Rents were received for the following: a messuage with a garden worth 10s yearly; 380 acres of land worth £12 13s 4d and at Odewell in Gestingthorpe 180 acres of land worth £6; 16 acres of meadow worth 32s; profits of underwood amounting to 8s; rents amounting £19 4s; a dovecote worth 3s 4d; perquisites of court and fines worth 20s; the tenth of the church of Maplestead, worth £6, and lands farmed for 100s at Bobbelonwe [the manor of Boblow near Helions Bumpstead] and for 66s at Assebrugg. Besides this, there was the *fraeria* or voluntary contribution from the neighbourhood, which amounted to £22. The total receipts for the year thus amounted to £77 16s 8d.

The expenses amounted to £37 16s 8d. Of this £7 16s 0d was paid for 52 quarters of wheat for baking bread; £5 4s 0d for 52 quarters of malt for brewing ale; £7 16s 0d for flesh, fish and other necessaries for the kitchen; £3 9s 4d for robes, mantles and other necessaries for the preceptor and brothers; 20s for the stipend of a chaplain, probably for the Round Church; 40s for the stipend of a chaplain celebrating thrice weekly in the chapel of Odewell; 13s 4d for the fee of the steward prosecuting the business of the house; 40s for the stipends of four clerks collecting the *fraeria*; 26s 8d for the stipends of a bailiff, a cook, a baker and a porter; 5s for the stipend of a palfreyman; 3s for a page for the stable; 40s for the visitation of the prior for two days; 40s on gifts to the sheriff, his clerks and others; 20s on the repair of the houses; 3s for rent paid for lands in Maplestead and 5s 2d for lands in Odewell; 6s 8d for suits at two courts and 8s 6d to the archdeacon for procuration. Thus some £40 remained to be paid into the treasury. John de Haulee, Esq, was preceptor or master of L'Hospital at this time.

THE GREAT MORTALITY

THE NEWS of the wars with France and of the unexpected and glorious victory at Crécy in 1346 would have filtered through to the inhabitants of Little Maplestead who, like every other village in the country, had been commanded to supply a soldier and arm him in preparation for the conflict. But the glory of this triumph was short-lived; the following year was the terrible year of the Great Mortality. In 1347-48 the rat-borne plague or Black Death arrived from the Far East via Europe arriving first at Melcombe in Dorset and carried from there to Southampton and Bristol before it spread all over the land. Its effect was devastating and there were four more major epidemics to follow, in 1349, 1361, 1368 and 1369. With the resistance of the malnourished people already low, almost one half of the population died in the space of a single generation. Statistics show that, countrywide, in monasteries and religious institutions such as L'Hospital, just under half the members of each community perished of the plague. The villagers, too, would have suffered although exactly to what extent we do not know; rural communities were probably not hit as hard as the towns but nowhere escaped unscathed. However in Little Maplestead both the village and preceptory do not appear to have been affected as badly as one might have expected and both had made a remarkable recovery by the end of the century.

But in the country as a whole, the severe and sudden depletion of the working population meant that there was a critical shortage of labour and ultimately landlords were forced to change their pattern of agriculture from labour-intensive arable farming to pastoral farming which did not demand the same manpower. The severing of feudal ties continued more rapidly now and competition arose between landlords to employ those workers who had survived and were available with the result that wages could not be held down. As the peasants' wages rose, the revenues to the lords of the manor fell. Records[7] show that most monasteries lost up to twenty percent of their revenues in the first half of the fourteenth century and despite its special status L'Hospital must have been affected too.

ALL THIS MEANT that at last, and for quite an unexpected reason, the peasant found for the first time in history, he held the upper hand, the labour market was his to exploit; now he was so sought after he felt free to protest about his place in society, he wanted to be free, in control of his destiny and no longer tied to the manor; indeed in some cases villagers destroyed the manorial records which laid down the rules and regulations of villeinage. And life for some peasants did improve - some were given the opportunity of buying the now unwanted excess land from their landlords and many small-holders benefited in this way, dramatically increasing their land-holding. After the Black Death the strips of land which had lost their proprietors could only be disposed of by the lords for money rent. This meant that some peasants on a manor now held land both as serf and as free tenant. The money raised by the peasants to buy the land mainly came from sheep farming, many peasant farmers rearing flocks on their land besides the usual arable crops. The sale of wool or cloth enabled the peasant to earn coinage and this raised him at last above subsistence level.

Now the terms yeoman, husbandman and gentleman began to come into use, to distinguish between the ever increasing layers of society. Ironically, certain of the poorest peasants received the biggest comparative increase in their wages; for example the thatcher, paid 1d a day normally, could now command more than double at 2½d a day.

Of course, most people at this time were still tied to the land and the peasant population still dominated numerically; in spite of all the changes, however, the peasant still had no real voice in government. But although during the first half of the fourteenth century the lot of many peasants had been greatly improved, those who had not been able to buy unwanted land or who did not have a trade in demand fell behind and were in fact worse off. So for many the inequality grew worse; this led to unrest and this time the peasants were determined to force change. Those in power realized that these ordinary men had become a body that could no longer be ignored. To this end Parliament in 1362 ordered all pleas to be heard in English so that they could be understood by the simplest folk and significantly this was reflected in the literature of the times. For the first time in English poetry the poor and the dispossessed became articulate through William Langland's *Vision of Piers Plowman*. Here the peasant had his say in his struggle along the road to perfection and his descriptions of some of the characters he encountered give us some idea of how the poorer peasants of Little Maplestead must have regarded such people. Particularly relevant is the 'monk on his palfrey, going from manor to manor with a heap of hounds following as if he were a lord' - a good description of the chaplain riding to and from Odewells chapel across the land of Byham Hall, or of the clerks visiting tenant farmers collecting rents for L'Hospital. There is also a description of the pilgrim, 'hung with medals from the shrines he had visited' and it is not difficult to visualize William Joy, proud of his successful journey to visit Jerusalem with all the spiritual benefits that this would confer upon him and his family. This new literary patriotism was echoed and emphasized by the works of Geoffrey Chaucer who wrote his *Canterbury Tales* in English at this time, establishing once and for all, for every man, the supremacy of English over Norman French.

AS ALREADY mentioned, it seems that Little Maplestead probably escaped the worst ravages of the epidemics of plague. The lay subsidy of 1380[8] does not show a decrease in the taxable population of Little Maplestead as one might expect but rather an increase. Interestingly there is no mention of L'Hospital. For the 'town of Little Maplestead' are listed William Nefen and his wife and six other illegible names. Grouped together under the heading of 'labourers' are William Peteway and wife, John Tuppyng and wife, John Schorthose and wife, Denise Schorthouse, Henry Toterych and wife, Henry Seman and wife, John Fynchyngfeld and wife, William Mot and wife, John Colyn and wife, Benet Panymere and Richard Wodeward.

This list suggests that the village somehow continued to grow and flourish. This might be explained by two factors; the village was isolated and rural, and therefore was less likely to be affected by plague epidemics, and farming methods were well organized and so food shortages would have been less likely; furthermore the Knights of St John of Jerusalem would have had excellent medical experience and would have known what simple precautions were necessary to avoid contracting disease.

One of the better-off villagers listed in the lay subsidy of 1380, perhaps even one of the labourers who had grasped the opportunity to buy up land after the epidemics of plague, may have built the ancient little cottage known now as Woodertons.

WOODERTONS

THE OLDEST PART of Woodertons still in existence was built in the late fourteenth century. It is timber-framed and parget plastered. It was once a hall house and the cross quadrant crown post and heavily sooted rafters, where the smoke filtered out through a hole in the roof, still remain. Originally there was a fifteenth-century jettied extension to the right, but this is now underbuilt. The floors were inserted in the sixteenth century and the modernized and enlarged cottage now incorporates a seventeenth-century farm building. There is also an eighteenth-century barn in the grounds[9].

Woodertons certainly spans all centuries down to the present day. At some time in its more recent history, while alterations were taking place such as the addition of a sitting-room and a back lean-to, the roof was taken off and turned through ninety degrees to face roughly east-west instead of its original orientation of north-south.

On the map of Little Maplestead dated 1600 a small house is depicted on the road from 'Crouchers Cross'[10] to Gestingthorpe', south of a larger house which is probably School Farm; this little house, labelled 'John Goddard's', is most probably Woodertons Farm.

In the Little Maplestead manor court book for 1693, we find the old name for Woodertons which is Aldricks[11], taken from an adjacent piece of land.

Copyhold of Joseph Crane for his cottage abutting upon land called Aldricks (1s 4d).

Copyhold cottage abutting onto land called Aldricks, Little Maplestead.

Copyhold parcels of land called Aldricks and Smiths in Gestingthorpe.

Woodertons 1600

In the 1817 survey of the village Mary Cornell was the landowner and Lot Borrows was the occupier and tenant. The cottage had no name in this survey.

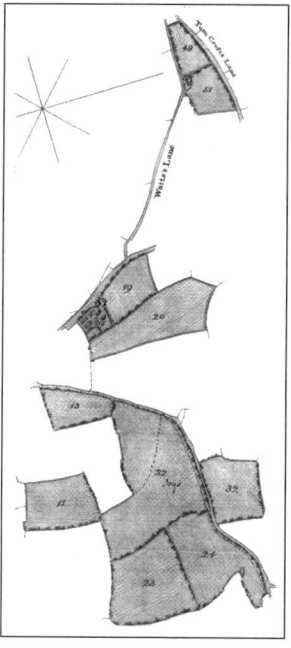

11	Tapers
13	The Bottom
18	House
19	Little Field
20	Long Field
22	Rush Grout, and Joys[12]
23	The Old Ley
24	Upper Ley
32	The Close
49, 51	Watts Field

The name Watts is reflected in the green lane running behind the Red House which in the 1817 survey of the village is called Watts Lane. A cottage, which no longer exists, on the other side of the green lane, opposite to what is now called Ethel's Cottage, was occupied in 1817 by James Watts, a gardener and his family who were still there at the 1841 census.

Woodertons 1817

In the tithe award of 1841, Joseph Baynes owned and occupied the farm, for the first time recorded as Woodertons, although a deed of 1826 calls it Woodingtons.

Woodertons

10 Tapersfield

12 The Bottom

17 Homestall

18   Little Field

19   Long Field

21   field

22   field

23   Old Ley

24   Upper Ley

32   The Close

48   Watts Field

40 acres   [see tithe map pages 218-219]

In the 1841 census we find Joseph Baynes a farmer, aged 45, his wife Mary and their six children living in Woodertons.

By 1861 the Baynes had moved on; the occupants of Woodertons were John Cooper, 54, described as a farmer of fifty acres employing three men and one boy, his wife Sarah and son Robert. Ten years later the Coopers were still there, though farming less land, now thirty acres, and employing two men and one boy. Their son, John, aged 39 is also listed, described as 'farmer's son'.

The 1881 census shows that the Coopers had been replaced by the Downs family at Woodertons Farm - James, farmer, and his wife Mary with their three children. Also listed at Woodertons Farm were the Argent family. They were a family of seven and the head of the family, William, was described as a farm labourer. It is likely that, at this time, the name Woodertons Farm was used for a group of buildings which included the farm-house and that of a labourer. It is obvious from the 1817 survey (see also 1841 census) that there had been a cottage and meeting house, now lost, next to Woodertons occupied by Joseph Watkinson, the deputy Independent minister, with his wife, Rhoda, and five sons and three daughters. It may be this group of buildings which was referred to as Woodertons Farm at this later date.

In 1891 James and Mary Downs were still living at Woodertons, with daughter Agnes and son James now described as a 'small farmer'.

A sale catalogue for Woodertons in 1896 describes it as

> *a valuable small freehold farm, well suited for a small dairy or poultry farm together with timber, plaster, slated and pan-tiled dwelling house - keeping room, parlour, passage, kitchen with brick oven therein, dairy and 2 bed-rooms. Weather boarded and thatch barn with lean-to pantiled pigs place, brick and pan-tiled stable, timber and pantiled meal house. Timber and thatched chaise house and hen house, with neat garden in front,*

orchard, back meadow and field of arable land. Now occupied by James Downs, yearly tenant, £16 year.

In a sale catalogue dated 27 January 1900 Woodertons Farm is described as freehold, let at £16; it was sold to James Mitchell for £350. In 1929 and 1937 Kelly's Directory informs us that Woodertons was occupied by Harold Hardy, poultry farmer and beekeeper.

As we have seen, Woodertons was possibly built by one of the better-off villagers listed in the 1380 lay subsidy. This list demonstrates that some of the Little Maplestead labourers must have benefited from the sudden decrease in population caused by the series of epidemics of plague and have taken advantage of the situation so successfully that they became rich enough to pay taxes on their property. And this new peasant generation which was beginning to emerge, with its material prosperity, was prepared to question and challenge old ideas and the established order.

MOTTS GARDEN

A SECOND LABOURER listed in the lay subsidy who had to pay tax was William Mot. His name is remembered today in the cottage called Motts Garden. We do not know what kind of a labourer he was but he paid a tax of 2s 6d on his moveable property.

The cottage today called Motts Garden is of seventeenth-century origins, perhaps earlier, timber-framed and parget plastered[13] but it does not appear in the records until the survey of the village in 1817 when the cottage, unnamed, was owned by John Sewell and occupied by Samuel Cockerton. The name Motts Garden refers in fact to an ancient piece of land adjacent to the cottage, described in 1817 as part of School House Farm, owned by Sir Lachlan McLean whose tenant was George Firmin. It is listed in the 1817 survey as a cottage and garden and it may have been the original piece of land owned by William Mot in the fourteenth century. It is also possible that the present day cottage called Motts Garden may stand on the site of William Mot's fourteenth-century dwelling.

At the 1841 tithe award we find Motts Cottage occupied by Samuel Cockerton, probably the son of the previous Samuel. The cottage was owned by John Sewell but the arable field called Motts Garden was owned by Sir Lachlan McLean and rented from him by John Cooper.

According to the 1841 census Samuel Cockerton was an agricultural labourer aged 58, and he lived at Motts with his wife Mary, a straw-plaiter, and family.

It is not easy to apply the census listings to Motts because no house names are used but in 1869 a deed shows that the land called Motts Garden was sold to Robert Hearn. Nevertheless it is probable that at the 1881 census the cottage was occupied by William Howlett, an agricultural labourer who like his father before him had farmed at Hurrells, his wife Charlotte who was a dressmaker and their son William, a factory assistant. In 1891 the cottage was still occupied by William and his wife Charlotte who had by then retired. Today it seems that the ancient patch of land called Motts Garden has been incorporated into the adjacent field and its name is remembered now in the name of the cottage alongside.

Motts Garden

NOT ALL PEASANTS had thrived and flourished like William Mot. And although William was taxed on his property it was not the only tax he had to pay. Even the very poorest in society were liable for a poll tax; that of 1381 was the third William had had to pay since the tax was first levied in 1377 to pay for the wars with France. This and the widening inequalities amongst the peasantry (as exemplified by the wealthy Little Maplestead labourers) led to widespread unrest which culminated in the Peasants' Revolt. This major uprising of peasants was particularly strong in East Anglia, Hertfordshire and Kent; Archbishop Sudbury of Sudbury was executed by peasants in such a riot. It started in Essex at Brentwood where the inhabitants of three villages led the way.

They had refused to allow the poll-tax collector into their villages and declaring 'that they would have no traffic with him, nor give him a penny' drove him away. This was the beginning of the rebellion which, headed by Wat Tyler, a Kentish peasant, invaded London and met with the boy king Richard II in a field at Mile End. Wat Tyler, face to face with the king, demanded the abolition of the poll tax, of villeinage and a fair rent on their land. Although Tyler was killed by the mayor of London in a fray and the mass of peasants returned home disillusioned with their apparent failure, the young king had listened to the grievances of the peasants and the poll tax was dropped.

The villagers of Little Maplestead would no doubt have known that one of the king's advisers at this time, who was by his side at Mile End to face the peasants, was Robert de Vere, Earl of Oxford, descendant of the Robert de Vere who had helped enforce the signing of Magna Carta. De Vere, the king's favourite, had much influence with Richard and eventually rose to great heights when he was created Duke of Ireland. But several other magnates became jealous of him and after committing various indiscretions the earl was forced to flee to Flanders and all his lands were confiscated. They were then restored to the next earl, Aubrey, Robert's uncle. The resulting uncertainty would again have caused concern and confusion amongst the farmers of Little Maplestead and even the knights at L'Hospital. They would certainly have been aware of the death of Earl Robert in Flanders in 1392 and some may have witnessed the magnificent spectacle of his funeral, held at Earls Colne church, performed by the Archbishop of Canterbury and attended by the king who had his favourite buried in a 'cypress case' apparelled in princely ornaments and robes, a gold chain placed round his neck and rings on his fingers according to the wishes of the grieving king.

Notes to Chapter IV

[1] Anon., 14th Century
[2] Document in Essex Record Office, T/A564
[3] Cartulary document no. 180
[4] P.H. Reaney, *The Place-names of Essex* (CUP, 1969)
[5] *The Lay Subsidy of 1327*, ed. Jennifer Ward, Essex Historical Documents, 1 (1983)
[6] *Report of the possessions of the Hospital in England* made by Prior Philip de Thame to the Grand Master, 1338.
[7] Asa Briggs, *A Social History of England* (London, 1983)
[8] Document in ERO, T/A 565
[9] Essex County Council Department of Planning, Listed Building Register
[10] Crouchers Cross seems to have been situated at the junction of the present-day Church Road and Gestingthorpe Road
[11] We can associate Woodertons with Aldricks because the two names, one gleaned from the trade directory and the other from the census, are at one time used concurrently.
[12] Named after the Joy family
[13] Essex County Council Department of Planning, Listed Building Register

FOURTEENTH-CENTURY EVENTS

1307 Edward II becomes king

1315 Start of seven years of agrarian recession

1327 Edward III becomes king

1337 Start of Hundred Years' War, Edward III claims French throne

1346 Edward III defeats French at Battle of Crécy

1347 The Black Death reaches England (1347-1348)

1356 Edward's son, the Black Prince, victorious at Poitiers

1361 Epidemic of Black Death

1368 Epidemic of Black Death (1368-1369)

1375 Epidemic of Black Death

1381 The Peasants' Revolt under Wat Tyler

1390 Epidemic of Black Death

CHAPTER V

THE FIFTEENTH CENTURY

Sheep have eaten up our meadows and our downs,
Our corn, our wood, whole villages and towns.
Yea, they have eaten up many wealthy men
Besides widows and orphan children,
Besides our statutes and our iron laws
Which they have swallowed down into their maws.
Till now I thought the proverb did but jest
Which said a black sheep was a biting beast.[1]

AS THE Hundred Years' War with France continued, straddling the fourteenth and fifteenth centuries, the extended military campaign abroad became a chronic financial drain on the country. This preoccupation with an expensive foreign war led to a sense of disorder and neglect at home and in the country at large and it was made worse by the breakdown of harmony between the Crown and the higher nobles at a time when the power, wealth and prestige of the great aristocratic families, such as the de Veres, had risen to their fullest extent.

But the social unrest in the first half of the century was felt most keenly amongst the labouring peasants. This eventually led in 1450 to a rural revolt in the south-east where Kentish peasants with Jack Cade as their leader took their rebellion into the heart of London. This uprising had at its core not economic grievances as before but political discontent. Above all, the peasants wanted the abolition of the hated Statute of Labours which enforced low wages and long hours on all poor labouring men, obliging them to work from dawn to dusk. The difficulties of the unpopular government which had lost the trust of the people were becoming acute; in particular and most importantly, the war with France was going badly. Although the peasants of Little Maplestead would no doubt have celebrated the victory, won against overwhelming odds, by Henry V at Agincourt in 1415, the last significant victory in the ongoing war had been won soon after this, in 1424. By 1453 most of the English possessions in France had one by one been lost, all except Calais. By then, England was once again isolated, once again on its own, an island. In the words of Jack Cade's rebels:

LITTLE MAPLESTEAD in

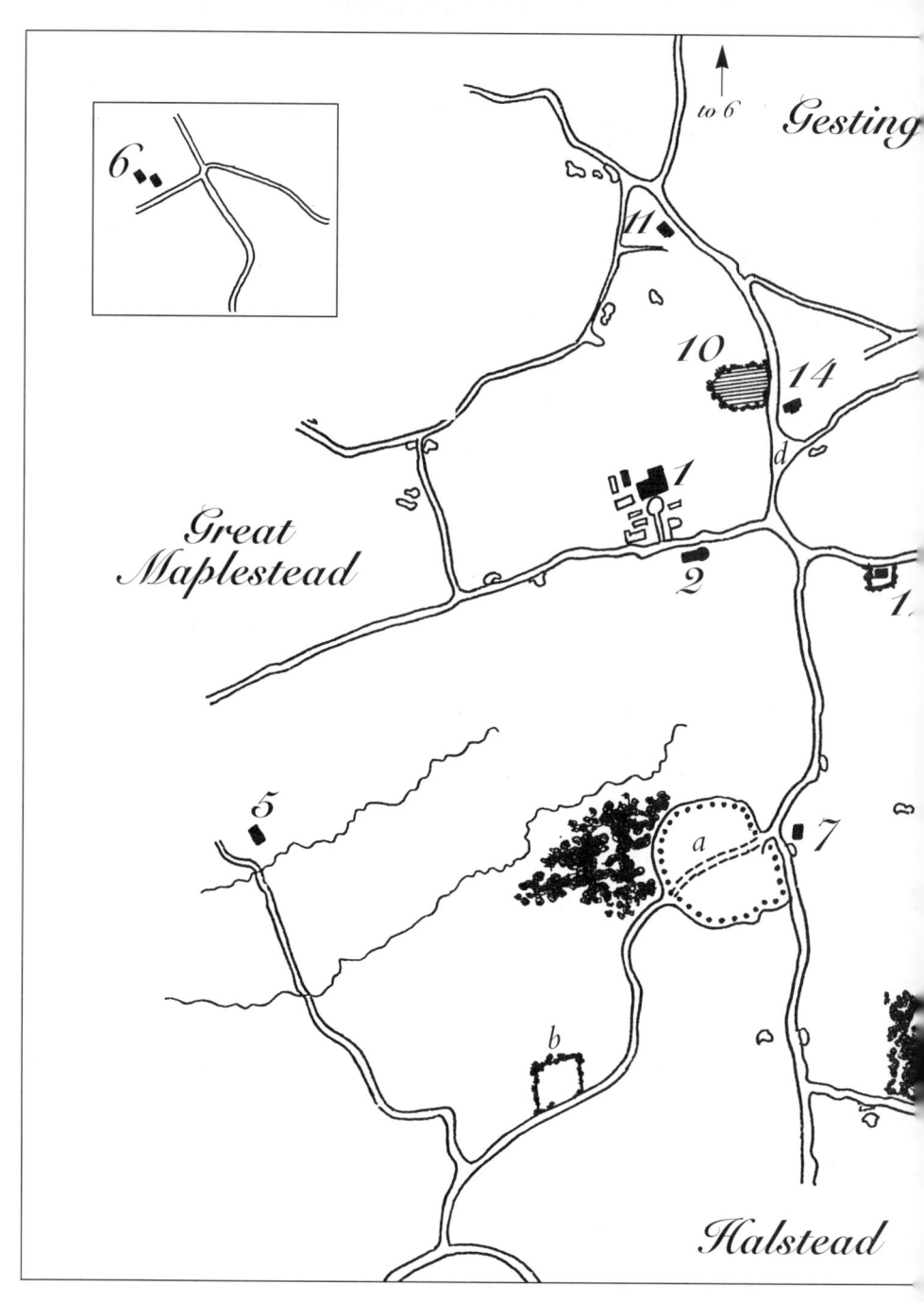

THE FIFTEENTH CENTURY

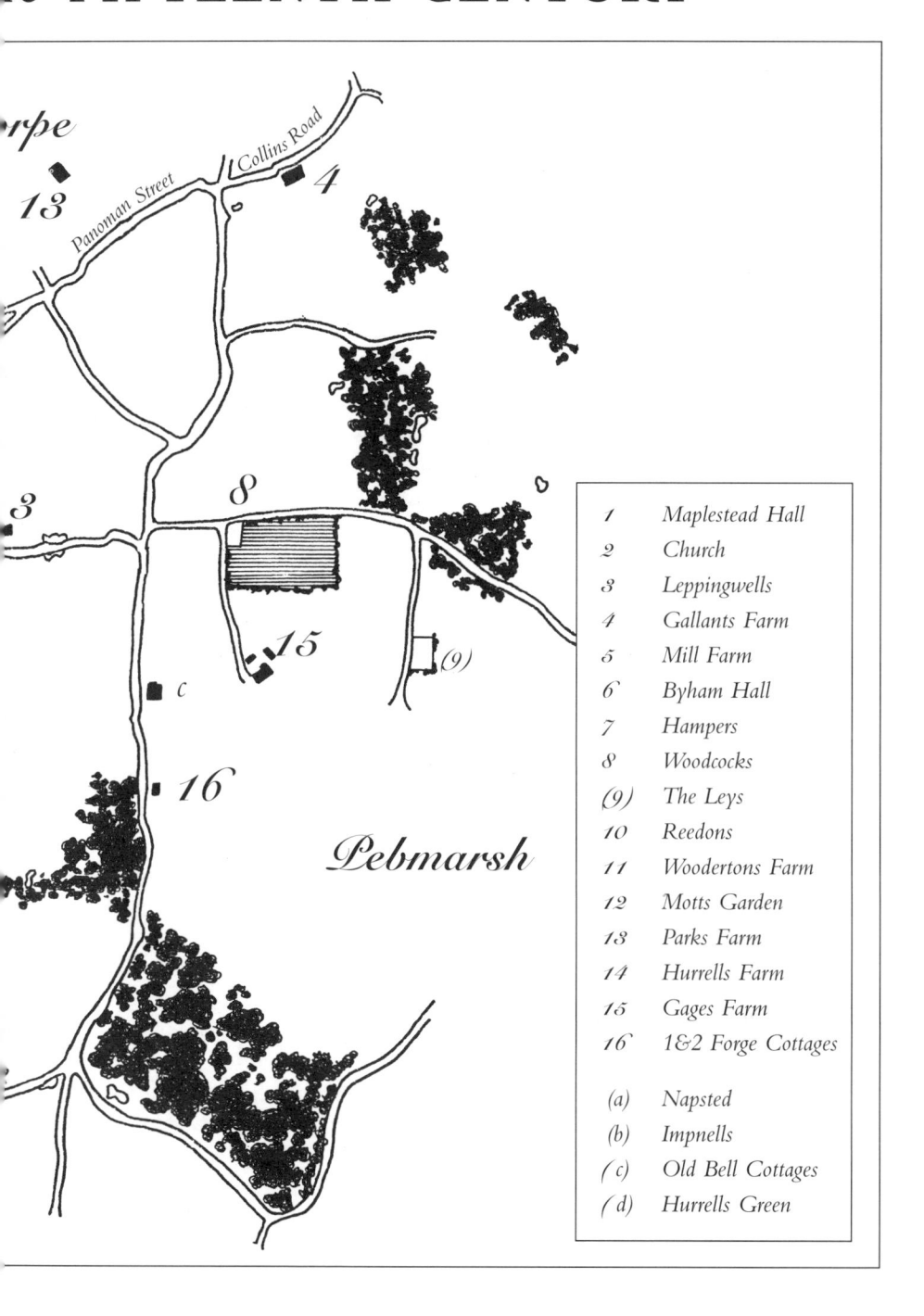

1	Maplestead Hall
2	Church
3	Leppingwells
4	Gallants Farm
5	Mill Farm
6	Byham Hall
7	Hampers
8	Woodcocks
(9)	The Leys
10	Reedons
11	Woodertons Farm
12	Motts Garden
13	Parks Farm
14	Hurrells Farm
15	Gages Farm
16	1&2 Forge Cottages
(a)	Napsted
(b)	Impnells
(c)	Old Bell Cottages
(d)	Hurrells Green

> *our sovereign lord [Henry VI] may understand that his false council has lost his law, his merchandise is lost, his common people is lost, the sea is lost, France is lost ... he owes more than any King of England ought ...*

Although life in Little Maplestead at this time was probably little disturbed by the struggles of the Kentish peasants, the villagers would have been aware of the unrest that had been simmering between the nobles which eventually escalated into the dynastic civil wars which came to be called the Wars of the Roses.

THE WARS OF THE ROSES

THESE WARS, fought over some thirty years from the 1450s to 1485 split the aristocracy between the red rose of the House of Lancaster and the white rose of York as the two factions battled for the throne. However, despite their impact on the monarchy, the Wars of the Roses did not affect large sections of the population and the numbers involved in the fighting were actually quite small. The nearest battles to Little Maplestead were at St Albans; there in 1455 the Duke of York, father of Edward IV who was to become king in 1461, with three thousand men defeated the forces of Henry VI under the command of the Duke of Somerset who only had two thousand men and who met his death on the battle-field.

The area of the country around Little Maplestead was probably of Lancastrian sympathy, John de Vere, the local magnate, probably greatest and richest of all the de Veres and a Lancastrian supporter, was the brother-in-law of Richard Neville, Earl of Warwick, known as the 'king-maker'. However, here as in the majority of communities countrywide life went on as usual against the background of conflict as people continued to farm their land or manage their estates.

IT WAS ABOUT this time that, for the second time in its history, the management of the estate at Little Maplestead, L'Hospital, was to undergo a fundamental change. After more than three hundred years the Knights Hospitallers of St John of Jerusalem withdrew from the manor of Little Maplestead. The Crusades were long over, the *raison d'être* for L'Hospital was no longer there. But, most importantly, in these post-plague years it had begun to be more profitable for the Order of the Knights of St John of Jerusalem to lease their manors out to farm; in fact, by the beginning of the fifteenth century Little Maplestead was one of the few manors still actively administered by the Knights Hospitallers. But by 1463 the 'hospital of St John of Little Mapulstede' was leased out to and farmed by John Syday[2]; however it was still administered by the head priory of the Knights Hospitallers of St John of Jerusalem at Clerkenwell in London and a chaplain was still provided for the church.

The departure of the Knights Hospitallers was a dramatic change at the heart of the village and Little Maplestead must have seemed diminished and empty without the busy community at its centre. It must have been hard for the villagers to accept that no more Hospitallers resided there, that they had withdrawn to live in other centres and that a rich source of employment and security had now dried up.

We do not know a great deal about John Syday except that he was a gentleman farmer and must have been busy with the management of his land which had grown to a very large estate in the hands of the Hospitallers. It is also very likely that he made alterations to the manor house at this time, while converting it back to secular use. It is also probable that he turned over much more of his land to sheep-farming. Many such landowners had grown rich by increasing the amount of pasture they owned so that they could graze sheep which was very profitable. It required less labour than arable farming, important in the post-plague years, and involved lower transport costs. It was not unusual for farmers to have as many as eight-thousand sheep and as more and more farmers turned to this way of life, the saying went that 'sheep began to devour men' as arable land turned to pasture. Although the way of life of shepherd and ploughman did not change much in the fifteenth century there was a continuing real though limited improvement for some in their material standard of life. Some peasants broke away from the crumbling feudal system and achieved the status of craftsmen or even yeoman farmers with their own land and houses held freehold.

Of course not all peasants could aspire to become yeomen; those were the lucky minority, the opportunists who had the foresight to take advantage of circumstances. Most continued to eke out a living, farming their patches of land, now often increased in acreage, for money rents, sweating to produce food for 'the gluttons to waste'[3]. Many still barely scraped a living, dwelling in hovels, farming small strips of land, some were even utterly dispossessed by their feudal landlords who had extended their own demesnes for grazing sheep. However, peasants in the eastern counties had always tended to be freer than those elsewhere, thanks to early Scandinavian influences, and they were able to exercise a freedom of choice not so readily available to others. Many peasants in Little Maplestead and the surrounding villages, already spinning and weaving small amounts of cloth in their own homes, were able to take advantage of the expansion in sheep-farming and increased their work at home so that it became a form of 'cottage industry'. Either on their own behalf or for their feudal lord, they manufactured the raw wool into cloth, a trade which embraced many other crafts such as dyeing and fulling, and opened up opportunities of employment to others. In fact as the sheep-farming gentry became more and more prosperous the countryside began to have a higher standard of living than the town. And as the amount of cloth woven at home and exported increased, the wealth generated for the region was reflected in some of the 'cloth towns' in the area; for instance in the mid-fifteenth century Lavenham was the fifteenth richest place in the country although it was still just a village governed by its manor court. Long Melford too was a rich cloth centre and so were Sudbury, Halstead and Hadleigh. As the cloth towns prospered the dealers in the manufactured cloth, the clothiers, became very wealthy; Thomas Spring, a clothier from Lavenham, was the richest man in Suffolk after the Duke of Norfolk. But the labouring spinners and weavers did not benefit to such an extent and inequality was still a grievance.

The economic depression that must have been felt by the village on the retreat of the Knights Hospitallers of St John of Jerusalem would have been ameliorated by the large-scale development of this new industry and no doubt John Syday became a very rich lord of the manor. In fact he was not alone in benefiting; a number of other farm-houses were built in Little Maplestead during the fifteenth century which reflected the new-found wealth of some of its inhabitants. Of these, probably the most important and a good example of a yeoman farmer's house is Parks Farm.

PARKS FARM

PARKS FARM was probably built between 1420 and 1460 and preserves many features from this date. The east end of the farm-house dates from 1420 and the central hall, west end, stairs and west wall chimney stack were built a little later, around 1460. It still retains the typical plan of a medieval hall house and the builders, good examples of those fortunate craftsmen whose wages had doubled between the Black Death and Agincourt, probably carved out all the beams and the framework from oak trees on the spot where they were felled; they then numbered them carefully and transported them to the site where they were reassembled into the skeleton of the house[4]. This process of construction reduced the need for expensive transporting. Parks Farm still shows evidence of the original layout of this fifteenth-century house; the positions of the buttery, hall and solar and serving passages still remain virtually unaltered. The interior walls of what was once the solar bear the remains of an intricate wall-painting of quatrefoils and rosettes from the early seventeenth century. Above this is a frieze of a series of inscriptions of religious text, unfortunately partly worn away, of the same date.

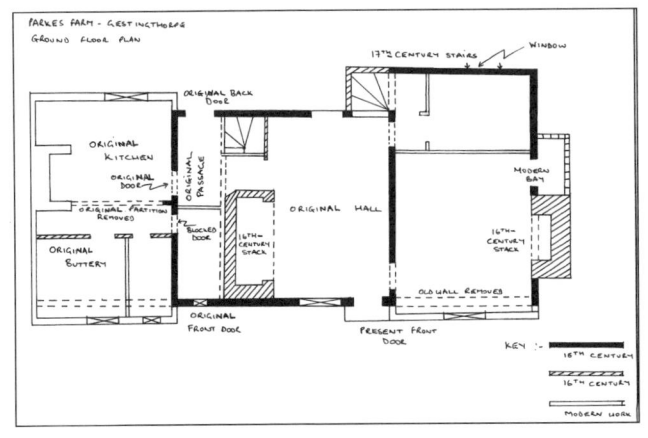

Floor plan of Parks Farm

The name of Parks Farm is probably derived from the Parke family. We have records of Thomas atte Park[5] in 1331, Robert atte Parke[6] in 1349 and we know that Julian atte Parke and Walter de Geldeford held here, from William de Ufford, Earl of Suffolk, the quarter part of a knight's fee in 1381[7]. From an early deed it appears that the name of the estate at this time may have been Morhall. Robert Parke, his wife Margaret and their son John, 'gentleman', are all buried in Gestingthorpe[8]. John's grandson, also John, married Alice Strutt from Little Maplestead. In 1553 John Parke was a steward at the manor court. He died in 1574 leaving another son, John, who was offered a knighthood but paid to be exempted from it - something many such men did to avoid the duties of knighthood which could be onerous. A map of part of the village in 1600 shows Parks Farm and its land.

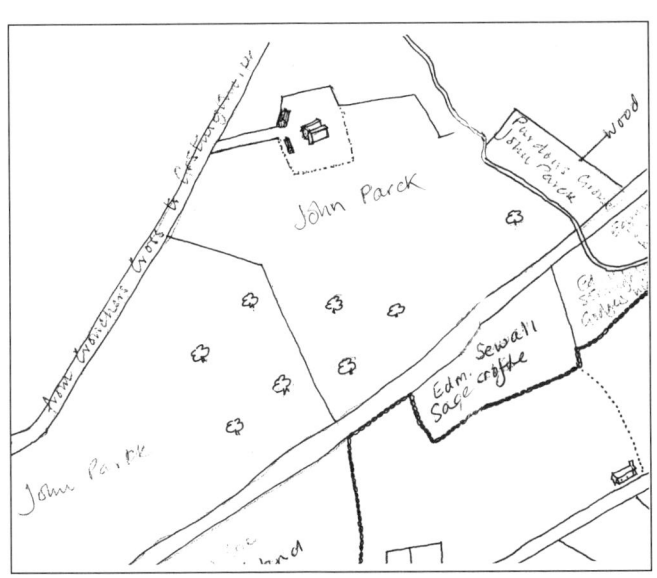

Parks Farm 1600

In 1629 Robert Parke, another member of the Parkes family, wrote the following letter[9]:

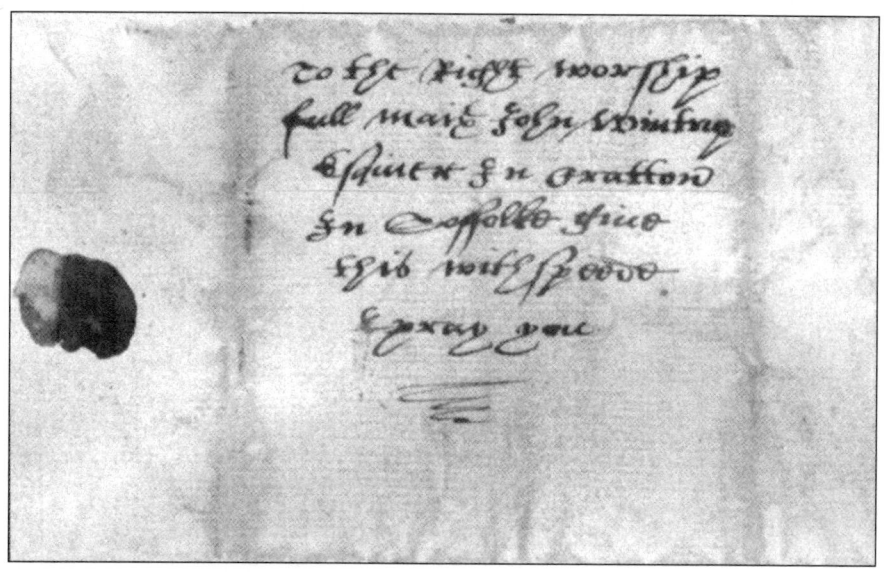

Envelope from Robert Parke's letter

> To the Right Worship
> full Maister John Wintrop
> Esquire in Gratton
> In Soffolke giue
> This with speede
> I pray you

To the Right Worshipfull,

Sir, I vnderstand by some of my frendes that
you are suddenly to goe into new England, if
it not be too laite for me, to provide my selfe with
cattel and shiping, I doe porpose to goe with you and
all my company, if please God to permit vs, life and
health, I haue sente my sonne and to Mathewe
Harrison to by for me six coues and three mayers
and a horse, soe I be seech you giue them directions
to take the beste coures for me that you shall thinke fit
for to be done; hoping you will doe the beste that you
can to fordere my jurny, furder I woulde desire
you to giue me directiones what househould I shall take

> with me and for howe lone we shalbe vittle us, and
> what day we shall set forwardes from London but
> as for our selfes we wilbe at Stratford the laste
> weke in February, and thus with my loue and seruis
> remembered in haiste I rest commiting you vnto the
> allmightie.
>
> In Lincolnshire
> from Easterkeale this your assured frend to
> xxviiith day of February 1629 commaunde, Ro: Parke

It seems that Robert Parke achieved his wish to go to New England; there is an American branch of the family that exists today.

Back in Little Maplestead, in 1634 the estate comprised Leppingwells, a messuage called Woodward and another called Aldertons which was in Joys Street. John Parkes' (the third) great-grandson, an attorney-at-law, died after being violently bruised from a fall from his horse and left the estate encumbered with debts. His daughter, Elizabeth, married Michael Drew who sank the estate even deeper into debt and eventually mortgaged it to a brewer, Thomas Morein, who then left it to his daughter, Mercy. It then passed into the Ashurst family[10].

At the 1841 census Parks Farm was occupied by John Claydon, a farmer aged 35, his wife Anna and daughter Mary. Ten years later John Baker Latimer, 17, described as the farmer's son, was living in the house together with Joseph Corder, 49, a farm labourer and 14-year-old Hannah Tyler, a household servant. At the 1861 census Nicholls Latimer, a farmer employing eight men, occupied Parks Farm with his wife Charlotte, and children Ellen, Nicholls and William, and Hannah Corder their servant. Then, in 1871, we find William Hearn, 71, as the farmer of 175 acres, employing seven men and three boys; he was married to Sarah, and living with them was their son William, 40, who was a farm labourer, and a domestic servant Mary Potter. By 1881 William Hearn was a widower and farmer of 200 acres employing seven labourers. He lived with his daughters, Sarah Ann, who was a widow, and Emma; his grand-daughter Rosa and servant Ellen Turner also occupied the house. The Hearns were still at Parks Farm in 1891 but the head of the family was now Emma, described as independent; she shared the house with her niece Rosa Ferris, 32, and three other younger nieces, Gladys, Dora and Hilda.

Parks farm-house was repaired and restored in the 1920s by its owner Mrs S. C. James. This was done in the most conservative manner possible so that the handiwork of all the ages through which the house had passed was retained. The house was then owned by Mr and Mrs Gosling who lived there until 1989. Even today, the house remains an wonderfully preserved example of a fifteenth-century farm-house.

OLD BELL COTTAGES

ANOTHER SUBSTANTIAL fifteenth-century house, which is now lost to the village, was known as The Bell House or Old Bell Cottages. We do not know who originally had the house built or the derivation of its name but it is possible that it may have been associated with the turnpike road upon which the house was situated - the main Sudbury to Halstead road - where it stood close to the road, almost directly in front of Gages Farm.

Old Bell Cottages were originally one house of two storeys, timber-framed and plastered with a tiled roof. Like Parks Farm, the house was built with a central hall and a buttery and a solar at either end. Later in the sixteenth century or early seventeenth century the hall was divided into two storeys and a chimney stack was inserted at the solar end. At each end of the west front, the upper storey was gabled and originally projected[11].

The Bell Cottage 1817

According to the 1817 survey, 'The Bell Cottage' was owned by a Mrs Oliver and occupied by her tenants Joseph Stokes and 'Widow French'. Later at the 1841 tithe award the house was listed as being owned by Mrs Sarah Martha Oliver and the tenants were Jacob Firmin and 'others'.

But the 1841 census shows that these 'others' were Elizabeth Felton and her daughter Emma who at the age of fifteen was a silk weaver, probably at the mill in Halstead. There were also two young sons, Robert, 8, and baby Thomas. The other part of the house was occupied by Arthur Stuck and another family, the Smiths - Edward, a carter, and his wife and children.

Twenty years later, in 1861, we find James Wicker, an agricultural labourer, in Old Bell Cottages with his wife Jane, a straw-plaiter, sons William and James, also agricultural labourers, and two small daughters. In the other cottage lived James Simmonds, agricultural labourer, his wife Mary, also a straw-plaiter, and two children. And a third family also seems to have lived in the cottages at this time, Edward Richer, an agricultural labourer, and his wife Mehetebel.

The Wickers were still living in Old Bell Cottages in 1881, when James Wicker was described as a stock-man, and also in 1891. The house is described in the volumes of the *The Monuments of North-West Essex*[12], published in the early twentieth century, and it was not therefore demolished until sometime after this.

A third village house dating from the fifteenth century, which still stands today, is Hurrells Farm. Originally probably a less important dwelling house than Parks Farm, Hurrells was always a small farm or small-holding.

HURRELLS FARM

THE NAME, Hurrells, probably derives from that of John Horrell[13] who was associated with Little Maplestead during the period between 1486 and 1515 and the surname Hurrell was still found in the village until relatively recently.

It is believed that the house was originally built around 1400 and that sometime in its early history it consisted of three joined houses. Importantly, it also had a well and pump which still remain. In the late seventeenth century the original houses were almost completely burnt down and all the old deeds and particulars were lost. We have an entry in the court book for the manor of Little Maplestead dated 1693 for some freehold land 'late of J. Freeborn called Hurrells' belonging to W. Lords, on which there was a tenement 'late burnt down and croft of land called Barres late of William Betts'. A later note appended to this entry links it to Hurrells. A single house dating from the early eighteenth century, the present-day Hurrells, was then constructed incorporating what was left of the old houses. The remains of the old houses can still be seen at the back of Hurrells where the original fifteenth-century walls with the old lathes and 'stuffing' are still standing.

Frequently Hurrells was written as Earls or Earles; this happened when the name was written down phonetically, as it was pronounced with the Essex accent. It was written Earles at a manor court in 1553, when John Merriton was lord of the manor of Little Maplestead. At this date it may have been owned or occupied by Elizabeth fflintham, Thomas Merriton, brother of John, and his wife Martha Merriton.

In the survey of the village in 1817 George Firmin owned Hurrells Farm which at this time comprised:

40 Reedons [the field where the house Reedons is now being built]

53 Barn field

54 House, homestead

55 encroachment on waste

58 Wood field

At the junction of Gestingthorpe Road with Cock Road, at the end of Hurrells' garden, was a large triangle of land which remained until the mid-nineteenth century when it was incorporated into the land on which now stand Lavender Cottage and Attadale. Some of this 'waste' land had already been encroached upon in 1817 to enlarge Hurrells' garden.

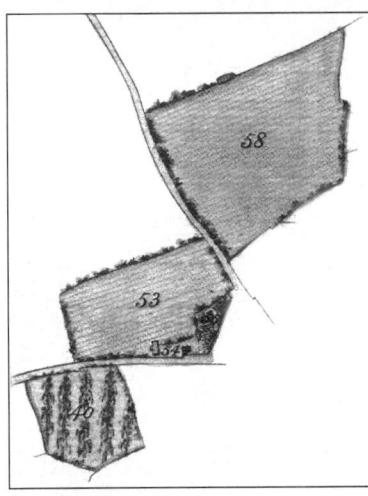

Hurrells Farm 1817

In the tithe award of 1841, we have George Firmin as the landowner and George Downes as the occupier of Hurrells which comprised:

39 Reedons

50 Barn Field

51 Homestall

52 garden

56 Wood Field

12 acres [see tithe map pages 218-219]

George Downes sub-let the property and in the 1841 census we find William Bush, 45, an agricultural labourer, and his wife, Hannah, and daughter, Susan, 15, living in Hurrells together with two other families, James Byford, agricultural labourer and Hannah his wife, and the Harringtons, Rose, 70, Hannah, 18, and Sarah, 12, all straw-plaiters.

By 1850, according to the trade directory, William Howlett, farmer, had come to live in Hurrells and in the 1851 census we find William Howlett, 79, farmer of eleven acres, Charlotte, 69, his wife and his son William who was a thatcher.

In 1861, listed under Earles, we find William Howlett, the son, now 37, listed as a farmer of twelve acres employing one boy.

By about 1864 William Howlett had left Hurrells and in the 1871 census Stephen Bridge, 34, an unemployed butcher, Eliza his wife, and two stepdaughters lived there. It must have been about this time that Hurrells' land was sold off. Ten years later in 1881 the Bridges were replaced by William English and Dinah his wife, both general servants, and Arthur their son, a printer. It is probable that William and his wife were servants at Maplestead Hall. In 1891 Hurrells was occupied by John Richbell, 28, a bricklayer, Kate his wife and their children, Frederick and Ivy.

In a sale catalogue for 1919 Hurrells Farm is described as a valuable freehold small agricultural property. It comprised:

> an Excellent Brick, Tiled, Slate and Plaster Dwelling House, Containing 4 Downstair Rooms, 6 Bedrooms, Dairy, oven and 2 coppers. Timber built and tiled Poultry House, brick and slated Chaise House, lean-to brick and iron roofed Shed, brick, timber and tiled Nag Stable, 3-bayed brick and tiled Shed, 4-bayed Shed and Cattle Yard with slate roof, brick and slate Loose Box with cement floor, thatched Barn with asphalt floor. Excellent water supply from a Pump and Well.

In the 1920s Mr and Mrs Dixey came to live in Hurrells and they remained there for many years; later the local district nurse lived there, subsequently it was rented out to Mrs Barrell and then her daughter and son-in-law, Carrie and Stanley Coe.

GAGES FARM

GAGES FARM is the fourth farm-house in Little Maplestead with fifteenth-century origins although the present-day house is essentially Victorian.

In a deed dated 1490 there is a reference to Clement Gauge owning land in Little Maplestead but there are also early references in the cartulary[14] to Gilberto le Geg around 1275 and, later, Wilhelmo Gegge in 1356 and 1381, both of whom appear as witnesses in grants of land and property in Little Maplestead. Gedges in Little Maplestead is mentioned in a rental of 1553 and Gawges in a deed of 1584. In the manorial court book for the village in 1693 we find the entry:

> ...parcel of land lying against Mountegreene in occupation of Thomas Tiffin [added later: near Braggs Farm now occupied by Samuel Hart]

This parcel of land belonged to Gages and is most likely the origin of the 'Mont' fields at Gages.

In a document dated 1718[15] Gedges was owned by Ambrose Raye and occupied by Thomas Tiffen who hands it to John Brandling. In the 1817 survey of the village Gages was owned by John Vaizey, an important local landowner, but only some of the land lay in Little Maplestead.

Part of Gages Farm

94	Lower Mont
104	Seven Acre Wood
105	Seven Acre field

106	Middle Mont
107	Upper Mont
160	Clay Pits
161	Dove House field
162	The Pightle
163	House and homestead
164	Cartlodge field
165	The Meadow
166	Nine Acre field
175	High Grove
176	p/o Stebbings
182	p/o Londons
197	encroachment, garden

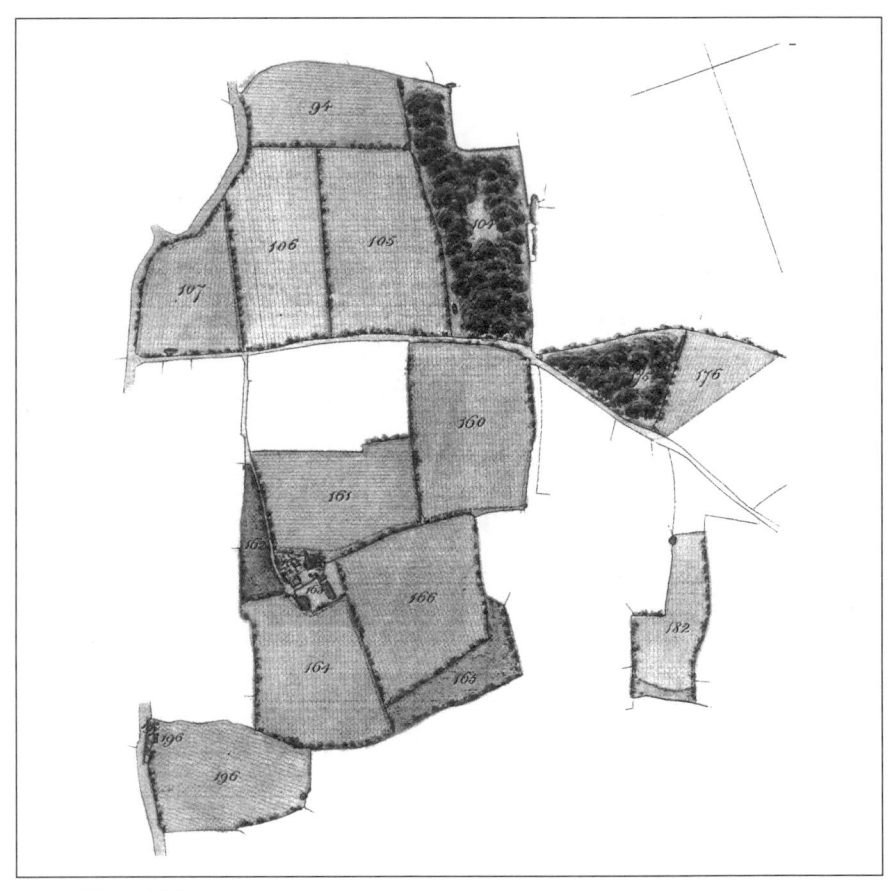

Gages Farm 1817

In the 1841 tithe award Gages Farm was owned by George de Horne Vaizey and comprised 93 acres:

89	Lower Moors
93	Seven Acre Wood
94	Seven Acre Field
95	Middle Wood
97	Upper Mont
145	Clay Pits
146	Dovehouse Field
147	orchard
148	pightle
149	Homestall
150	Cartlodge Field
151	The Meadow
152	Mill Acre Field
153	pasture
161	High Grove
162	part of Stebbing Field
166	part of London Field
181	part of Old Field
182	Old Pasture

[see tithe map pages 218-219]

In the 1841 census Isaac Harrington, an agricultural labourer aged 58, Mary his wife, and children, Susanna, 23, Joseph, 14, an agricultural labourer, Elizabeth, 10, John, 5 and David, 3, all lived at Gages Farm together with Susannah Parker, 45, a straw-plaiter.

Isaac Harrington, then described as a pauper, was still at Gages in 1851 together with his wife Mary but their son Joseph, still a farm labourer, was presumably earning enough money to support them and his younger brother and sister Elizabeth and David. In 1861 Isaac was again described as an agricultural labourer and he lived at Gages with his wife and James, his grandson.

After this, the farm-house may have been left unoccupied for some time, however we know that in 1870 the land was farmed by C. A. Bentall and owned by George de Horne Vaizey. Together with The Leys it was leased to C. A. Bentall for sixteen years.

He was still farming the land in 1888 but by 1891 Gages Farm was occupied by Henry Shave, a farmer, and his wife Phoebe.

On 16 October 1899 the following document[16] was enacted 'Duchy of Lancaster [with a great seal attached] for the Queen, to George De Horne Vaizey, of Crosly Sq, City of London, wine merchant, enfranchisement of Gedges and land held of the Honor of Clare in the county of Essex, 86 acres of arable and pasture and 20 acres of wood.' This document shows that historically Gages Farm had not always been part of the manor of Little Maplestead but once been held of the manor of Clare.

Henry Shave continued to farm Gages until 1912 when he was succeeded by Wilfred Wright who farmed there until 1937 when Mrs Wilfred Wright was listed as the farmer. Mr Wright had a herd of prize red-poll cattle and he also had a milk round. Cecil Cook relates in his *Memories* how Mr Wright lost five heifers in a thunder storm when they were all sheltering under a tree which was struck by lightning. They were found lying in a circle round the tree all touching one another.

ONE AND TWO FORGE COTTAGES

AT THE TIME of the 1817 survey Gages Farm also included an 'old field and a cottage'; this cottage is now known as One and Two Forge Cottages.

In 1817 Forge Cottages were occupied by Joseph Bryant and James Lot. They were probably farm workers on Gages Farm. Although these cottages may not be as ancient in origin as Gages Farm, they were part and parcel of the property. They were certainly there in 1777 on the Chapman & André map and legend has it that highwaymen would hide there waiting for their victims to pass on the turnpike road.

They would gather information from accomplices about the people staying at the Cock Inn with a view to robbing them as they came along the road by coach and horse. It is known that the houses had belonged to the farm and the Vaizey trust for more than one hundred years and there are some original doors and very old locks, keys, beams and ceilings. There is also a water pump, essential for the smithy and perhaps one of the reasons for the early siting here of the forge. It is possible that, like Gages Farm, these cottages may have fifteenth-century origins.

The tithe map shows that in 1841 Forge Cottages were occupied by Henry Drane, the blacksmith, and his wife Mary and the census shows us that the cottages were also home to the Bartholomew family, Charles and Mary and their young son John. Charles was an agricultural labourer, working at Gages Farm.

In the census for 1851 Henry Drane was still there with his wife, 'formerly a dressmaker', and another two families - the Bishops and Thomas Catley and his wife; Catley was a wheelwright. According to Kelly's Directory, Henry Drane was still at Forge Cottages in 1855 but by 1862 we find another blacksmith there, Thomas Smith. Smith was followed by Albert White, whose large family all worked in the forge, and then, in 1895, by the appropriately named Arthur Sparkes who remained there as blacksmith until 1929. Cecil Cook remembers pumping his bellows for him.

TUDOR ENGLAND

AS THE FIFTEENTH CENTURY drew to a close the Wars of the Roses were ended in 1485 by the Battle of Bosworth when Richard was defeated and killed by the forces of Henry Tudor who became King Henry VII. But in Little Maplestead, as in similar villages all over the country, for the most part economic, social and religious life went on unhindered and, in fact, the end result of the conflict made little difference, even to the structure of politics. For the inhabitants of Little Maplestead it was the departure of the Knights Hospitallers of St John of Jerusalem which would have had the greatest impact on their lives. At the same time, all around the village, a new-found wealth for the fortunate few led to a spate of building of substantial farm-houses and the villagers themselves began to benefit from the rapidly increasing wool trade.

For the country at large Henry Tudor completed the recovery of the Crown and kingdom from the wars of Lancaster and York and by the time he died in 1509 he had set the stage for the political, social and cultural achievements of the Tudor monarchy in the sixteenth century. These cultural achievements were of course to include the works of England's greatest playwright, William Shakespeare, whose *A Midsummer Night's Dream* is brought to mind by the fifteenth-century name for the hill in Little Maplestead which is today called Pearman's Hill. First mentioned in 1446[17], it derives from Pucksale or Puxells which means 'hill of the goblin' or Puck's Hill.

Notes to Chapter V

1. *Epigram*, Thomas Bastard
2. De Banco, Mich. 3 Edw. IV, 362
3. Anonymous quote from Asa Briggs, *A Social History of England* (London, 1983)
4. *Transactions of the Essex Archaeological Society*, vol xix (1927-28), p 193
5. P.H. Reaney, *The Place-names of Essex* (CUP, 1969)
6. Cartulary document, no. 838
7. Reverend Philip Morant, *History and Antiquities of the County of Essex* (reprinted 1978, Wakefield)
8. *Transactions of the Essex Archaeological Society*, vol xix (1927-28) p 194
9. The copy of this letter kindly provided by Gary Parks, a member of the American branch of the Parks family
10. Reverend Philip Morant, *History and Antiquities of the County of Essex*
11. The Royal Commission for Historical Monuments, *The Monuments of North-West Essex* (HMSO, 1922)
12. The Royal Commission for Historical Monuments, *The Monuments of North West Essex*
13. P Reaney, *The Place-names of Essex;* information from Early Chancery Proceedings, Public Record Office
14. Cartulary document, no. 114
15. From Deed in ERO
16. From Deed in ERO
17. *The East Anglian* (1858-1910)

FIFTEENTH-CENTURY EVENTS

1413 Henry V becomes king

1415 Henry V invades France and wins Battle of Agincourt

1422 Henry VI becomes king

1428 English troops besiege Orleans

1431 Joan of Arc burned at stake

1453 Hundred Years' War ends as England loses France except for Calais

1455 Start of Wars of the Roses

1461 Edward IV becomes king

1483 Death of princes in the Tower of London; Richard III becomes king

1485 Richard III killed at Bosworth; Henry VII becomes king

1492 Columbus discovers New World

There were regular epidemics of the plague throughout the fifteenth century

CHAPTER VI

THE SIXTEENTH CENTURY

*Never so much oke hath been spent in a hundred years before
as in ten years of our time, for everyman almost is a builder,
and he that hath bought any small parcel of ground,
be it ever so little, will not be quiet
till he have pulled downe his old house,
if any were there standing, and set up a new after his own device.*[1]

AS WE HAVE SEEN, during the last half of the fifteenth century the villagers of Little Maplestead had witnessed a fundamental change in the use and occupancy of their manor house, Maplestead Hall. For three hundred years it had been a priory hospital run by the Knights Hospitallers and now it had become the rented property of a single tenant farmer, John Syday. Nevertheless, the link with the past was still preserved; the manor was farmed as before and the landlord remained the Order of the Knights of St John of Jerusalem: the relationship with the knights, though altered, was not truly broken.

THE SPLIT WITH ROME

THE SIXTEENTH CENTURY, however, had more changes in store for the manor of Little Maplestead and its inhabitants. Henry VIII had come to the throne in 1509 and his schism with the Catholic church over his desired divorce from Catherine of Aragon led inexorably to the dissolution of the monasteries. Because of the split with Rome, Henry ordered a complete reformation of the church in England and the first step was the disbanding of all existing religious communities. Countrywide, the first steps were taken in 1536 and the dissolution was carried out in two stages. At first, in 1536, only the 374 lesser houses with an annual income of less than two hundred thousand pounds were dissolved but between 1538 and 1540 the remaining 186 'great and solemn monasteries' were closed down. This latter dissolution included all the houses of the Order of St John of Jerusalem in England including their manor of Little Maplestead. But for a while the Knights Hospitallers were allowed to continue in their possession of the manor as landlords and nothing appeared to change. However in 1540, a receiver was sent down by the king to take account of the

LITTLE MAPLESTEAD in

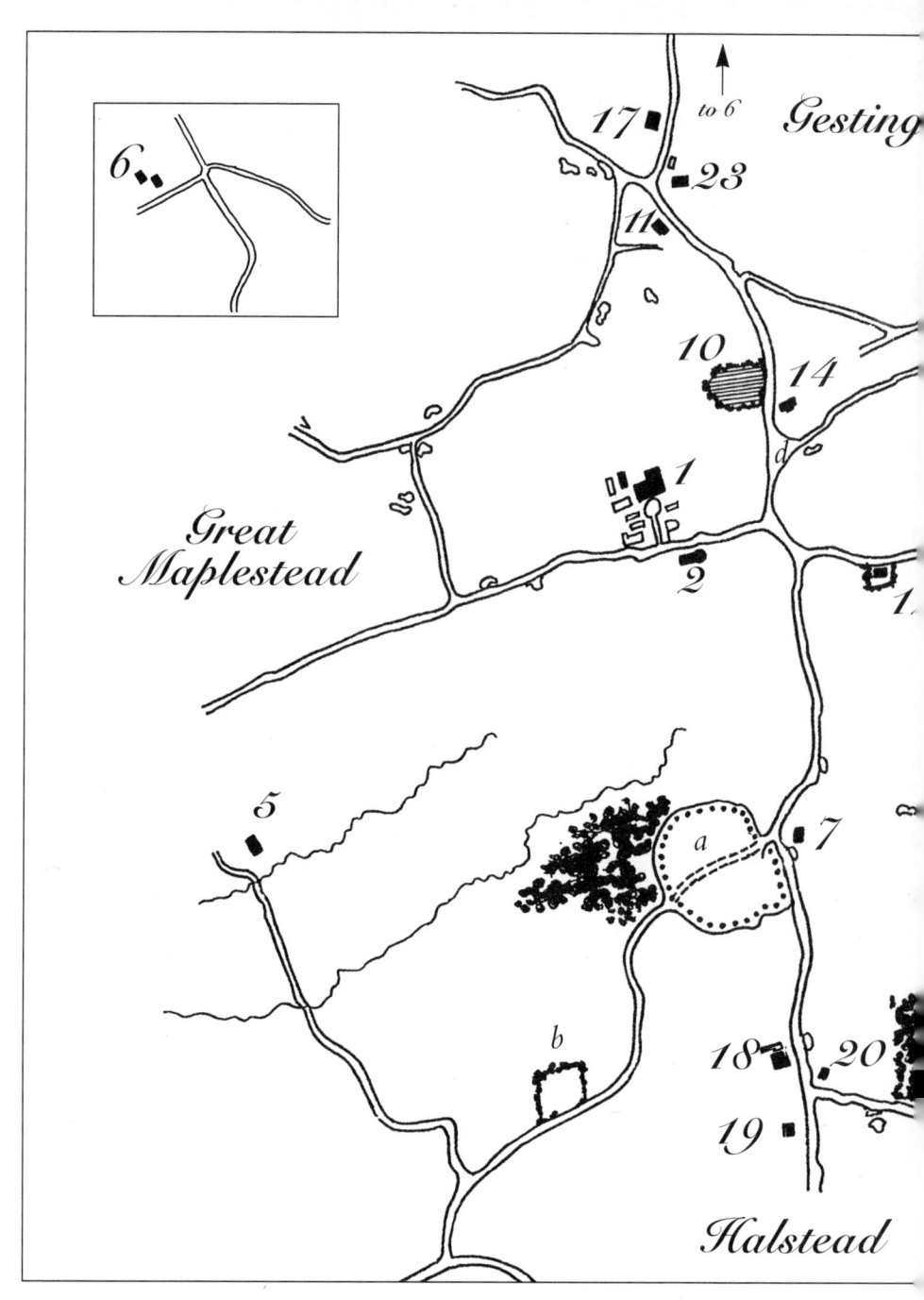

SIXTEENTH CENTURY

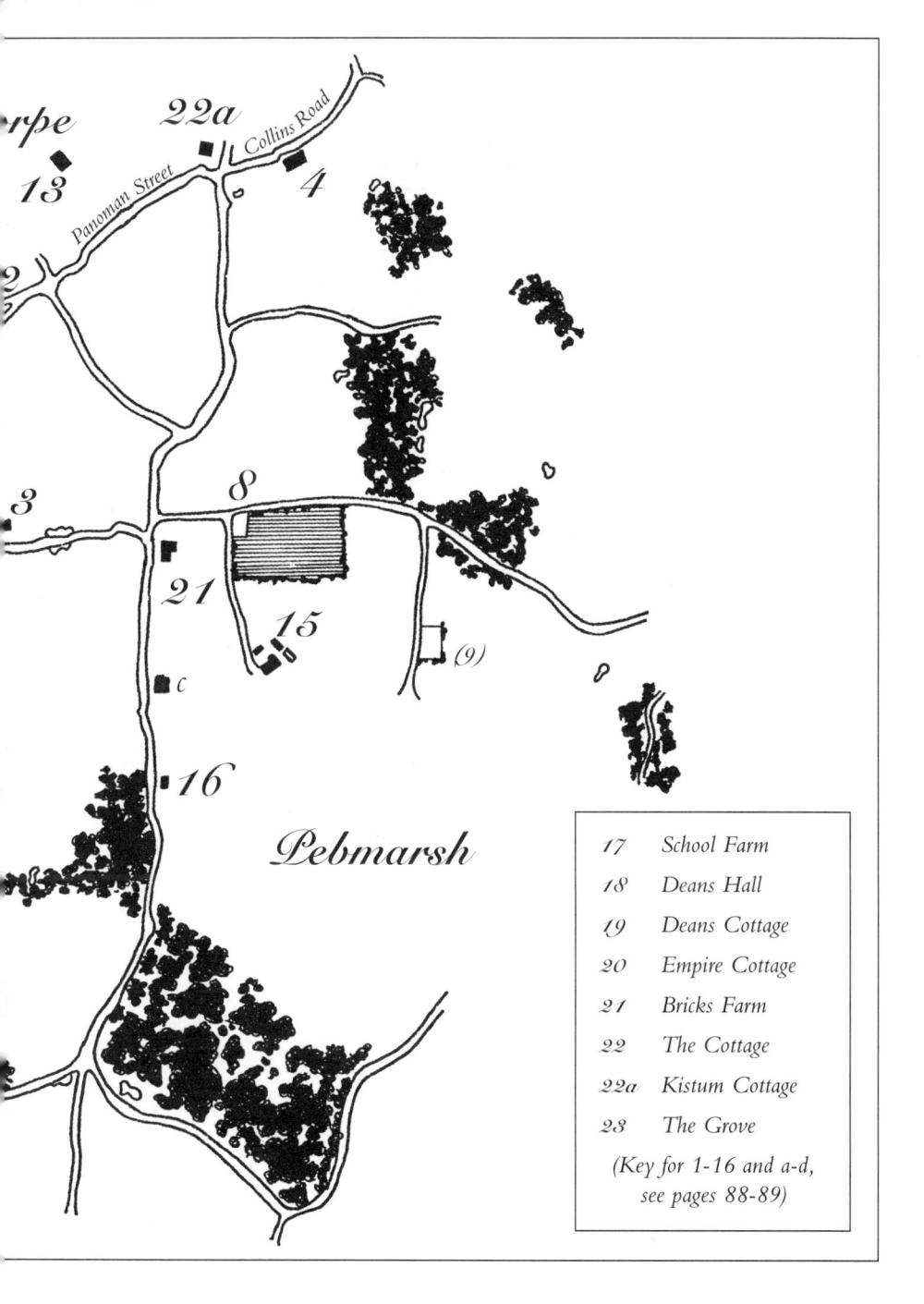

Pebmarsh

17	School Farm
18	Deans Hall
19	Deans Cottage
20	Empire Cottage
21	Bricks Farm
22	The Cottage
22a	Kistum Cottage
23	The Grove

(Key for 1-16 and a-d, see pages 88-89)

manor which was now being farmed by the tenant, Henry Hale. The receiver records under the heading of:

> Late Priory or Hospital of St John of Jerusalem in England

> Manor of Little Maplestead in the County of Essex, the account of the farmer Henry Hale there. A rent of £10 13s 4d from the aforesaid Henry Hale for the farm of the Manor of Maplestead aforesaid, with all the lands and tenements, meadows, feedings and pastures, rents and services, with all profits and commodities of whatsoever kind appertaining and belonging...[2]

Up until this time all the many monastic foundations in the country had been responsible for bringing in a substantial amount of money to the church - in fact, about half its total income. Now this money was due to the king. Henry Hale no longer paid his £10 13s 4d to the Order of the Knights of St John of Jerusalem but to a Court of Augmentation which had been set up to deal with the considerable new royal income from these monastic lands; but the Crown was careful not to keep what it had acquired. A large part of the land it had gained was leased or sold at market prices, some was exchanged and a small part of the land was given away subject to knights' feudal service. This last is what happened to Maplestead Hall. On 28 April 1541, the manor of L'Hospital at Little Maplestead was granted, along with other of the order's possessions, by King Henry VIII to George Harper, Esq to hold by knight's service :

> The manors of Sutton Temple, Chawreth, and Maplestead, and the Rectory and advowson of the vicarage of Chawreth, which belonged to St John's of Jerusalem ...[3]

Shortly afterwards George Harper disposed of the property to John Wiseman, Esq[4], one of the auditors of the king's revenues.

We have a record of the wealthier inhabitants of the Little Maplestead just before the dissolution began, in the lay subsidy tax of 1525[5]:

Master of the College in Sudbury	12d
Henry Hale	5s 6d
William Strutt	18d
Thomas Carter	18d
Thomas Garlynge	18d
Richard Lytell	12d
Thomas Paternoster	12d
Thomas Johnson	4d
John Reyner	4d

- 108 -

John Strutt	*4d*
Robert Walshes	*4d*
Robert Loone	*4d*
Thomas Clement	*4d*
John Mylkesop	*4d*

Here we see Henry Hale paying his tax but we also learn that the 'Master of the College in Sudbury' held some land in the village at this time. This land in Little Maplestead was most probably given to the college as a gift in alms. The college was the religious college founded by Archbishop Sudbury in the town of Sudbury in 1375. Its gateway can still be seen south-west of the mother church of St Gregory in Sudbury. Archbishop Sudbury was executed in 1381 during a peasants' uprising when resentment at the wealth of the church turned to violence. His skull can be seen today, preserved in the vestry of St Gregory's Church.

Like L'Hospital at Little Maplestead, the college at Sudbury was affected by Henry's dissolution of the monasteries which was the catalyst for its evolution from a religious foundation to a secular school.

SCHOOL FARM

THE PLOT of land owned by the Master of the College in Sudbury in 1525 is that on which School Farm now stands. Interestingly, the name Robert Walshes appears in the 1525 lay subsidy list; the name Walshes was also associated with School Farm[6] and it is possible that there is a connection.

In the primitive map of the village dated 1600 it is very likely that the substantial house shown on the road from Crouchers Cross to Gestingthorpe is School Farm (see Woodertons, page 80).

In 1693 the manorial court book of Little Maplestead lists:

> the school master of Sudbury for certain freehold land belonging to the college of Sudbury in the occupation of William Carter

and again

> Freehold lands belonging to College of Sudbury in Great and Little Maplestead.

The reference to the 'school master' is explained by the fact that the original religious foundation continued as a school after the dissolution of the monasteries and this association is the origin of the name School Farm. In the 1817 survey of the village 'School House Farm' comprises land only and barns; the farm-house is absent and suggests that the name of the farm at this time may have been confused with the school house situated close by in what is now The Grove. The absence of a house at School Farm in 1817 is puzzling as the present house is listed as seventeenth century. However if we accept that the survey is accurate then it may be that an earlier house on the site was pulled down before the survey and rebuilt, possibly with improvements, perhaps incorporating some of the original materials.

In the 1817 survey, School House Farm was owned by Sir Lachlan McLean and the tenant was George Firmin but we know that McLean held the property on behalf of the trustees of the school at Sudbury. The extent of the farm in 1817 was:

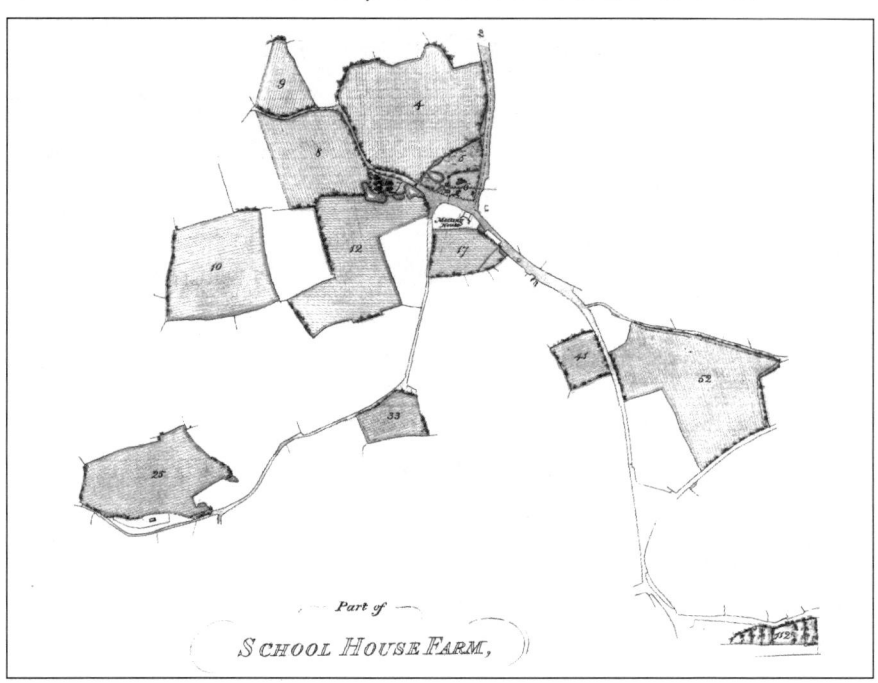

School Farm 1817

4	Home field
5	Pightle
6	Yard and outbuilding
7	orchard
8	Skippers
9	Small Croft
10	Cross Path field
12	Pond field
17	Little field
25	High field
33	Wood field
41	Burtons
52	Joyes
112	Motts Garden

Some of the School Farm field names are of ancient origin, for instance Joyes field is so called after the thirteenth-century Joy family and Motts Garden here refers to the field originally given that name. Skippers may have been 'the parcel of land called Scurborks, late William Harrington (8d)' recorded in the manorial book of 1693. Similarly Burtons may have been derived from the 'copyhold of Luke Lawrence, now David Stone, of a tenement and lands late of William Smith after John Burton'.

At the 1841 tithe award a new tenant paid rent to Sir Lachlan McLean, he was John Weybrew. By this date, on the tithe map, a house was shown on the present-day site of School Farm. The farm consisted of:

4	Homefield
5	Homestall
7	Orchard and pightle
7(a)	Chase
8	Skippers
9	Crosspath Field
11	a field
16	Little Field
25	High Field

33	Wood Field
40	Burtons
49	Joyes

54 acres [see tithe map pages 218-219]

In the 1841 census John Weybrew was replaced by George Weybrew at School Farm; he was described as a farmer, aged 40, and living with him were his mother Anne, his daughter Elizabeth, 7, and son George, 2. In 1851 we find John Sadler at School Farm, 'farmer of 53 acres employing 2 men', with his wife Phoebe. He was replaced ten years later by Robert Hearn, 27 and unmarried, who employed two men and three boys on the farm. He was looked after by 60-year-old Mary Hunt, his servant. In 1871 Robert Hearn was still farming at School Farm with four men and three boys; his sister Emma was also living with him and a young servant, Ann Wright. In 1878 the trade directory lists George Hearn as farming School Farm but by 1881 we find John Fenner, stockman, who occupied the house with his wife Sarah. In the 1891 census Arthur Chinery, farm bailiff, and his wife Jane resided at School Farm with their four daughters Edith, Maud, Ethel and Flora.

The 1889-1902 accounts for Byham Hall[7] include School Farm. Both properties at this time belonged to the Maplestead Hall estate, School Farm having been sold by the governors of Sudbury Grammar School to Charles Brewster in 1891 thus ending its long and historic association with this foundation.

At the 1919 auction, School House Farm was described as 'The very attractive freehold property', a good brick, plaster and tiled residence comprising:

> 3 Downstair rooms, 5 Bedrooms, Landing, Scullery with Brewing copper, washing copper and sink, also good underground cellar.
>
> The Ample Farm Premises which are in good condition comprise:
>
> Brick and tiled 5-bayed Cart Lodge, brick and tiled Chaise House, brick, timber and thatched Corn Barn with ashphalte floor throughout, slated lean-to Granary adjoining, timber-built and thatched Poultry Houses, 2-stall Nag Stable with mangers and rack fitted, Harness room, thatched brick and timber Barn with clinker floors and middlestree, slated brick and timber-built 2-bayed lean-to Cattle Shed and yard, 4-bayed Cattle Shed with thatched roof and brick back with fixed mangers and Cattle Yard, Cow Yard, brick and tiled Cowhouse, 2-bayed brick and tiled Cow Shed adjoining, brick and tiled large Loose Box brick and tiled Cart Horse Stable for 6 horses with mangers as fixed and Chaff House, Horse Yard, brick and tiled 4-bayed lean-to Horse Shed, brick back and tiled 2-bayed Horse Shed.

In 1923 School Farm was sold to Mr Brandon, a butcher, who sold it in turn to Henry Goodey. Goodey sold in 1927 to Mr R. Pearce (who called the farm Walshes) and in 1943 the farm was sold to Mr Wilfred Williams, who had occupied it since 1937; it then reverted to its usual name of School Farm. Mr Williams and his brother had set up as poultry breeders and by 1954 they were leasing some of Byham Hall's land for their business. After he retired Mr Williams continued to live at School Farm until 1986. It is now lived in by Mr and Mrs Sunnucks and their children.

GENTRIFICATION AND REFORMATION

MOST OF THE newly freed lands in the country, such as the manor of Little Maplestead, passed into the hands of existing landowners, the peerage or the established gentry rather than 'new men' or speculators and both George Harper and John Wiseman, the new owners of the manor of Little Maplestead, had royal connections. At last, after nearly four hundred years, the manor of Little Maplestead had had its links with the Order of St John severed and the estate was now in the hands of the gentry who owned the land but who, in return, owed a nominal knight's service to the Crown.

Throughout the sixteenth century entry into the ranks of the gentry had become increasingly flexible - the main requirement being ownership of land which bestowed the greatest social status. As the numbers of gentlemen increased feudalism lapsed to become almost dead by 1600. And as the dissolution of the monastic properties proceeded and the buildings became 'gentrified' there was a 'wide-scale conversion of naves into farm-houses, chantries into parlours, and towers into kitchens'[8] as religious buildings were converted to homes by their new owners. Maplestead Hall had already been secularized to a certain necessary extent before this, when the first tenant farmer John Syday came to reside there in 1463, but the property at that time still belonged to the Knights. Now in 1541 they no longer had any responsibility for it and as a result many manorial tenants may have been evicted. There would have also been an end to any charitable provisions for the poor still provided by the Knights and it is also possible that the villagers of Little Maplestead may have lost the priest provided for them by the order. We know that in 1563 there was no vicar in Little Maplestead.

These changes certainly happened in the country at large and inevitably led to increasing social change since monasteries had been important employers, exercising many charitable functions, especially in rural areas. There is no doubt that the dissolution of the monasteries caused much suffering to the villagers of Little Maplestead and, as in other rural communities, there would have been resistance to the new ways of the Reformation. The traditional religion and faith had been part and parcel of the village life since the twelfth century. The reforming 'new ways', resulting from the split with the Catholic church, included the destruction of church images, the replacing of medieval wall paintings with white walls and stark religious texts and the selling of church plate.

The walls of the Round Church were probably whited out in this way and remain so to this day. The new clergy of the Reformation were allowed to marry and no longer said the mass in Latin. But the old religious beliefs and customs, now often linked to folklore and superstition, were hard to eradicate. Thus the reformers in their new-found zeal for a simpler way of worshipping spawned a witch craze; this was particularly severe in Essex and in the last half of the sixteenth century around 170 people were indicted for black witchcraft, a capital offence, and half of them were executed. Many of the witches were buried at cross-roads, an example of this is the reputed witch's burying place on the lane leading to Castle Hedingham from Great Maplestead.

As we have seen, for the villagers of Little Maplestead, the sixteenth century saw the final dissolution of L'Hospital. Countrywide the resulting demand for monastic land pushed up land prices and rents. The fortunes of landowners and high aristocracy varied but many, such as the owners of Maplestead Hall, built up their estates and wealth and while the 'simple English labourers had houses made of sticks and dirt'[9] it is to the builders of this period that we owe some of our most characteristic English domestic building. In Essex more new country houses were built between 1570 and 1620 than in any other half century and with this came a similar spate of simpler houses. Dynes Hall, Great Maplestead, is a splendid example of such a country house built in 1575 by William Dean Esq, lord of the manor of Hosedens in Great Maplestead. However it was one of William Dean's antecedents, John Deane, who gave his name to Dean's Hall in Little Maplestead, first recorded as Denes in a rental in 1538.

DEANS HALL AND DEANS COTTAGE

Deans Hall

DEANS HALL as we see it today was built in the early 1800s. According to the 1817 survey of the village the whole estate was owned by John Greenwood and it was described in two parts.

The first part, 'part of Deans Hall' was let to the tenant, Robert Haiden, and comprised the following fields:

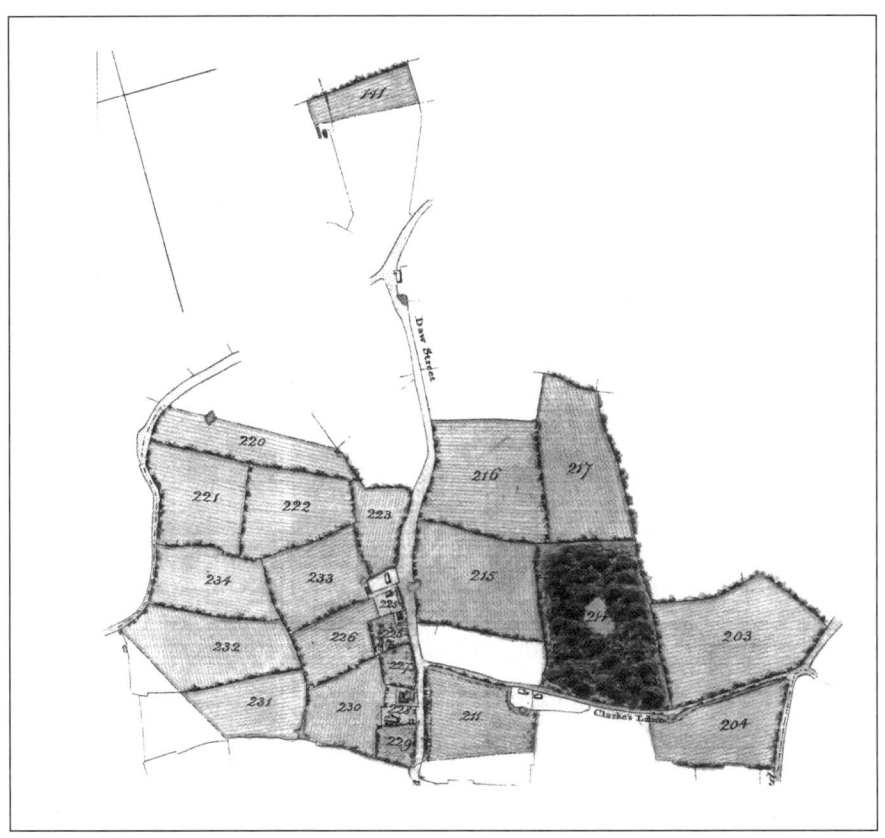

Deans Hall 1817

    203   White Post field

    215   Cart Lodge field

    216   Upper Bowditch

    217   Lower Bowditch

    232   p/o Pond field

    233   Cart Lodge field

    234   Three Acres

This part of the property also included the house and homestead, Deans Hall, together with the fields behind the house, numbered 225 and 226. It was occupied at this time by a sub-tenant, John Chaplin.

The other part of the property, 'part of Rows Hill', was let to tenant John Gunn and it consisted of the 'house and homestead', in this case Deans Cottage, numbered 228, and fields:

> 141 p/o Great Etheridge
> 204 Mites
> 211 p/o Fore field
> 220 p/o Felts Folly
> 221 Hill field
> 222 Middle field
> 223 "   "
> 227 "   "
> 229 Barn Pightle
> 230 Upper Stable field
> 231 p/o Lower Stable field

Rows Hill was the name for the area around Deans Hall and Deans Cottage. Deans Cottage is included here not only because of its link to Deans Hall through the name of John Deane. The cottage we see today predates Deans Hall and is late sixteenth century or early seventeenth century in origin and retains some of the original features. Originally two farm cottages, Deans Cottage was converted into one house in 1965 to 1966. However, although we have no records to prove this, it is probable that Deans Hall was built on the site of an pre-existing older building. Historically it was a small farm with a simple farm cottage, Deans Cottage, next to it.

At the tithe award of 1841 Firmin de Tastet was the owner of Deans Hall and had sub-let it to James Brewster of Maplestead Hall so that it had become part of the Maplestead Hall estate.

128	part of Grove Field
130	part of Mead Field
131	part of Etheridge Field
132	Barn Field
188	White Post Field
189	part of Ashford Lodge
191	Orchard

194	Spanish Field
196	part of Fore Field
198	part of Cart Lodge Field
199	Deans Wood Field
200	Bowditch
203	Barn Field
206	Homestall, Deans Hall
207	Orchard
209	pasture
209(a)	part of field
210	Pond Field
235	part of Sandpit Field

102 acres   [see tithe map pages 218-219]

According to the 1841 census, James Brewster had let Deans Hall to his gamekeeper, James Moss, 35, and his wife Harriet, with their children William, 12, already working as an agricultural labourer, Robert, Sarah, James, Emma and a baby son.

Deans Cottage was occupied by Isaac Dodd, an agricultural labourer, and Sarah his wife, with their son, also an agricultural labourer, and a young daughter.

By 1851 Samuel Moss lived in Deans Hall with his wife Rebecca. He was a farm labourer and his three grown-up daughters were all straw-plaiters. It is unclear who occupied Deans Cottage at this time.

Deans Cottage

Ten years later, in 1861, Deans Hall was occupied by William Hustler, his wife Caroline and their large family of five sons and four daughters. William Hustler was described as clerk of Halstead Poor Law Union. Deans Cottage was occupied by John Curtis, an agricultural labourer, Elizabeth his wife and their five children; one son was an agricultural labourer and a twelve-year-old daughter was a silk twister, probably for the Halstead silk trade.

In 1871 William Cant lived at Deans Hall farm; he was a farming bailiff for Mr Brewster and lived with his wife Jane and daughter Susan. In Deans Cottage we find William Coe, an agricultural labourer, with his wife Susan who was a house domestic and their baby, Lucy. John Stuck, stockman, his wife Ellen and baby lived in Deans Hall in 1881, while William Cant and his daughter and two grandsons had moved to Deans Cottage.

By 1891, William Cant's son, another William, lived in Deans Hall with his wife Julia and baby son Edward. William was described as farm bailiff to Mr Brewster. In Deans Cottage we find John Bishop, an agricultural labourer, his wife Emily and son-in-law Ebenezer Watkinson, also an agricultural labourer.

A year later, in 1892 the freehold of Deans Hall and Hampers Farm was sold to Charles Brewster by Owen Williams, Decimus Sewell and the grandly named Firmin Antonio de Tastet.

In a sale catalogue dated 1919, Deans Hall was sold along with Hampers Farm and Deans Cottage in one lot of 235 acres. Deans Hall was described as:

> a substantial and well-built farmhouse of brick and plaster construction with slate roof containing on first floor 5 bedrooms and good cupboards and landing: and on ground floor entrance hall and two reception rooms. The offices consist of a kitchen with cupboards fitted, larder, dairy and good cellar. There is a brick and tiled wash-house fitted with copper, sink and soft water tank. Brick and tiled building adjoining now used for poultry is suitable for a nag stable. Good garden partly walled in. Never failing supply of excellent water from pump and well.

> The Farm premises comprised of brick and slate horse shed, brick, timber and slate cart horse stable for 8 horses, chaff house, timber tiled loose box, slated lean-to horse shed, large brick timber built and tiled barn with weather-boarded and slated lean-to Granary adjoining. Cattle yards, brick, slated and weather-boarded shed, brick stone and slate bullock house, brick and slate cowhouse, calf pens, brick and slate mixing and root house, cowshed, loose boxes, brick and slate barn, slated lean-to granary adjoining, cart shed opening on to road, coal shed, cattle yard, implement shed.

The description of Deans Cottage read:

> Double tenement brick, plaster and tiled cottage containing in each tenement 2 rooms on ground floor, and 1 bedroom (6 rooms in all), brick and tiled washhouse with copper for joint use. One tenement let to James Patrick at £3 15s per annum and the other to Samuel Bishop. Water from Deans Hall pump.

The buyer was Mr Percy, a London businessman, and some years later, about 1926, Mr Percy, who was living at Deans Hall, opened a small factory in one of his barns (see page 207). The site of the factory can be seen on the 1817 survey map together with Empire Cottage and another cottage now lost.

EMPIRE COTTAGE

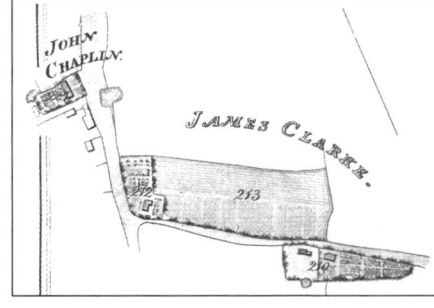

Empire Cottage 1817

THIS SMALL COTTAGE may also date from the sixteenth century; however there are no early records to confirm this. In the survey of 1817 it was described as a cottage and garden, number 212, owned by James Clarke and occupied by Thomas Clarke. At the 1841 tithe award the proprietor was Firmin de Tastet and the occupier was Ann Clarke. The 1841 census recorded Hannah

Clarke, 75, and Sarah Freebold, 35, living in the cottage but after this the records are unclear.

ALTHOUGH in the sixteenth century landowners built up their estates and the wealthy prospered, those people with fixed incomes and people with insecure land tenures were at a disadvantage. These were the cottage and wage workers, simple peasants such as the inhabitants of Deans Cottage, and they suffered seriously as wages lagged behind prices because they had no other ways of supplementing meagre incomes.

Things were made worse during the years 1557-59 which were years of epidemic disease. At the same time a series of bad harvests had weakened the most vulnerable, usually the poor, and burials were more than double the average in number. Life expectancy was very low. Over half the population was under twenty-five (only eight to ten percent were over sixty years old). Very young children from poorer families were expected to work from six or seven years of age and infant and child mortality were high.

THE REIGN OF ELIZABETH I

IT WAS IN THE MIDST of these epidemics and bad harvests that England's most glorious monarch came to the throne and although the poorer inhabitants of Little Maplestead, like peasants everywhere, were busy struggling for survival, the fact cannot have escaped them that now England had a young girl as queen. But they could never have foretold, after all the religious and economic unrest of her father's reign, that this was going to be the nation's golden age. Golden in discovery, seafaring, music, drama, poetry and in many aspects of social life, the reign of Elizabeth I was destined to be an age of harmony and creative power.

This flowering of a new age of possibility and achievement was in part enabled by the evolution of a new class system which took the place of the old feudalism. According to William Harrison, a country parson at that time, people were now divided into four sorts. First and foremost were the nobility, the knights and the gentlemen, and at Little Maplestead the owner of Maplestead Hall was a gentleman with a knight's tenure. Secondly came the citizens and burgesses, men who held office. Essentially these people were town-dwellers.

The third class were the yeomen of the countryside and into this class would have fallen the owners of Parks Farm and Byham Hall. Below this in rank would have been the lesser yeomen or 'working husbandmen' who farmed such properties as Hampers, Woodertons, Hurrells, Leppingwells, Gages and Gallants and also School Farm, Deans Hall and Bricks Farm.

The fourth and last group of people were 'those to be ruled and not to rule others'. These included day labourers, poor husbandmen and 'all artificers' such as carpenters and tailors. For these people the golden age was still far off. Although the population recovered from the bad years and between 1563 and 1603 grew by fifty percent until it exceeded four million, the first time it had reached this number since the epidemics of the plague in the fourteenth century, the rise in population meant that the labourers lost their bargaining advantage and wages continued to fall.

During the first half of the sixteenth century the rise in the price of wool had continued to cause an expansion in flocks and pasturage. 'Of all stock rearing sheep are the most profitable' says Fitzherbert in his *Book of Husbandry* dated 1579. Despite legislation in 1489, arable land was still being converted to pasture. Farmers enclosed their land for 'improvement' and rich men enclosed other men's common land; simple greed seemed to be the prime motivation and this gave rise to serious anti-enclosure riots in 1548 and 1549.

No doubt the villagers of Little Maplestead would have had great sympathy with Robert Kett who in 1549 led a rebel army of peasants through Norfolk urging the king, Edward VI, for relief for 'your poor commons'. Word would surely have reached them that Kett's rising had camped on Mousehold Heath near Norwich and slaughtered over twenty thousand sheep as a protest against the landlords who had now begun to enclose some of the common land, needed so badly by the poor, to graze their ever-increasing flocks.

However, after 1551 the economy saw wool prices rise which led to a sudden decrease in demand for raw wool and this meant unemployment for many of the peasants working in the cottage spinning industry. Following this, there was a fall in the sheep population as farmers began to shift to meat production. But despite this, woven textiles were still England's most valuable export. Fortunately for the villagers of Little Maplestead, by 1580 the spinning and weaving cottage industry was revived and increased in the villages around Halstead. The reason for this revival was the 'bay and say' textile trade which had begun to flourish in Halstead. 'Bay' was a coarse woollen cloth with a teazeled nap, 'say' was lighter and was used for aprons, shirts and linings. Both these newly produced fabrics, 'the new drapery', were in great demand and had been originally introduced by Dutch immigrants who had come to live locally. They had set up production of the fabrics using English wool and employing local peasant cottage workers which had provided a welcome boost to the peasants' dwindling wages.

An entry dated 11 May 1596[10] in the records of the quarter sessions refers to the theft of some 'Dutch wool' which was probably a newly woven bale of bay or say:

> William Goslynge of Little Maplestead, labourer, from breaking into the house of Robert Swayne at the same, in the night, the said Robert and all his household being there, and stealing 2 women's petticoats worth 20s, a woman's gown worth 13s 4d, divers parcels of linen worth 20s, a hat worth 5s, 14 cheeses worth 4s 8d, 30lb of Dutch wool worth 20s, a jerkin and a pair of stockings worth 10s and 9s 6d in money.

BRICKS FARM

WHILE DEANS COTTAGE was probably always a simple labourer's cottage, as its name suggests Bricks Farm, although originally a double cottage, seems to have had land. In *The Monuments of North-West Essex*[11] Bricks farm-house is described as being two storey, timber-framed and plastered with thatched roof. Built in the late sixteenth century, the original central chimney stack remains. The Bricks Farm land, however, was eventually amalgamated with that of Maplestead Hall farm. In fact Bricks Farm seems to have been part of the Maplestead Hall estate from at least 1730 when 'a survey of this manor' gives us these particulars;

> *The capital messuage [Maplestead Hall] with the outhouses and yards 5 acres, 31 perches. Several closes of meadow and pasture containing 90 acres, 3 roods, 38 perches. Several closes of arable land, about 140 acres 1 rood 38 perches. Woods containing 51 acres and 2 roods. In all 295 acres 2 roods 29 perches. A farm called Bricks containing in arable and pasture 60 acres*

In 1817 Joseph Slater, trustee for James Brewster, owned Bricks Farm as a trustee as part of the Maplestead Hall estate. The tenant at the time was George Nott. The following fields were listed as belonging to Bricks Farm:

91	Little Fallshams	
92	Great Fallshams	
96	Pulley land spring, wood	
97	" " "	
98	" " "	

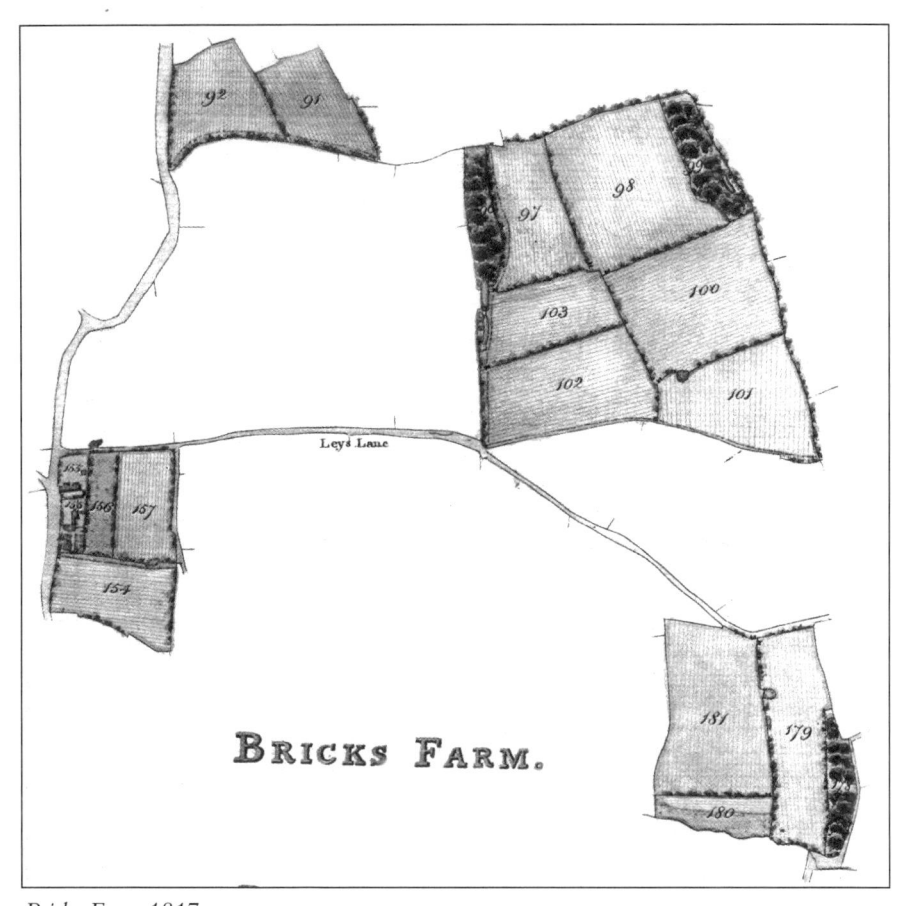

Bricks Farm 1817

99-103	Pulley land spring, wood
154	Lower Bricks field
155	house, homestead
156	Bricks field
157	Upper Bricks field
178	Baysland Wood
179	Little Baysland
180	Baysland Bottom
181	Great Baysland

[64 acres]

In the tithe award for 1841 Bricks Farm comprised:

    88   Fallshams
    91   Pulley lands
    92   Hither lands
    140   Lower Bricks Field
    141   Homestall
    142   Bricks Pasture
    164   Bays Land Wood
    165   Bays Land Field   [see tithe map pages 218-219]

The fields called the Pulley lands have a very ancient origin and derive from the ancient manor of Pooley whose manor house was Hunts Hall in Pebmarsh.

At the time of the 1841 census Bricks Farm was occupied by James Lott, an agricultural labourer, Mary Ann his wife and four children. A second family also shared the house. By 1861 Bricks Farm was occupied by Edward Golding who was a 'colt breaker' and in 1881 and 1891 by Samuel Butcher, farm bailiff for Maplestead Hall estate, his wife Charlotte and their daughter.

In 1919 Maplestead Hall estate advertised Bricks Farm for sale. At that time it was described as:

> *a useful small-holding with an old-fashioned farm-house, now used as cottages containing 3 sitting rooms, kitchen and 4 bedrooms. There is also a cart shed, open shed and yard, loose box, good barn, stabling for four and a cart-lodge.*

However, despite the attempt to sell, Bricks Farm still seems to have been part of the Maplestead Hall estate in 1937.

The barn at Bricks Farm is listed as late eighteenth century. Cecil Cook remembers this barn during the Second World War, when two Hanley Page bombers made emergency landings close by in the Ley Field. They were lost in bad weather on their way to their base at Stradishall. There was a crew of four in each plane and they were put up for the night in Bricks barn. According to Cecil, people came up from Halstead in buses to see the sight and next day the school children were taken to watch as the aeroplanes took off again safely!

THE COTTAGE

POSSIBLY OF EVEN earlier origins than any of the other sixteenth-century buildings in Little Maplestead is The Cottage. A simple cottage, timber-framed with plastering and displaying early pargetting, it was built in the sixteenth century and possibly earlier. It would have been in a cottage such as this that the peasant inhabitant might have worked as part of the wool and clothing trade, spinning the wool and, later, weaving it into the 'new drapery'.

The Cottage

It is precisely because it was such a simple dwelling that the records are sparse for The Cottage. We know that in 1817 it was owned by Samuel Wenden but the name of his tenant, the occupier of The Cottage, which was described in that year's survey as 'a cottage and garden, double' is not recorded.

In the 1841 tithe award, The Cottage, described as tenements, was owned by William Rayner and occupied by Thomas Henderson. From the 1841 census we find that Thomas Henderson, 40, an agricultural labourer lived at The Cottage with his wife Jane and daughter Mary. The Cottage was probably shared with at least one other family at this time but it is not clear from the census exactly who they were.

In 1871 The Cottage was occupied by Elizabeth Bishop, a widow of 78, a straw-plaiter, with her lodger James Corkerton, farm servant. The other tenement was probably occupied by John Dixey, horse-keeper, and his wife and family of six children. In 1881 William Binks, a farm labourer, and his wife Mary lived at The Cottage and by 1891 John Binks, a thatcher, and his wife Mary and daughter Margaret lived there.

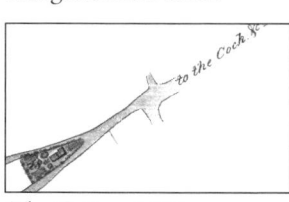

The Cottage 1817

In the nineteenth and early twentieth centuries The Cottage was always occupied by agricultural labourers, many of whom worked at Maplestead Hall farm, the last being Bill Simmonds, cowman for Mr Joe Blomfield at the Hall until the early 1980s, and his wife Mary.

According to Cecil Cook, in the 1920s the tramp, Bill Turp, lived for a while in the small building in the grounds of The Cottage which served as a shed and was known by some as Shoulder-stick Hall!

KISTUM COTTAGE

THIS COTTAGE is included here because its plot is clearly marked out on the 1600 plan of the village. However, the records for Kistum Cottage are few and only the description in the 1919 sale catalogue is certain when the cottage was described as a 'Double tenement cottage, plaster, slate and tiled':

> 1. South end, 2 bedrooms, dining room, kitchen, copper and sink fixed, pantry, good garden. Let to Mr Henry Pearson, a monthly tenant at the annual rent of £4 10s.
>
> 2. North cottage - 1 dining room, 2 bedrooms, pantry, slate roof, wash house, with copper and oven, let to Mrs Susannah Mayes, on a monthly tenancy at the low rent of £4 per annum.

THE GROVE

THE GROVE used to be in Gestingthorpe but, after the parish boundaries were redrawn in the 1980s, it was transferred to Little Maplestead. It is included in this chapter because it was first mentioned in a manorial document dated 1592.

A map dated 1804 made for the rector of Gestingthorpe shows a single building on a small plot of land which appears to have been enclosed from the highway, not an uncommon practice at this time. The house does not appear on the 1817 survey of the village because The Grove was then still in Gestingthorpe but the word 'school' is pencilled in on the site.

By the tithe map of 1841 an extension had been built on to the existing building (most likely a simple 'two up two down' cottage) and a separate building was placed to the north which is most likely the present Gothick cottage. The tithe map also shows changes to the boundaries of the property which reduced the obstruction to the highway. At that time the property belonged to Joseph Thomas Bethel Jones who had bought it in 1832; he was an academician who used The Grove as a small school for boys.

From a newspaper cutting of 1833[12]:

> *At Maplestead Academy ...the Terms are only 5 guineas per quarter including every expense (if under 10 years of age). This respectable establishment has been conducted by Mr J T B Jones for the last 15 years and being his own property has rendered it unequalled for comfort and convenience. The Premises, Play and Pleasure Grounds are spacious and the treatment kind and liberal in every respect.*

On census night in 1841 Grove House, as it was then referred to, accommodated a family of five, a governess, an assistant teacher, a servant and seventeen boys. The head or academician, Joseph Jones, had a wife and three daughters. The governess was Mary Ann Downs.

In 1847 J. T. B. Jones sold the property to Edward Mason, a coal merchant from Berkshire. The following year Mason leased the property, now called Poplar Grove, for seven years to Reverend William Clements of Halstead, a dissenting minister. The property is described as comprising a dwelling house, stable, coach house, cow house and other outbuildings, plus an adjoining dwelling house called West House, a bakehouse, brew-house, lawn, garden, orchard and meadow. The West House (probably the original cottage of the north-west wing) was let to a tenant who shared the use of the bakehouse and brew-house.

Although Reverend Clements held the lease from 1843 to 1855 the 1851 census records George and Sarah Underwood, a jobbing labourer and his wife, living there with their two children.

At the time of the 1861 census the property may have been empty. The 1864 conveyance from Edward Mason (deceased) to George Hearn describes two brick and slate messuages and a detached stable and coach house as being unoccupied. In 1867 George Hearn sold the property to Reverend John Harward of Little Maplestead. A mortgage which the Reverend Harward took out on the property at this time mentions that the two brick and slate messuages had lately been converted into one dwelling. By the time of the 1871 census The Grove was occupied by the vicar, his wife, son, daughter, step-daughter and a housemaid. On the same census enumerator's schedule the uninhabited 'Old House Cottage' is recorded.

By the 1881 census, Poplar Grove was occupied by the Reverend Harward, and also an agricultural labourer and his wife, their two children and a boarder. The same year Reverend Harward sold the property to George Hearn of Hepworth Hall, Halstead, who was a farmer; he appears to have let the property to the curate of Lamarsh, the Reverend Joseph Cornah; the 1891 census shows it was lived in by his family of eight, two boarders and a general servant. Joseph Cornah occupied Poplar Grove until 1895.

When George Hearn died in 1900, The Grove was sold to F. E. Barnes of Mincing Lane, London, a drug broker. In 1918 the house was sold to C. E. Brewster of Maplestead Hall. By this time it was being described as including 'garden, grounds and all outbuildings, groom's cottage, stable, chaise house and loft, and pasture land adjoining.' Shortly after this, around 1922, Mr and Mrs Lyon came to live at The Grove. Mr Lyon set up an egg-packing business there collecting local eggs and selling to London in association with his neighbours the Williams brothers. Cecil Cook remembers that Mr Lyon employed several people from the village, amongst them Jack Felton, who used to do the London rounds in an old Ford van. Even in 1979, when The Grove was mentioned to any long-time inhabitant of Little Maplestead or Halstead, they would still refer to it as the 'egg-packing station'. Mr Lyon also dealt in scrap metal and The Grove became a store-house for his purchases - a number of enormous Nissen huts, now demolished, were erected in the grounds. The Lyons sold The Grove in 1964 but Miss Ivy Lyon continued to live nearby in Halstead until her death when her funeral was held at the Round Church.

WILLIAM SHAKESPEARE

NO MENTION of the sixteenth century would be complete without reference to William Shakespeare and the villagers of Little Maplestead may have an unexpectedly close association with England's greatest literary genius. The exact date when Shakespeare wrote *A Midsummer Night's Dream* is not known but it is thought to have been in 1597. Locally there is a story that Shakespeare wrote the play while staying in a lodge or guest-house of the castle at Castle Hedingham, although there is no hard evidence for this, and it has also been suggested that it may have been first performed for Queen Elizabeth I at Hedingham. But only a short distance away in Little Maplestead, just off one of the pretty lanes that Shakespeare might have ridden along, is the secluded hill called Pearman's Hill. First mentioned in 1446 as *una crofte terre vocata Puksale juxta terras vocatas Fitz Johns*, its name derives from Pucksale or Puxells which means 'hill of the goblin' or Puck's Hill. It is tempting to indulge in a flight of fancy and wonder whether Shakespeare might have found inspiration for his most famous spirit in this part of the village. Of all his plays, *A Midsummer Night's Dream* is his most individual creation.

In Shakespeare the English language had touched its moment of fullest beauty and power. Englishmen were not yet bound to the service of machines and had the potential to be craftsmen and creators at will. Peace and order at last prevailed in the land and politics, so long a fear and oppression, were for a few decades simplified into a service paid to a woman, Elizabeth I, who was to her subjects the symbol of their hopes for unity, prosperity and freedom.

Notes to Chapter VI

[1] William Harrison in Holinshed's *Chronicle*, 1577
[2] Document in Essex Record Office, T/A427/1/1
[3] Stow's *Annals*, p 579. In a deed from George Harper 1530; George Harper's seal is affixed.
[4] Document in ERO, D/DU 463/5
[5] Document in ERO, T/A427
[6] Deeds of School Farm
[7] Document in ERO, D/DU 1558
[8] Asa Briggs, *A Social History of England*, (London, 1983)
[9] Asa Briggs, *A Social History of England*
[10] Document in ERO, Ass 35/102/1/29
[11] The Royal Commission for Historical Manuscripts, *The Monuments of North-West Essex* (HMSO, 1922)
[12] *Halstead Gazette:* Maplestead Academy had been founded in 1819 but exactly where is not clear. It might have been held in the Meeting House.

SIXTEENTH-CENTURY EVENTS

1509 Henry VIII becomes king

1517 Martin Luther condemns the Church of Rome and begins the spread of Protestantism

1529 Henry VIII fails to obtain divorce from Catherine of Aragon from the Pope

1534 Henry VIII proclaims himself head of the Church in England and begins the dissolution of the monasteries

1535 Execution of Thomas More

1547 Edward VI becomes king

1553 Queen Mary becomes queen and begins religious persecution against Protestants

1558 Queen Elizabeth becomes queen

1587 Mary Queen of Scots executed

1588 Victory by the English fleet over the Spanish Armada

The Round Church, 1999

CHAPTER VII

THE SEVENTEENTH CENTURY

Houses are built to Live in, and not to Looke on:
Therefore let Use be preferred before Uniformity;
Except where both may be had.[1]

AS THE SIXTEENTH century passed into the seventeenth century English society and culture continued to flourish. But after the death of Elizabeth I and the accession of James I the country found itself on the brink of dramatic changes.

During the first few years of the seventeenth century the population growth had begun to slow down, price rises were stabilizing and, at the same time, by 1614, exports of cloth had never been higher. All this, of course, benefited the country as a whole but it was of especial value to those involved in the cottage wool industry and the local bays and says industry, supplied by the spinners and weavers of Halstead and the surrounding villages, went from strength to strength. Such employees in the wool trade, which included many villagers from Little Maplestead, must have entered the new century confident that their livelihoods were secure. This confidence must also have been felt by the sheep-farming landowners of both great estates and smaller farms. So great was their optimism for the future that they felt able to expand and improve their properties and it was during this century that Maplestead Hall had a substantial 'rebuild' for its new farming owners. This seventeenth-century work re-used many of L'Hospital's original and ancient timbers, including some uprights and tie beams with mortices for five-pegged arch braces and some heavily sooted roof rafters, reminders of its beginnings as a hall house[2].

During the seventeenth century Maplestead Hall had four lords of the manor[3]. The first, in 1602, was Edmund Wiseman, John Wiseman's youngest living son. Edmund had been a soldier in the Low Countries and a follower of the fortunes of Robert Devereux, Earl of Essex.

After Edmund's death his brother William took his place as lord of the manor of Little Maplestead followed by Sir Mark Guyon from Coggeshall who also owned and rebuilt Dynes Hall. In Guyon's will he left the manor of Little Maplestead and the Great Maplestead manors of Dynes, Caxtons and Hosedens to his son William. But William died without heirs and in 1693 his sister Elizabeth brought the manor of Little Maplestead to Edward Bullock as dowry in her marriage.

LITTLE MAPLESTEAD in th

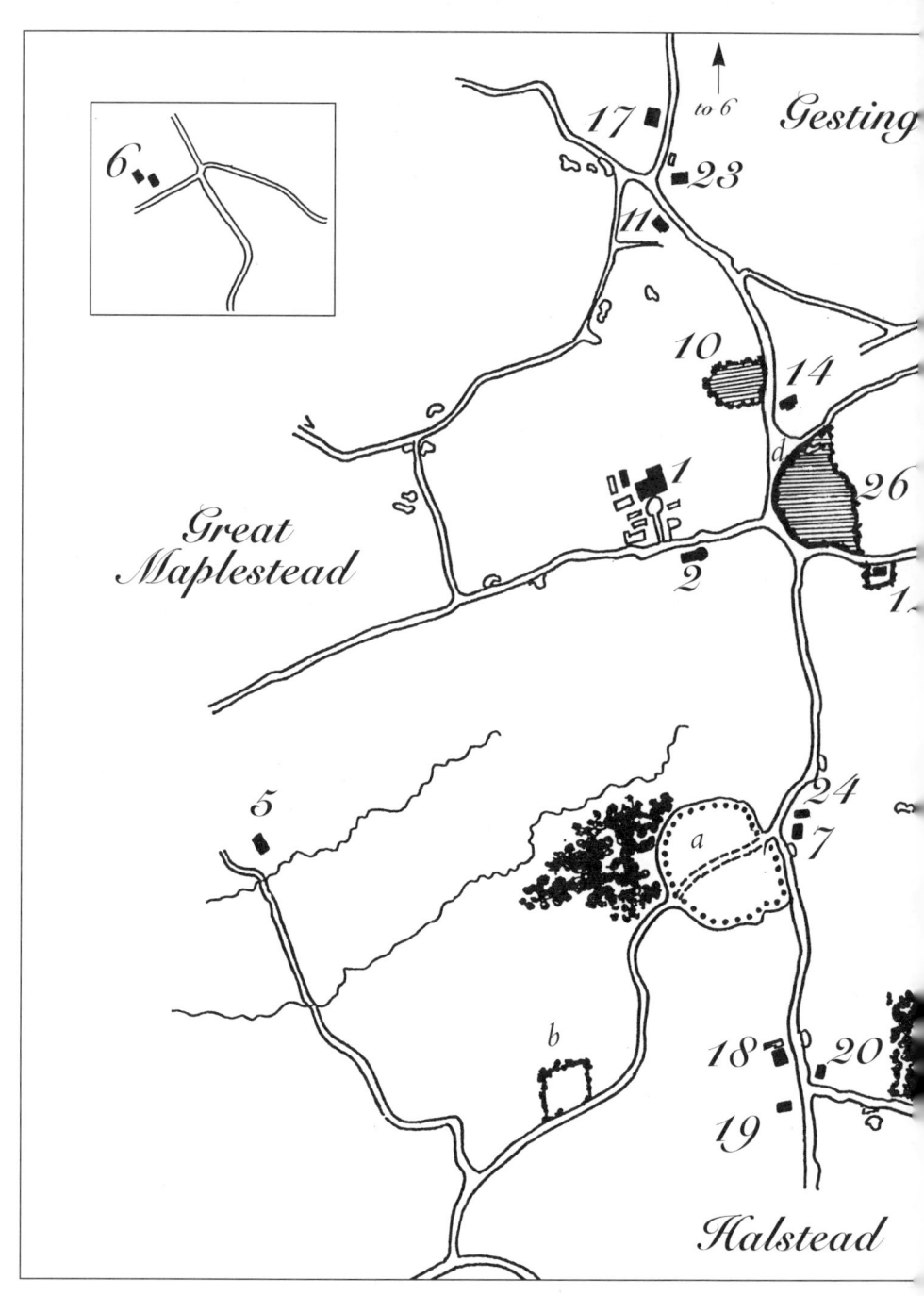

SEVENTEENTH CENTURY

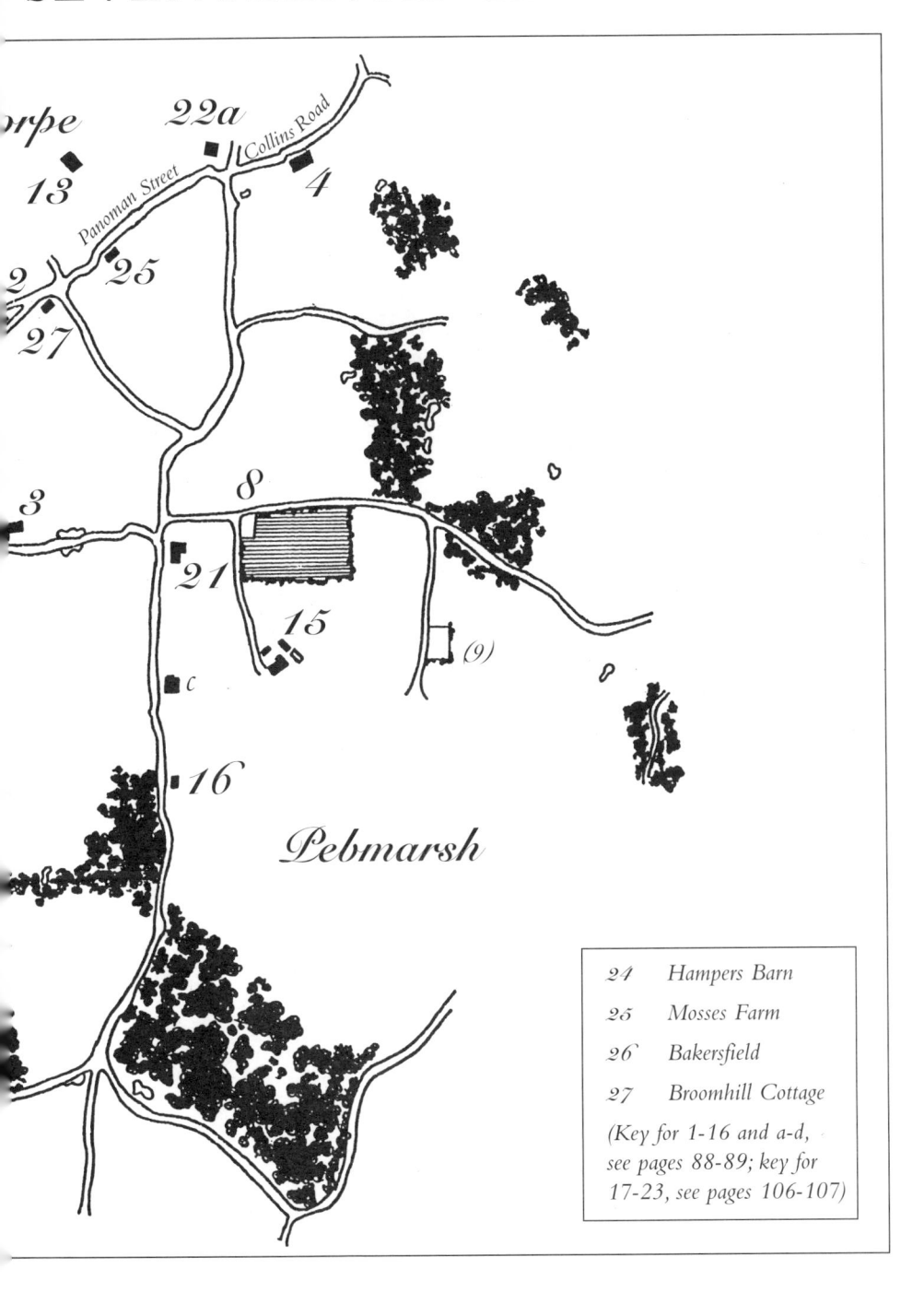

Pebmarsh

24	Hampers Barn
25	Mosses Farm
26	Bakersfield
27	Broomhill Cottage

(Key for 1-16 and a-d, see pages 88-89; key for 17-23, see pages 106-107)

Besides the land-owning gentry, even the smaller yeomen farmers shared in the general optimism and many improved their properties at this time by building barns to house animals, or to store grain and agricultural tools. Such a yeoman's farm was Hampers whose owner set about building a large thatched barn beside the farm-house.

HAMPERS BARN

FEW BARNS have a recorded history of their own but we do know a little about the barn at Hampers Farm. It was built in the early seventeenth century and ceased agricultural use in 1973. It was converted into a house in 1974, retaining its thatched roof and many of the original interior timber features.

The barn is mentioned in the 1919 sales catalogue as a two-bayed thatched barn with cement bays and floors and a large 'middlestree', the bay of a barn containing the main entrance for carts. This has been preserved in the house as a magnificent domestic window reaching from ground to roof.

Bill Turp, the village tramp who was a familiar sight in the 1920s with his donkey and cart, spent his last night of freedom in Hampers Barn. Homeless, he used to live rough around the village and made a little money, as his father had done, by getting lime from the pits at Sudbury and making it into balls to sell to people for whitewashing their ceilings. Eventually his hard life resulted in illness and when at last he became too ill to be on his own Bill Simmonds, from The Cottage, took him to Haverhill workhouse on a bed of hay in the back of a farm truck.[4]

POLITICS AND CIVIL WAR

DESPITE a promising start, turmoil and dramatic events were to characterize the seventeenth century and early on, in 1605, the Gunpowder Plot, a failed attempt by the Catholic Guy Fawkes to blow up James I and parliament, was a troubling portent of things to come. Greatly increased literacy amongst the general public was enabled and encouraged by the wide use of the printing press (in 1665 the first newspaper, *The London Gazette*, was to be published). This meant that religious and political pamphlets could inform many of the villagers of Little Maplestead of the latest developments in the country at large.

By the 1620s a variety of natural and economic problems coincided which dramatically changed the economic outlook and adversely affected the lives of all those working in the wool and cloth trades. Bad harvests, repeated epidemics of plague and an adverse balance of trade led to a rapid reduction of cloth exports and a need by the treasury to rely upon its gold reserves to pay for necessary imports of grain. A raft of new taxes were imposed - even upon beer - and life no longer seemed so good for the weavers, spinners and sheep farmers of Little Maplestead. Peasants and landowners alike began to make their grievances heard, focusing their anger on what they saw as unjust taxation.

Many grievances were expressed in terms of 'court' and 'country' - the court, under the new king Charles I, appeared to spend money extravagantly and 'the average man' saw favoured people elevated to high office and consequently to great wealth and status. The lord of the manor of Little Maplestead, William Wiseman, was in the service of Charles I and was created baronet by him in 1641. The old established country landowners, who had worked hard to create their own independence, found this favouritism unacceptable. The grave situation was made worse when the king dismissed parliament and continued to rule without it, being forced to impose martial law and unregulated powers of imprisonment upon the country. He had further incurred the wrath of the country gentlemen and yeomen farmers when he greatly increased the amount of tithes they had to pay. It was probably a yeoman farmer like this who lived in the farm called Mosses.

MOSSES FARM

MOSSES SEEMS always to have been a small farm. The farm-house, timber-framed and plastered, is listed as seventeenth century or earlier and this is confirmed by the map of part of the village dated 1600 on which Mosses is clearly shown.

It stands on two patches of land, one of which bears the tenant's name, Henry Edwards, and is called Terriers Croft. The other seems to belong to Maplestead Hall and bears the tenant's name Sampson.

Mosses Farm

An early deed shows that in 1718 William Sewell surrendered Mosses to William Moss senior, and that a tenant, John Crysal, was living there. The name Mosses Farm probably comes from the surname Moss. Moss's son, William junior, seems to have inherited the three acres of land called Terriers and one acre called Groyn acre; this had 'one chamber with appurtenances'. The land was rented first to John Ayleworth, then to John Crysal. According to a rental of 1723 Mosses possessed land belonging to the manors of Little Maplestead and Borley Hall and some woodland which was in the manor of Pebmarsh.

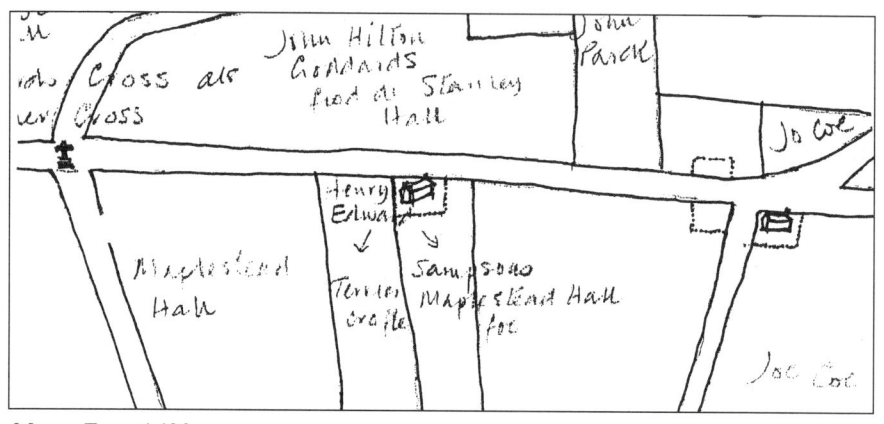

Mosses Farm 1600

In an interesting will of 1735, William Moss, described as a carpenter of Bulmer, gave his wife Sarah his property in Belchamp Walter, also the property in Bulmer where they lived, as long as she provided for the maintenance and education of their children, son William and daughters Sarah, Mary and Elizabeth. He gave to his son William the property in Little Maplestead occupied by John Crysal - Mosses Farm - and William was to use the rents to educate himself and his sisters. A brother-in-law, Robert Butcher, was executor. William Moss senior obviously realized the value of a good education and was keen that his children achieve their full potential.

In the mid-eighteenth century, Mosses Farm was bought by George de Horne Vaizey for £28 3s 6d and was let back to the Moss family. In 1788 we find William Moss named as a copyhold tenant of Mosses. This was probably William Moss junior. His only child, Mary, married John Baker and lived in Mosses Farm; she surrendered it to her daughter Rachel in 1796.

In 1800, in an abstract of title, Mosses Farm is confirmed as owned by George de Horne Vaizey but the 1817 survey of the village lists John Gunn, victualler and dealer in pigs, as proprietor; however, he was probably a sub-tenant. Four fields are recorded but none has a name; in all, the land amounts to just under fifteen acres.

In 1825 Gunn was succeeded by H. J. Bentall and by 1827 the tenant was William Webber from Woolwich, a watch-maker. Webber appears to have sub-let Mosses to William Moss Baker, great-grandson of the first William Moss, but by 1837 Moss had left. In that year, a gardener from Halstead called James Fairbank is recorded as leasing Mosses from George Vaizey, paying £40 for the fifteen acres. In a rental for the

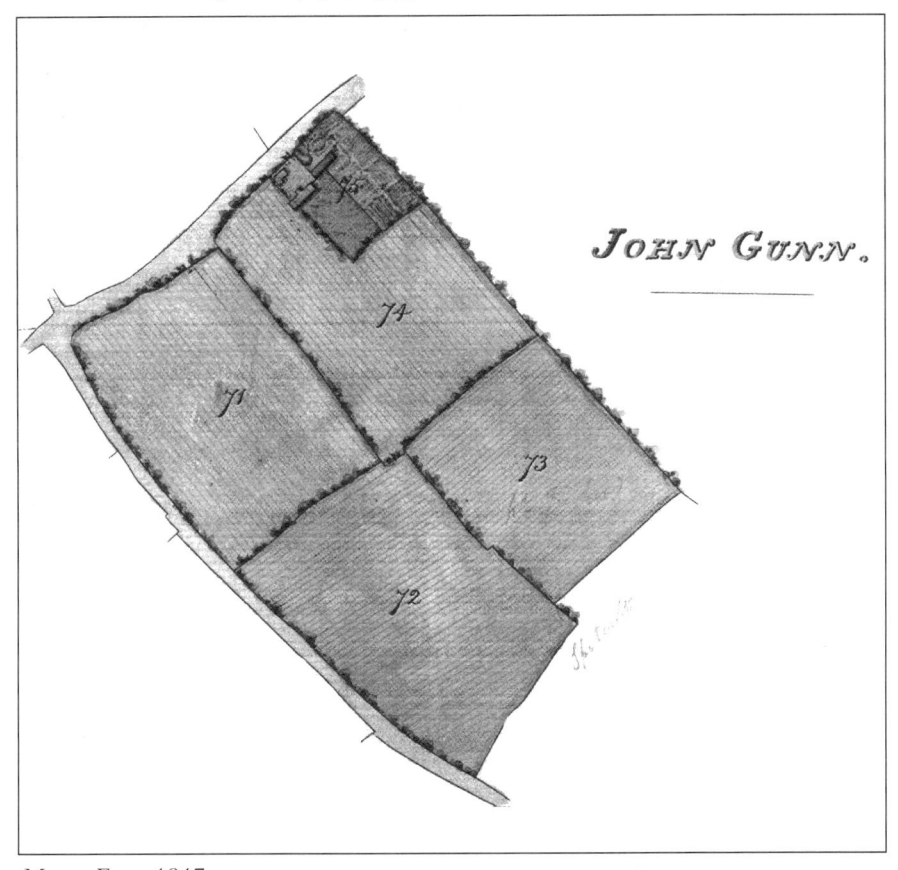

Mosses Farm 1817

manor of Little Maplestead of the same year Mosses Farm is described as 'all that customary messuage or tenement with barn, stable yard, garden, land …'

At the 1841 tithe award William Hearn farmed the fourteen acres of land belonging to Mosses Farm, and still rented from George Vaizey.

68	field arable
69	field arable
70	field arable
71	field arable
72	Homestall arable 14 acres [see tithe map pages 218-219]

The 1841 census shows that Hearn, described as a farmer, occupied the house with his wife Sarah and children William, Herbert, George, Sarah and John, aged between ten and two years old. William Hearn, farmer, is listed in an 1850 trade directory and, in an 1855 directory, William Hearn senior and junior are listed, as farmer and pork butcher. But in the 1859 directory only William Hearn junior, pork butcher, remains.

Mosses still held land from the manor of Borley in 1867, as a deed shows. Another deed, dated 1870, states that William Gatward of Castle Hedingham is tenant of Mosses for one year, renewed annually; the land belonging to the farm is shown as the three-acre Spitcroft, one part of Leppingwells, and the Rents of nine acres, across the road from the farm-house. Although Gatward was the tenant, the house was still occupied by William Hearn.

However, by the time of the 1871 census William Gatward was living at Mosses himself with Temperance, his wife, and his four children. He is described as a farmer employing one man and a boy with a holding of twenty-six acres, so land had obviously been added to the farm. Two years later, in 1873, Mosses formed part of the estate of the late Dr M. Vaizey of Star Stile, Halstead. In 1881 William and Temperance Gatward still lived at and farmed Mosses with their sons, Charles, William and Alfred, and George, William senior's brother, who was a butcher. In 1891 Charles Burdor, described as a small farmer, lived at Mosses with his wife Maria and their son Walter, a farm labourer. The house continued to pass from tenant to tenant until, in 1953, Mr and Mrs Cornell came to live in Mosses.

IN 1641, parliament at last seized back control from Charles I who moved out of London to Oxford; with him went those men loyal to him and these included the lord of the manor of Little Maplestead, Sir William Wiseman. A civil war was now set to take place between Charles and the forces of parliament led by Oliver Cromwell. His new model army represented the 'average man' - these were country landowners, yeomen, small farmers, merchants and craftsmen. Although, in general terms, the south-east of England tended to support the parliamentary cause, the villagers of Little

Maplestead may have remained loyal to the lord of their manor and supported the king, provided, of course, that William Wiseman had been a good manorial lord -and there is no reason to suppose that he was not. However, although over one hundred thousand men were killed in the ensuing series of battles, as in the Wars of the Roses many small communities remained unaffected. Little Maplestead, however, lost its lord of the manor; William Wiseman was killed fighting for the king. And when Charles surrendered into Cromwell's hands and was executed in 1649 the word of his manner of death must have spread like wildfire into the smallest of villages who would have learnt that England had become a protectorate with Cromwell as lord protector.

During the protectorate the vicar of Earls Colne, from 1641 to 1683, was Ralph Josselin, who kept a diary; in some entries he mentioned Little Maplestead[5]. These give some idea of country life in Essex at the end of the seventeenth century.

> *27/2/1644 Preached at Maplestead. God good to me in the going and returning, in the word preached, in the company of good friends, in the mercies of family, and in my strength notwithstanding my more than ordinary labour ...*

> *12/5/1645 Mr Shepheard of Maplestead accused by his maid for endeavouring to abuse her, his patience was so moved that he struck her on the mouth whereupon she bled much. It made much against him. The Lord discover truth, shame us in ourselves and preserve us from reproach ...* [*This was Edward Sheppard, vicar of Maplestead, who did not please the majority of his parishioners. He accused his maid Elizabeth Spurgeon of stealing various possessions while she and others accused him of being a common 'barrator' and disturber of the peace. The matter came to court but both sides were acquitted. By 1650 Sheppard still farmed some of the tithes in the village but the parish had found another preacher.*]

> *13/6/1649 I had a very comfortable and contentfull journey to visit some friends at Maplestead.*

> *23/12/1649 I went at night to Mr Harrington's at Maplestead where I was kindly entertained. I found his son ill, but in my opinion somewhat better than formerly.*

> *8/3/50 I went this day to Maplestead. I found Mr Harrington had made over the school to his kinsman Elliston and so had broken his promise and ingagement to me. This is the world. His son was taken up four days after his burial in the chancel and buried in the churchyard.* [*Elliston was probably Joseph Elliston, 1605-1663, son of Matthew and William Harrington's sister, Anne. The school referred to was probably held in the church. Both the Harrington family and the Elliston family are referred to later in the 1693 survey of the village.*]

FROM PROTECTORATE TO RESTORATION

CROMWELL'S new model army had included several radical republican groups – Cromwell himself was an Independent – and these groups now began to exert an influence upon the country. Fiercely puritanical, they began to impose their views everywhere and the villagers of Little Maplestead would have been all too aware of the new anti-gambling rules, the closed ale-houses in the village and the rules to suppress dancing and even such celebrations as Christmas. These radical groups diversified into the various bands of religious dissenters which evolved at this time – the Quakers, the Independents, the Baptists, the Unitarians and most significantly for Little Maplestead, the Sabbatarians. The Sabbatarians were a sect of dissenters who maintained an excessively strict observance of Sunday and it was a group of Sabbatarians led by Joseph Davis, a textile merchant from London, who later, in 1705, purchased the manor of Little Maplestead from Edward Bullock in the name of the Davis Charity to provide an income for his church. It was probably at this time too that the first seeds were sown for what was to be quite a strong nonconformist following in Little Maplestead.

During Cromwell's protectorate thousands of acres of royalist and church land were confiscated and redistributed – only to be returned to their rightful owners after the restoration of Charles II. And so, in the end, the civil war did not achieve any significant change in land ownership and certainly, for the poor, who had suffered from the dwindling wool trade, there was no improvement in their lot. By the end of the century, despite many set-backs, agricultural estates were continuing to expand and the possession of private property was more firmly established than before. Because of this feeling of stability among large landowners, particularly those who had not been totally dependent on the wool trade and who had diversified in their farming, great interest was developing in all manner of agricultural improvements which could now lead to higher crop yields. An extensive range of publications on profitable husbandry became available to progressive landowners who began to put the new theories into practice while many more experimented with their own ideas.

At this time there were about one hundred and sixty peers in existence and below them in status were another one hundred non-noble families who owned 10,000 acres of land or more[6]. The old barriers to hereditary peerage had been removed and these groups now began to intermarry to mutual benefit ensuring the survival of England's great estates. The gentry below these groups – as exemplified by Edward Bullock, lord of the manor of Little Maplestead – was called the 'squirearchy'; smaller landowners they may have been, nevertheless, between them they owned about half the land in the country. They were also much closer to the local community; many had been made justices of the peace and many were also in charge of the local militia volunteer defence force – the only armed force in the country – all of which gave them substantial power and in many ways made them the most influential class of people in seventeenth-century society.

THE VILLAGE IN 1693[7]

THE FOLLOWING transcript of a rental taken from the court book of the manor of Little Maplestead gives an over-view of the village at this time.

A Yearly Rentall made by and with the Consent of the whole Homage At a Court Baron of Edward Bullock Esq held on Tuesday the first day of August Anno 1693 for the Mannor of little Maplesteed Hall.

Copyhold Mr John Baker for a certain field called Impnells 5 acres late Samuel Richardson near the Starch-house gate.

Freehold of [?] Hurrell for land late of J Freeborn called Hurrells.

Copyhold John Bridge and Sarah his wife for a customary tenement and croft called Merrymans late Robert Jefferson also for his customary land part of Willsons late William Syday's.

Copyhold of Anna Bingham for a customary tenement called Willsons late Edmund Syday's after Edmund Harrington.

Copyhold of Joseph Crane for his cottage abutting upon land called Adricks.

Freehold of John Cooke and now John Cooke his son for certain lands called Leppingwells.

Freehold of the same for a parcel of land late Parkes afterwards Joseph Cookes.

Freehold of the same for a parcel of land called Hillards late William Harrington's.

Copyhold of Abraham Cooke for a parcel of land called Scurborks late William Harrington.

Freehold of the same for a croft of land called Stonards late Ambrose Biggs after William Harrington.

Freehold of John Dodd for a tenement and croft of land abutting upon Hillard Wood late John Cooke's called Little Pasture [added later: pulled down and wood stubbed by old Rob. Deal about 1730 - lies in lane leading to Cock by Joys Wood. Broomhill].

Freehold of John Deane certain parcel of land lying at High Wood late John Makin's.

Freehold of the same parcel of land called Barne Croft late Susanna [?Wistods].

Freehold of John Dearsh certain wood called Hillards late Thomas Searsly's.

Freehold of Mr Elliston Freehold tenement called Crane's and a parcel of land called Little Brockolls occupied by John Aylwood [added later: in green lane leading to Cock from Maplestead church].

Freehold of William [?F...ham] Tenement called Little Pasture.

Copyhold of Richard French Tenement and orchard abutting upon messuage of John Spearepoints late W Lord's.

Copyhold of John Harrington Part of a tenement and certain lands customary late of John Edwards and afterwards of Thomas Harrington father of John Harrington.

Copyhold of George Kempe Portwells late of Nicholas Clarke's.

Freehold of John King, now John Baker's Tenement and customary lands late of John Garwood's.

Freehold of the same tenement and certain parcels of land late of John Garwood's.

Freehold of W Lords For tenement late burnt down and croft of land called Barres late of William Betts [added later: on Hurrells Green].

Copyhold of Luke Lawrance now David Stone Tenement and lands late of William Smith after John Burton.

Freehold of John Maynard Tenement late Mr Hilton's.

Copyhold of Robert Moore Certain tenement late of Edmund Harrington.

Copyhold of same Tenement late William Hill's after purchased of the Lord of the Manor by Edmund Harrington.

Freehold Thomas Otley Tenement late Thomas Miller's.

Copyhold Samuel Parmenter Customary tenement abutting on house of Richard French.

Copyhold of Mr James Robinson Braggs, the Links, Goodins Meadow and part of Bushy and Joys Wood late Mr Hilton's [Bushes, now lost, was on the 1777 Chapman & André map on the lane to Parks Farm].

Freehold Mr Ray parcel called Harwoods late Ambrose Biggs.

Freehold the same Parcel of land lying against Mountegreene in occupation of Thomas Tiffin [added later: near Braggs Farm now occupied by Samuel Hart. This could be origin of Mont fields at Gages].

Copyhold Jeremiah [?Sh ...ingley] Parcel of customary land lying in High Field.

Copyhold John Sparepoint Customary messuage.

Freehold of Samuel Sparrow now John Wade parcel of land called High Field joining to Link Hills late John Cooke then John Parker.

Freehold the same, now John Wade, for parcel of marsh ground lying by Link Hills late John Cooke, John Baker.

Freehold Thomas Sewell parcel of land called Bakers late William Layzell's.

Freehold of the school master of Sudbury, for certain freehold land belonging to the college of Sudbury in the occupation of William Carter, School Farm

Freehold Elizabeth Siday, widow, tenement and one croft of land

Copyhold of the Widow Walker, Turpitts.

The manor of Little Maplestead also included an almshouse, tenements and land in Sible Hedingham, properties and land in Halstead, tenements, lands and marshland in Gestingthorpe, land in Belchamp Walter, and land and marshland in Great Maplestead.

BAKERSFIELD

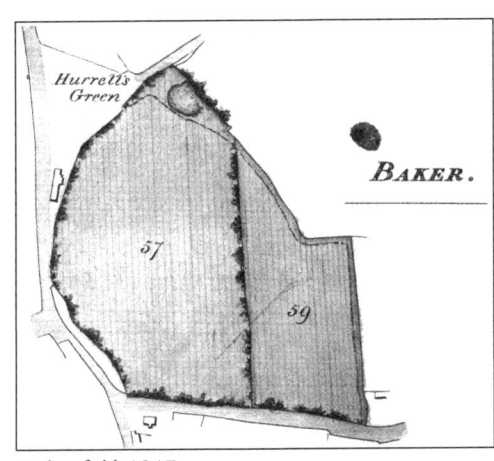

THE HOUSE built in 1977 for Mr and Mrs Wicks called Bakersfield was named after the land on which it stood. The earliest record of this field name is in the 1693 rental and the land was part of the parcel of land called Bakers owned freehold by Thomas Sewell, and probably rented by the Baker family

But by the 1817 survey of the village John Baker owned the field which was called Mrs Baker's field and the tenant was George Firmin.

Bakersfield 1817

THE PICTURE of the manor of Little Maplestead shown in the 1693 rental seems to portray a relatively affluent village which no doubt was due to its stable and prosperous history. Here we see the villagers secure in their freehold or copyhold houses and cottages almost all occupied on the land, many involved in sheep-farming and the wool industry. But it provides no evidence for the existence of the poor - at this time about half the families in the country. Many of these were living below subsistence level and would have had the meanest of dwellings that would not have been listed as part of any manor. In the 'dearth' of 1659, a year of great famine and hardship, the poor suffered greatly. They were also affected by the game laws passed in 1671 where no freeholder of less than one hundred pounds income a year (which meant most people) could kill any game even on their own property. This of course took away a vital source of food. Things became so bad that a futile attempt was made to 'divert the poor' by reviving those lately banned recreations such as dancing, Christmas and 'May' festivities. The poor law which had been introduced as a system of public relief was barely adequate to cope with the situation. Care of the poor was now in the hands of each parish and the 1632 act of settlement had enabled a parish to eject any newcomer who could not support himself back to the parish from whence he had come.

BROOMHILL COTTAGE

ORIGINALLY THIS cottage was probably occupied by those at the poorer end of the social scale but by those lucky enough to be employed and so by no means poverty stricken. Broomhill is listed as seventeenth century or earlier. It is timber-framed and plastered with later alterations and recent extensions.

There is a mention of Bromehill in an early rental of 1603 but no details; however in the 1693 rental of the village there is a record of a tenement and croft of land called Little Pasture abutting upon Hillard Wood in the lane leading to the Cock by Joys wood. This tenement is probably Broomhill so it would seem that Broomhill was built sometime before 1693 and possibly as early as 1603, but it is not present on the 1600 map of the village. It seems to have been pulled down in about 1730 and rebuilt again for by 1753 a deed dated 3 January states that Stephen Bridge of Pebmarsh, then of Colne Engaine, and his wife Mary convey Broomhill to a Mr Cook.

A deed dated 1800 mentions Broomhill, described as a cottage, in earlier occupation by 'Matthew Otley, Thomas Wyatt, Abraham Bocking, John French the younger and now of John Cook of Great Maplestead'. It is being handed over to Aaron Lamprell, the younger, of Little Maplestead. The property comprises one acre of land and a cottage.

In 1812 Aaron Lamprell (who could not write but made his mark) handed Broomhill on to John Sewell. But in the 1817 survey of the village we find Aaron Lamprell named as the owner with no tenant named; the entry reads '69, 70 cottage and garden'.

Broomhill 1817

It seems that there may have been two cottages on the plot of Broomhill at this time. In a later sale catalogue dated 1874 we find Broomhill described as 'all those 2 timber built, lath and plaster and tiled freehold cottages in a good state of repair with outbuildings and a new WC. 1 acre of highly productive garden ground.'

At the 1841 tithe award the cottage was owned by Joseph Spurgeon but the census shows that Samuel Davey lived there with his wife Henrietta, two sons and a daughter, together with Samuel Salmon, his wife Harriet and their baby. John Davey his wife and young children may also have lived there. The 1851 census shows that Samuel Davey still lived at Broomhill with his wife and one daughter but in 1871 the cottage was shared by Joseph Walls and his family; George Walls, his wife and children, John Watkinson and his wife and the Potter family. In 1881 Jeffery Summers lived there with the Walls. The latter were still at Broomhill in 1891, by which time the cottage was owned by George Vaizey of Star Stile.

The 1874 sales catalogue recorded that Broomhill was 'Now in occupation of George Walls, Walter Downes, and Robert Potter at the Low rent of 9s per annum'. And the property was described in 1879 as having been 'one old cottage and 2 plots of land'. A barn had stood on one plot and this had been pulled down and the double cottage built. In 1926, when Broomhill was home to Mr and Mrs W. and Mr and Mrs J. Felton it was referred to as the 'end of lane' cottage.

BY THE LATTER HALF of the seventeenth century, eleven percent of the population of England lived either in London or in one of the towns with a population of more than five thousand[8]. The nearest large town to Little Maplestead, apart from London, was Norwich 'a rich thriving industrious place'[9] whose population had doubled between 1600 and 1650; one in nine people lived in London in 1700 when its population was more than four hundred thousand[10]. It was calculated that of

- 145 -

an English population of over five million, more than four million lived in the villages and hamlets of rural England[11].

As the seventeenth century drew to a close, the economic situation grew so bad that in 1694 the ever-increasing government expenditure resulted in the setting up of the Bank of England. Trade and industry had been badly affected by the fluctuating economy and it was the country landowners who were the most secure. 'Trade and Credit were less solid than the land' and it was the landed gentlemen, yeomen and farmers who were the 'most settled inhabitants and the bulk of the nation'[12]. At the end of the century it was these men, men like the lords of the manor of Little Maplestead, who were described as the 'true owners of the political vessel, the money'd men no more than mere passengers in it'.[13]

Notes to Chapter VII

[1] Francis Bacon, *The Essays of Bacon*, (OUP)
[2] Essex County Council Department of Planning, Listed Building Register
[3] Reverend Philip Morant, *History and Antiquities of the County of Essex* (reprinted 1978, Wakefield)
[4] Information supplied by Miss Helen Blomfield
[5] *The Diaries of Ralph Josselin*, published by Alan McFarlane
[6] Statistics from Asa Briggs, *A Social History of England (London, 1983)*
[7] Document in ERO, D/DDd M6
[8] Statistics from Asa Briggs, *A Social History of England*
[9] Daniel Defoe, *Tour through the whole Island of Great Britain*
[10] Statistics from Asa Briggs, *A Social History of England*
[11] Winston Churchill, *A History of the English Speaking Peoples* (Purnell)
[12] Trade pamplet quoted by Asa Briggs. *A Social History of England*
[13] Viscount Bolingbroke (1678-1751)

SEVENTEENTH-CENTURY EVENTS

1601 Beheading of the Earl of Essex

1603 James I becomes king of England and Scotland

1605 Gunpowder plot discovered

1620 Mayflower sets sail for New England

1625 Charles I becomes king

1642 English civil war begins

1649 Charles I executed; beginning of the Commonwealth

1653 Cromwell becomes protector

1660 Monarchy restored; Charles II become king

1665 Great plague of London

1666 Great fire of London

1685 James II becomes king

1689 William and Mary come to the throne

CHAPTER VIII

THE EIGHTEENTH CENTURY

> *They hang the man and flog the woman*
> *That steals a goose from off the common*
> *But leave the greater criminal loose*
> *That steals the common from the goose.*[1]

THE EIGHTEENTH CENTURY was a century of remarkable growth, adventure and innovation. First and foremost was the growth of the British empire which affected all Englishmen whatever their status - rich or poor, lord or peasant - and changed the way they perceived the world. At the beginning of the century, by 1713, Britain had twenty-five possessions including Newfoundland, Nova Scotia, Barbados, Jamaica, Gibraltar, Bombay, Madras and Calcutta. By 1763 nine more had been added which included Canada, the Falkland Islands, Minorca and St Louis. And, by 1815, twenty-eight more territories recognized British rule, among them Trinidad and Tobago, Malta, the Seychelles, the Maldives, Ceylon, Singapore, New South Wales, New Zealand and Sierra Leone. The possibility of high profits, including those from the developing slave trade, had drawn British adventurers to all corners of the globe and between 1700 and 1780 British foreign trade had doubled and with it shipping. Suddenly the horizons of ordinary folk were expanded beyond their imagination.

THE VALUE OF LAND

BUT ALONGSIDE the growth of the British empire was another source of wealth and power which was being exploited and one which was close to the lives of those who lived in Little Maplestead. Throughout the eighteenth century the quest for riches was being pursued as successfully inside England as it was abroad. Land was this major source of wealth, status and power and it was through land that the great landlords continued to expand, improve and secure their economic position within the country.

In 1700 peers had owned about twenty percent of England's wealth in land and by 1800 they owned about twenty-five percent[2]. Below them in social status, the landed gentry, which included the lords of the manor of Maplestead Hall, were also

LITTLE MAPLESTEAD in

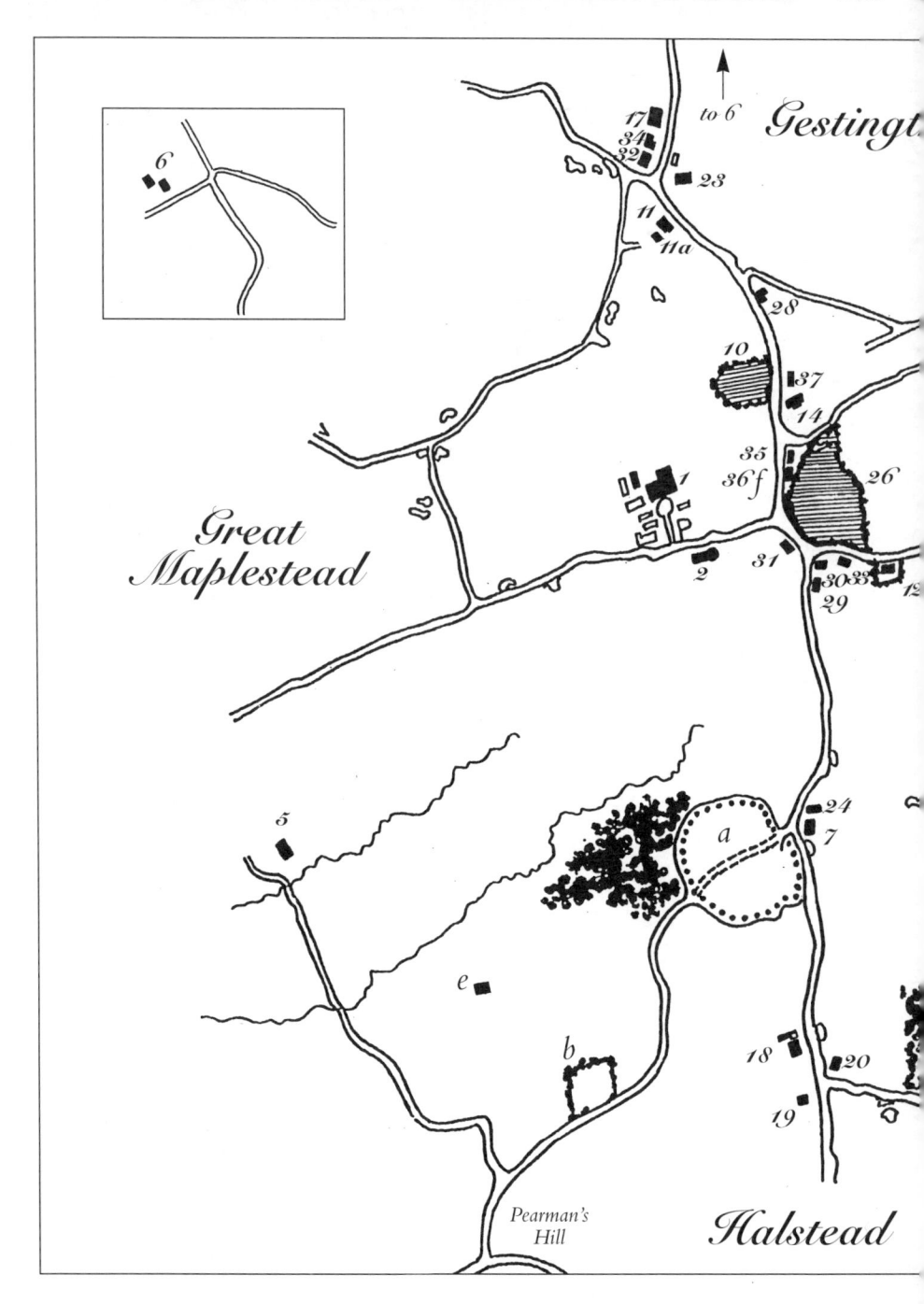

EIGHTEENTH CENTURY

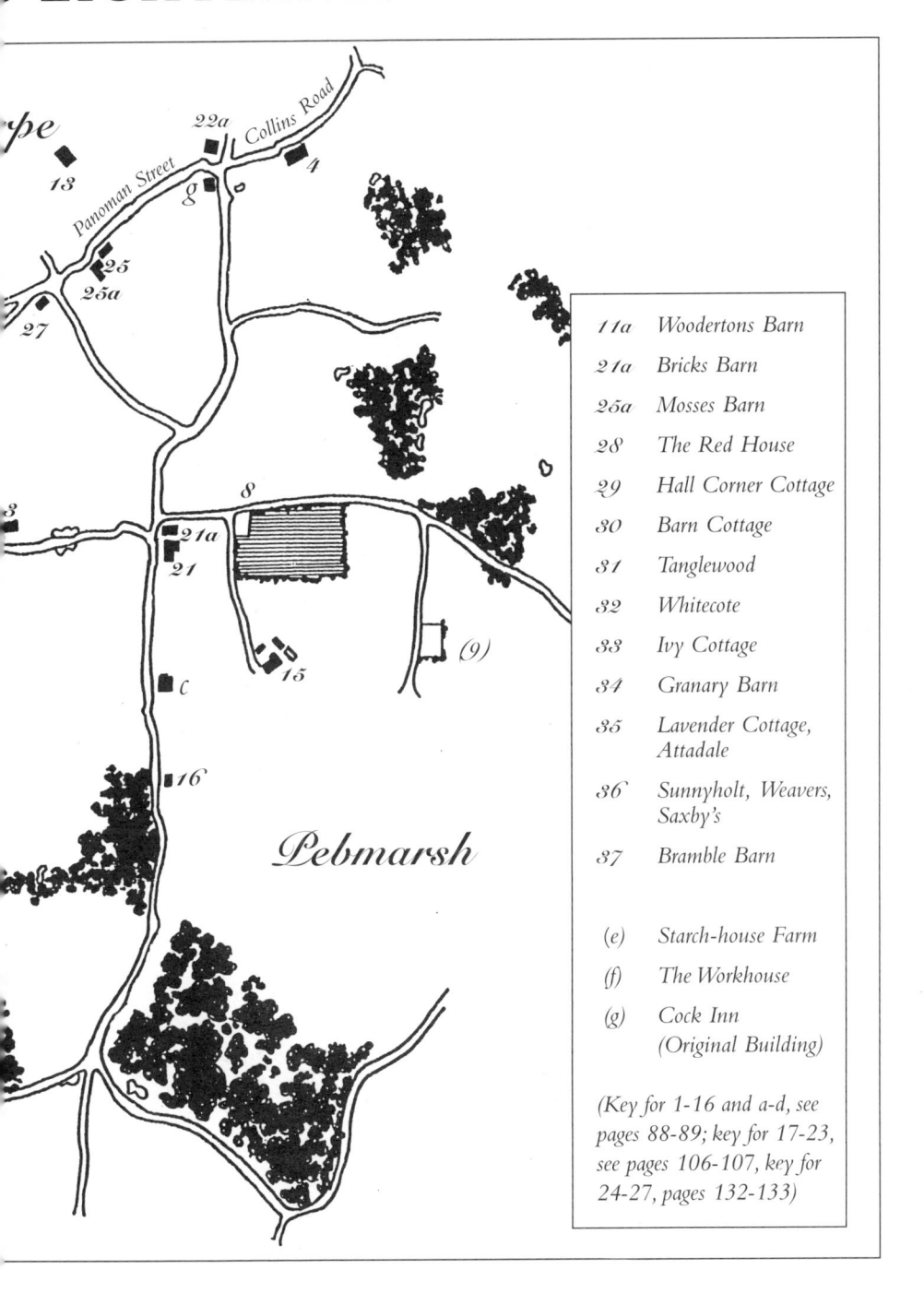

11a	Woodertons Barn
21a	Bricks Barn
25a	Mosses Barn
28	The Red House
29	Hall Corner Cottage
30	Barn Cottage
31	Tanglewood
32	Whitecote
33	Ivy Cottage
34	Granary Barn
35	Lavender Cottage, Attadale
36	Sunnyholt, Weavers, Saxby's
37	Bramble Barn
(e)	Starch-house Farm
(f)	The Workhouse
(g)	Cock Inn (Original Building)

(Key for 1-16 and a-d, see pages 88-89; key for 17-23, see pages 106-107, key for 24-27, pages 132-133)

interested in improving their agricultural practices and increasing their revenues. It was generally acknowledged that 'merchants were commonly ambitious of becoming country gentlemen[3]'. Even Daniel Defoe's Robinson Crusoe bought land in Bedfordshire when he returned from his desert island and, in Little Maplestead, Joseph Davis the textile merchant from London purchased the manor of Little Maplestead in 1705 - although it must be said, in his case, he had bought the estate as a means of supporting his church rather than creating wealth for himself. His son Joseph inherited the manor at the death of his father in 1707 and continued to use the rents to support his church and so the Little Maplestead lords of the manor at this time were honourable exceptions to the general rule.

Certain documents give us glimpses into the daily running of Little Maplestead manor at this time: the lord of the manor continued in his responsibilities towards the village priest. In a document entitled: *Conveyance of Great Tithes of Little Maplestead to be held in trust for Joseph Davis' Charity for Sabbatarian Protestant Dissenters (1777)* there is a conveyance of tithe rent charge and perpetual annual stipend of £10 payable to the curate of the Round Church. Dated 29 November 1777 it includes 'articles to secure a stipend of £10 per annum. Rev Thomas Orchard, clerk and curate of Maplestead Parva'.

In the gamekeepers' books for the manor of Little Maplestead the gamekeepers are registered and listed for each lord of the manor:

> *Joseph Davis Lord of the Manor, Maplestead, Edward Morley Gamekeeper, Date of authority 12 Jan 1713, date of entry 25 March 1713*[4].
>
> *William Stead, Lord of the Manor of Little Maplestead, Matthew Sargent, Gamekeeper, Dated 7 Sept 1762, Entered 11 September 1762*[5].
>
> *Daniel Noble, gent., Lord of the Manor of Little Maplestead, Gamekeeper, John Sewell the younger, Dated 24 June 1778, Entered 11 July 1778*[6].

These lords of the manor held their titles from the Davis Charity. Recorded in the court book for the manor of Little Maplestead in 1781 is an entry concerning John Sewell when his father and mother, originally from the neighbouring village of Earls Colne, were admitted tenants to a piece of land in the village called Joyswood. Ten years later, his parents having died, John Sewell, their son and heir, was admitted tenant to Joyswood in the same way. He was now also the owner of Lodge Farm and Goldmillers or Strongmillers (now lost); his father had inherited these estates from his uncle and by 1797 Maplestead Hall itself was occupied by John Sewell as a tenant on lease.

John Sewell was to make a name for himself with his interest in agricultural improvements and he became quite famous in certain local circles. But he was not alone. Starch-house Farm was occupied by another local celebrity.

STARCH-HOUSE FARM AND PEARMAN'S HILL

STARCH HOUSE FARM, pulled down early in the twentieth century, was once owned by the famous John Morley of Halstead, originally a butcher by trade who probably lived there when he was first married.

Starch-house Farm

Morley was born in Halstead in 1655 and married into money. After his marriage he lived at Starch-house and when Edward his second son was baptized at Little Maplestead on 20 April 1690 he presented the register book to the parish. A third son was baptized there in 1697. John Morley was fortunate to meet and come under the patronage of Sir Josiah Child and was so skilled at buying and selling land that he soon amassed a large fortune and was admitted to the friendship of many influential people including Robert Harley, the Earl of Oxford, the Duke of Newcastle and the poet Alexander Pope. Morley's son Edward owned Starch-house Farm from 1723 although he lived at Hepworth Hall near Sible Hedingham. Edward's son, John, lived at Starch-house until 1776. From Starch-house, John Morley senior moved to the prestigious Blue Bridge House in Halstead where the Butchers' Company coat of arms can be seen over the gate to this day. He died in 1733 and is buried in a vault in the Bourchier chapel in St Andrew's Church, Halstead. Despite his wealth and status John Morley never forgot his humble origins as a butcher and, having paid for the paving of Halstead market-place, he slaughtered a pig there every year to demonstrate his pride in his trade.

By the 1817 survey of the village Starch-house Farm was divided up into three parts. John Sperling Esq, from Dynes Hall, owned the main part:

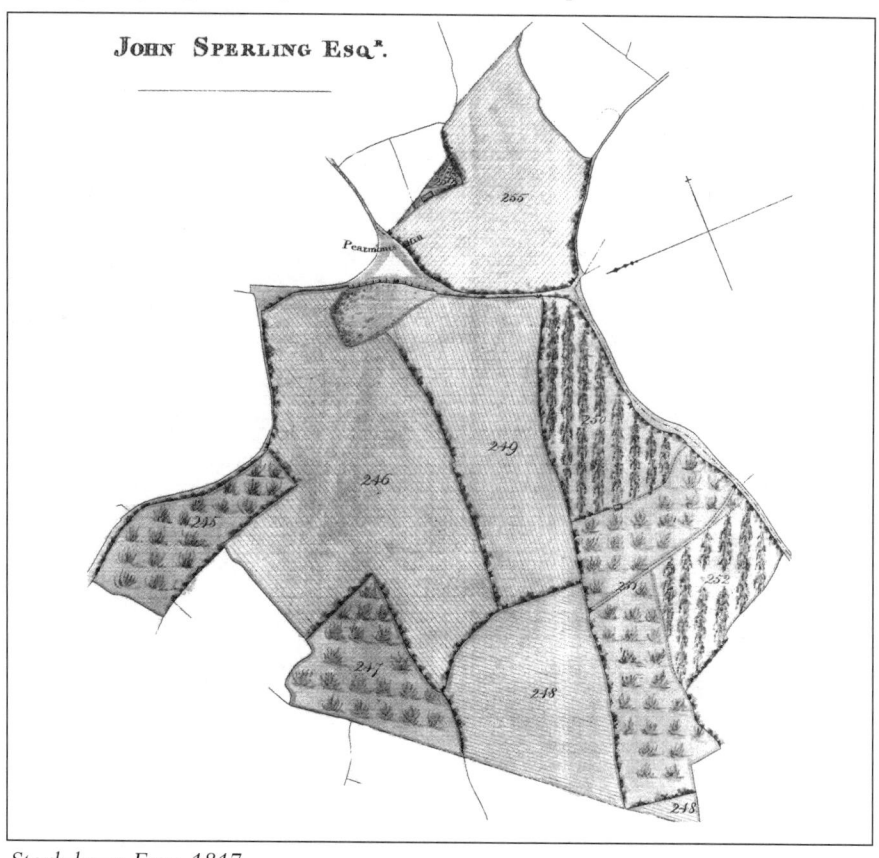

Starch-house Farm 1817

245 Starch house ash ground, ash wood
246 The Ley
247 p/o Fen Ash Ground, ash wood
248 p/o Great Harlow
249 Stony Ley
250 Tavenders Hop Ground, hops
251 Harlow Ash Ground, ash wood
252 Old Hop Ground, hops
255 p/o Pearmonts [Pearman's] Hill field

256 Cottage and garden at Pearmont's Hill

Secondly Ambrose Myall owned:

238 Down wood meadow
239 Ash Ground, ash wood
240 Yard and buildings
241 Starch House Cottage and pightle
242 Long Panamas
243 Panamas
244 Plantation, firs

Thirdly John Turner owned (235) and (236) part of Barn field.

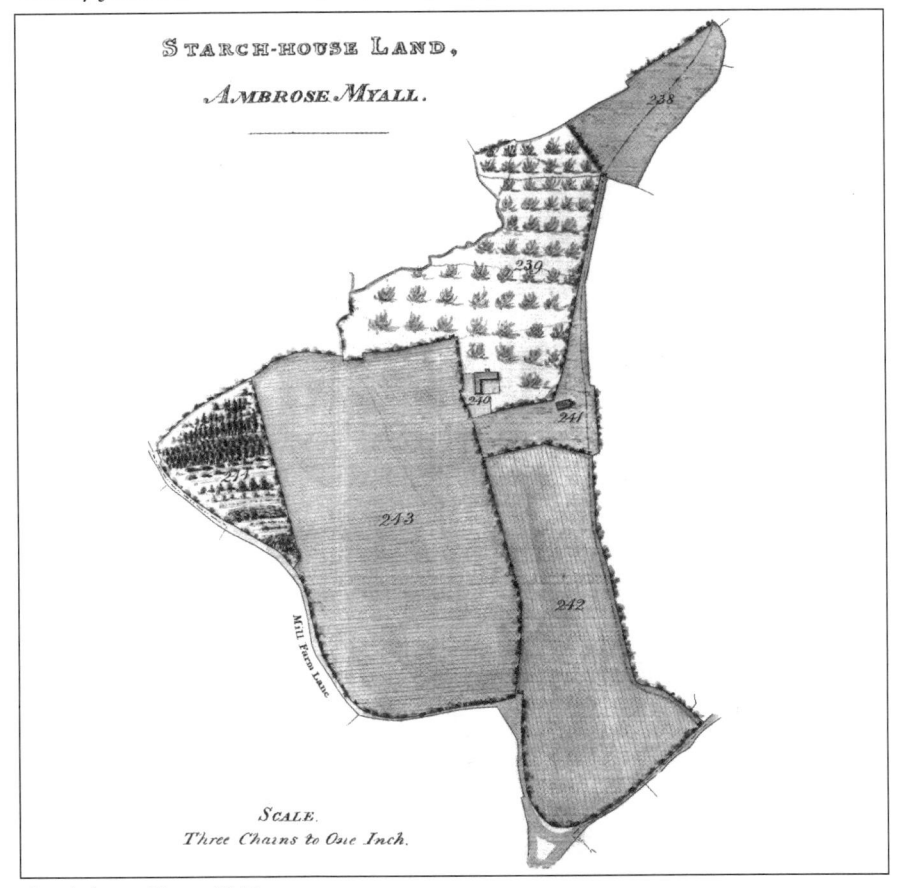

Starch-house Farm 1817

- 153 -

In the 1841 tithe award Starch-house Farm was owned by Henry Sperling and sublet to William Emberson. The land was greatly reduced in acreage:

215	Pasture grass
216	arable piece arable
218	arable piece arable
219	yards and buildings grass
220	cottage and pasture grass
222	Panamas arable
223	Panamas arable

22 acres [see tithe map pages 218-219]

In the 1841 census we find Mary Radley, 53, straw-plaiter, at Starch-house together with James Richer, 60, an agricultural labourer, his wife Mary and children James, 15, an agricultural labourer and William 10. Mary Radley still occupied what was then called Starch-house Cottage in 1851 but she was a lodger, described as a pauper. She shared the house with Joseph Partridge, 39, a farm labourer, his wife Mary and children Frederick, Mary-Ann and Hannah. Later, in 1871, we find James Warren, 55, a farm labourer, and Judith his wife, a straw-plaiter, daughters Jane and Charlotte, son William and grandson Walter. Mary Radley was still there aged 86. In 1881 the Warren family were still at Starch-house with their daughter Charlotte and a lodger Mary Potter. By 1891 Starch-house was unoccupied and eventually it was pulled down, like the cottages at Pearmont's or Pearman's Hill, in the early 1900s.

The 1861 census listed three cottages on Pearman's Hill. The families that occupied them were Isaac Emberson, 54, agricultural labourer and his wife Elizabeth and children Emma, 17, a crêpe weaver, and Mark, 15, an agricultural labourer; George Patrick, 50, an agricultural labourer and his wife Louisa, sons Charles, 16, and James, 14, agricultural labourers, and young children Eliza, Henry and Ann; Samuel Mole, 79, an agricultural labourer, his wife Rebecca and unmarried daughter Harriet, 48, a straw-plaiter. In the 1871 census we find James Patrick, 24, a horse keeper, Jane his wife, a straw-plaiter, and baby Clara; George Patrick, 60, agricultural labourer, his wife Louisa, a straw-plaiter, and children Eliza, 23, a straw-plaiter and son Henry, 20, a stock-man; Rebecca Mole, a widow of 86, a house domestic, and daughter Harriet, a needle-worker. Ten years later, in 1881 Harriet was living alone. James Patrick, 35, was now a farm labourer and Jane was still a straw-plaiter, they had four young sons James, William, Henry and Charles and a daughter, Eliza. Henry Patrick, 30, a labourer, lived with his sister Eliza, a straw-plaiter, and his niece Sarah, 13. In 1891 James Patrick, 20, an agricultural labourer lived there with his wife Sarah, a silk-weaver. Harriet Mole, now 77, lived with her niece Eliza, 43, a laundress.

BETWEEN THE beginning and the end of the eighteenth century land values doubled as more land - about four million acres - came into cultivation. Unlike the industrial revolution yet to come the agricultural revolution was not a sudden change but more like a tide of slow growth. In 1700 each person involved in farming fed 1.7 persons, by 1800 each fed 2.5 persons[7]. England ceased to export wheat flour in 1750 using it all for home consumption and from this date regularly had to import extra wheat as the population grew.

Necessity is the mother of invention and this was nowhere more evident than in the improvement of farming. Increased demands for food led to experiments to increase yields. Much attention was given to the better use of soil, the suitability of various strains of crops, the invention of new and more efficient tools and the best breeds of cattle for beef and milk. The names of the pioneer agricultural improvers from this time are familiar; Jethro Tull, Turnip Townsend, and Thomas Coke of Holkham in Norfolk. When in 1760 George III came to the throne his involvement in agriculture led him to style himself as the Farmer King. This great interest in agricultural improvement was encouraged by Arthur Young who in 1768 published his *Six Weeks Tour through the Southern Counties of England*, a discussion of methods of farming. There was lively controversy about all aspects of agriculture ranging from livestock to potatoes. Paintings were made for landowners of their prize bulls, pigs, sheep and horses and these were hung among the portraits and landscapes in the great houses and in many of the 'new' eighteenth-century houses which had come into being. Many of these started life as farm-houses and like Maplestead Hall were brought up to date and improved by varying measures of rebuilding.

THE RED HOUSE

THE RED HOUSE is a classic example of a small eighteenth-century country house. The earliest information we have about this house is from the 1817 survey of the village. The proprietor was Joseph Orbell and it was occupied by James Chatters. The property consisted of a house, shop and garden and there were outbuildings on the site of what is now Ethel's Cottage. These may have housed the shop.

At the 1841 tithe award the Red House, described as house and gardens, is owned as well as occupied by James Chatters and in the 1841 census we find that James Chatters, 38, farmer, and his wife Mary and her cousin lived there. Ten years later in 1851 Mary Stuck, his niece, a widow, was running the shop with her unmarried cousin Mary Chatters. By 1861, however, the Chatters had moved; Ann Callow, a widow of 69, described as a beer-seller and grocer lived at the Red House with Walter, her son of 28, a grocer, his wife Mary Ann and their young daughter Emily. In 1871 Ann Callow was still the shopkeeper and beer-seller at the Red House. She lived with her son Walter, now a dealer, his wife Ann, an assistant in the shop, and

Ellen and Charles, their young children. Ann Callow, nearly 90 in 1881, was still running the shop but by 1891 her son Walter had taken over; described as a baker and shopkeeper, he lived in the Red House with Mary-Ann, his wife, and their son George.

The Red House

By 1919 the house was no longer used as a shop but was owned and occupied by the Henderson sisters. They were artists and painted water-colours. They had private means and spent the winters painting in Italy. The sisters set up the Henderson Trust, which provided a district nurse for the village[8], had a library in the house for the use of the village children, and donated the wooden folding chairs, now in the church but which were originally to be used in the village hall. The beneficent Henderson sisters lived in the Red House until 1937 when it was sold.

According to the records we know that in 1780 there were two shops in the village and although we have no record of the Red House before 1817 one of these was probably that at the Red House. The Little Maplestead shopkeepers approved in the official weights and measures list for this date were William Bland, flour-seller, Ann Firman, flour-seller, and Robert Nash, victualler.

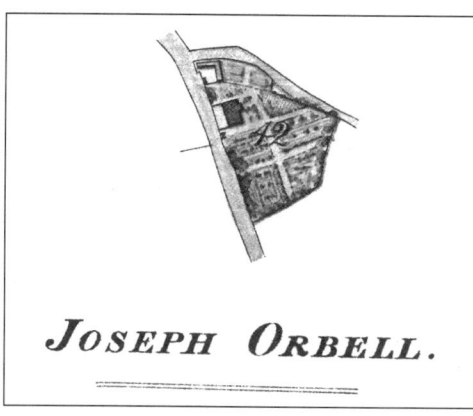

The Red House 1817

ANNALS OF AGRICULTURE

ARTHUR YOUNG'S *Annals of Agriculture*, a journal dedicated to the new husbandry, was first published in 1784. Norfolk led the country with experiments in crop rotation, a practice pioneered by Thomas Coke, Earl of Leicester, of Holkham Hall, Norfolk, which allowed continuous cultivation with no fallow period. This way farmers could provide hay and winter feed for sheep and cattle so that more livestock could be reared and at the same time more manure created to fertilize the land. Up until then half the county of Norfolk had yielded nothing but pasture for sheep and now the land could be used to grow good quality barley, rye and wheat. Coke enjoyed so much success that under his management the value of produce from his estate increased fourfold within fifteen years. Not all counties carried out such experiments and improvements but the East Anglian farmers, including those of Essex, who did so turned increasingly more of their land to arable farming and this was reflected in Little Maplestead under John Sewell who came to Maplestead Hall in 1797. However even before this mixed farming, recommended as being the most flexible type of agriculture, was the policy at Maplestead Hall; this included the growing of hops.

The hops that were grown in Little Maplestead were used by local brewers in Halstead and Sudbury and in 1819 Little Maplestead had forty-two acres under this crop. The hops were harvested in the autumn and many villagers would have helped, regarding the hop-picking as a kind of well-paid out-door holiday. Each person would get about ten days' work at 7d a day, with the bonus of a half pint of beer once or twice during the picking period. It was a busy time, made even more so by the presence of children of tradespeople and even of the gentry who were often sent into the hop-gardens during the picking because the aroma of the hops was considered good for their health.

At this time the planting of hops in Essex was confined to comparatively few parishes. The principal of these were the following: the two Hedinghams, the two Maplesteads, Halstead, the Colnes, Chelmsford, Moulsham, Shalford, Wethersfield, Finchingfield and Great Bardfield.

HALL CORNER COTTAGE AND BARN COTTAGE

HALL CORNER COTTAGE began life as a single-storey building which may have been a thatched granary. The cottage takes its name from Hall Corner, the turning to Maplestead Hall nearby, to which the cottage and its land once belonged but this name is relatively recent. The original smaller cottage stood on a different site - set well back from the road in what is now the garden of the present house - and was probably built about 1770 but this was pulled down and the granary converted into the present house sometime in the early eighteenth century.

Hall Corner Cottage

In the 1817 survey, Hall Corner Cottage is shown as plot number 115 and is a 'Part of Lodge Farm and of Goldmillers, In hand', proprietor John Sewell, and is described as 'Granary, Hopkiln and Cottage' with 'garden etc'. The large field next to the property, Barn Field, was a hop field. There was a potash office next door to the cottage which also belonged to Maplestead Hall. This was a small barn where the potash, probably derived from the wood ash left in the hop kiln, was processed and stored. This potash office was eventually converted into a barn and implement shed and much later, in 1973, to a dwelling, Barn Cottage. The hop kiln at Hall Corner Cottage was used to dry the hops grown in Barn Field next to the property.

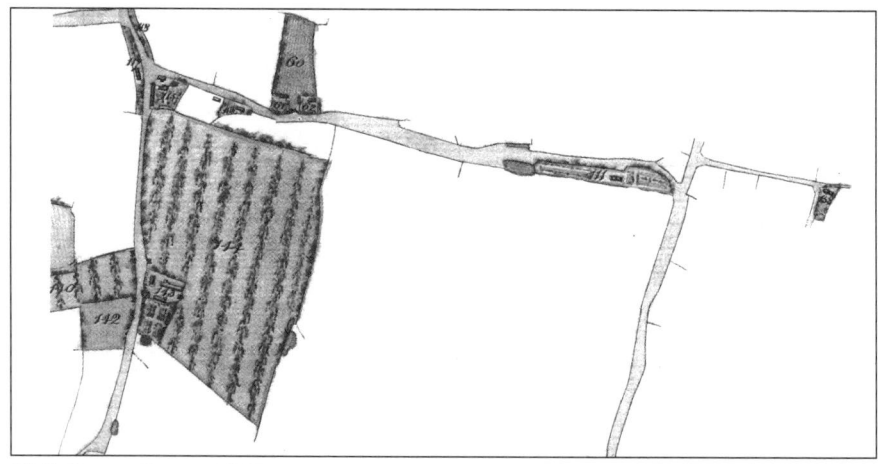

Hall Corner Cottage 1817

On 7 June 1836 at the court of the manor of Little Maplestead, Hall Corner Cottage was surrendered to John Allen, of Pebmarsh, yeoman, for a sum of £110.

Barn Cottage

In 1841, according to the tithe award, the copyhold ownership of Hall Corner Cottage changed hands once again. Joseph Thomas Bethel Jones of The Grove was now named as owner of the tenements and hop kiln and they were occupied by William Root. By this date it is probable that hop production had ceased.

The 1841 census for Hall Corner Cottage shows that William Root, aged 50, was a shoemaker, and lived there with his wife Mary and daughters Susan and Eliza. William Root was one of four shoemakers in the village at this time and several Victorian iron shoe heels, nails and shoe buttons have been found in the garden of Hall Corner Cottage. The house was probably shared with William Howlett, 25, agricultural labourer and his wife Anne and baby sons William and Samuel. A few years later, in the 1851 census, we still find William Root in Hall Corner Cottage but also Jabez Bishop and his family. The entries read as follows: Jabez Bishop, 57, farm labourer, his wife Elizabeth, adult sons George, Thomas, Benjamin and younger children Samuel and Elizabeth. None apart from Jabez was recorded as having employment and he probably worked at Maplestead Hall farm. William Root was still working as a village shoemaker; he lived with his wife Mary and two other daughters, Ann and Ellen.

In the 1861 census we find only one part of the house occupied, by Joseph Stuck, 36, an agricultural labourer and his wife Charlotte, a straw-plaiter.

In the 1871 census we find both the tenements of Hall Corner Cottage occupied again. In the south tenement lived James Simmons, 40, an agricultural labourer, Mary his wife, their son William aged 14, who was a groom, and daughters Alice, Clara and Ada. Both James and his son William probably worked at Maplestead Hall farm. In the north tenement we find John Dixey, 38, horsekeeper, Charlotte his wife, a straw-plaiter, their son John, 14, a labourer, and younger children Elizabeth, Sarah, Alice, George and baby James. Again, it is most likely that John Dixey and his son John worked at Maplestead Hall farm.

By 1881, there was a change of use for the south tenement of Hall Corner Cottage which also gave the cottage a name for the first time in its history. It became a post office and the cottage began to be known as Post Office Cottages. In the 1881 census, listed as occupants of the newly named Post Office Cottages, are James Simmonds, farm labourer, and his wife Mary who had taken on the considerable responsibility of postmistress. John Dixey, horseman, still lived there with his wife Charlotte, his daughters Sarah, 17, and Alice 15, factory-hands, his son George, 13, a groom and younger children James, David, Harry and baby Celia. The south tenement continued to be used as a post office and in 1891, the latest census available, we find James Simmonds was still working as an agricultural labourer and his wife was still the postmistress; they still shared the house with John Dixey and his wife and sons George, 23, unemployed, David, 15, and Harry, 13, both agricultural labourers, and young daughter, Eliza.

In Kelly's Directory, James Simmons was officially listed as sub-postmaster for Little Maplestead from 1882 to 1914 but his wife carried out the duties while both James and John Dixey, her neighbour, probably worked for Charles Brewster at Maplestead Hall Farm.

In 1919, after the death of Charles Brewster, the house now called Old Post Office Cottages was sold to Alfred Blomfield as part of the Maplestead Hall estate. The price agreed was £135. In the deeds the property was described thus:

> *All that double tenement or cottage situated in the parish of Little Maplestead in the County of Essex on the road leading from Halstead to Maplestead and known as Old Post Office Cottages, with the timber built and thatched building and implement shed and small paddock and now in the occupation of James Simmons and Mistress Mayes ....*

In the 1919 auction particulars Hall Corner Cottage was described as: 'a brick, stone and tiled double tenement cottage each tenement consisting of living room, kitchen, 2 bedrooms, wash-house and bake house with oven and copper fixed ....'

When Alfred Blomfield died in 1934 his son Joseph Sankey Blomfield took over the estate and became the owner of Old Post Office Cottages. Mr Blomfield improved the cottages installing a water supply which had hitherto been obtained from a village pump at Hall Corner.

After the First World War Old Post Office Cottages continued to be occupied by families who were mostly employed by Mr Blomfield as farm workers or domestic staff; between 1919 and 1936 these included Mr and Mrs Mayes with their four children (Mrs Emma Mayes was postmistress and the south part of Hall Corner Cottage continued as a sub-post office), Mr and Mrs W. Simmonds with their nine children (Mr Simmonds was head cowman at Maplestead Hall) and Cecil Cook who moved to Hall Corner Cottage in 1936 and worked for Mr Blomfield at Maplestead Hall bottling milk in the dairy. Mr Cook also did milk rounds in Halstead and Sudbury and delivered free milk to local schools daily. After the war the Cooks remained in the south end of the house but there was a rapid turnover of rents in the north half of the house including the Brittons (Mr Britton was foreman at Maplestead Hall farm) and the Akroyds (Mr Akroyd was the blacksmith at Maplestead Hall farm). This use of the house for employees of Mr Blomfield continued until 1973.

In 1973 the house, now called 2 and 4 Hall Corner Cottages after the post-office was transferred elsewhere in the village, was finally freed from its feudal ties after nearly two hundred years and was sold privately away from the Maplestead Hall estate. The thatched barn was bought privately, converted to a small cottage, now called Barn Cottage, and was sold.

TANGLEWOOD

LISTED AS 'probably eighteenth century', the earliest information we have about Tanglewood is from the 1817 survey of the village (see map page 158). Its name was given to it by the owners in the 1970s. Like Hall Corner Cottage opposite, it was built to house the farm labourers who worked at Maplestead Hall and in 1817 it was described a cottage and gardens owned by John Sewell as part of the Maplestead Hall estate and occupied by Stephen Root and others.

At the tithe award of 1841 the tenements were owned by John Allen and occupied by George Lavender 'and others'.

In the 1841 census we find that Tanglewood was home to George Lavender, 60, a pensioner, Sarah Hurrell, 60, who worked as a servant, and probably also Edward Willsmore, 52, a dealer, Mary his wife, sons Edward 19, Samuel, 15, William, 13, John, 9, and George, 7, all agricultural labourers. In 1851 George Lavender was still at Tanglewood with John Cooper, shoemaker, his wife Sarah, his sons John and Robert, farm labourers, and Josiah and John Bishop, lodgers. The house was shared with Samuel Willsmore, a farm labourer, Hannah his wife and William, their baby son.

It is very difficult to determine who lived in Tanglewood for most of the later censuses. Its position in the village at the intersection of several roads caused its entries to vary in order and like most of the other village properties it had no name.

In a deed dated 1880, held by Maplestead Hall estate, the property is described as a timber and tiled messuage with a detached bake-office and a large garden. The house had been in the occupation of John Cooper or his sub-tenant and was now occupied by Samuel Turner and George Mayes. Both George Mayes and Samuel Turner were farm labourers.

At the 1919 auction Tanglewood was described as a plaster and tiled double tenement cottage.

> No 1 North End contains 2 living rooms, 3 bedrooms, storeroom, brick and tiled wash-house with copper and wood oven. Let to Mrs Jane Felton at £5 per annum.
>
> No 2 South End contains sitting room, 2 bedrooms, good storeroom, brick and tiled wash-house and copper. Let to Mr Carrington £6 10s per annum.

In 1926 Mr and Mrs W. Nichols occupied the south end of Tanglewood and Mrs Felton remained in the north. Like many other properties which had belonged to Maplestead Hall the house was sold in the 1970s.

WHITECOTE

IT IS BELIEVED that Whitecote was built between 1720 and 1780 and that it was originally three cottages. It is thought that the south cottage was constructed first with the later addition of the northern pair. There is evidence of a house on the site from the 1777 Chapman and André map but the 1817 survey of the village reveals only a barn or outbuilding on the site of Whitecote; this is shown as part of School Farm. There is also a note to say that the plot was 'waste granted in 13 November 1805' and was owned by Mr Tucker. If the 1817 survey is accurate (and there is no reason to suppose it is not) then the explanation must be that either Whitecote was temporarily run down and was being used for farm storage or the property was converted after 1817 from a existing farm building. There is no mention of a cottage in the description of the property and land in the 1817 survey which does not include a house at School Farm either.

Whitecote

In the 1817 survey the building, which would now seem to be Whitecote, was owned like School Farm by Dr Lachlan McLean with sub-tenant George Firmin and was described as a yard and outbuildings.

However by 1841, at the tithe award, the cottages are clearly shown on the tithe map and are described as tenements owned by Joseph Thomas Bethel Jones of The Grove and occupied by Daniel Cottar. In the census for this date we find Joseph Cottar, 30, a carpenter, his wife Mary and three daughters, also Daniel Cottar, 65, also a carpenter and Sarah his wife, all living at Whitecote. Two uninhabited tenements are listed with this entry.

It is not easy to interpret the censuses for Whitecote; several families would have occupied the house but it is likely that the following information, although probably incomplete, is correct. At the time of the 1851 census Daniel Cottar, 75, was still at Whitecote with his wife Sarah and Rachel Wenden, 25, a lodger and straw-plaiter. In 1871 James Searles, 56, farm servant and his wife Eliza lived at Whitecote with their son Henry, a gardener. Also at Whitecote were Henrietta Davey, a widow of 82 and her daughter, a tailoress. By 1881 William Dixey, a farm labourer, occupied Whitecote with his wife, Eliza, a straw-plaiter, and their son. In 1891 we find Charles Bocking,

25, a farm labourer, at Whitecote with his wife Jane and son Charles together with Charles's sister, Jane, who was a silk-weaver. Robert Winch, 37, a farm labourer, also lived at Whitecote with his wife Rhoda and young sons Frank, Charles and Robert.

ENCLOSURE AND RURAL POVERTY

CONTINUING ENCLOSURE of common land was a part of the process of agricultural improvement by landowners and during the eighteenth century it was carried out mainly by Act of Parliament rather than voluntary agreement. The Enclosure Commissioners surveyed the land under consideration and were supposed to be independent but they usually supported the farmer wishing to enclose. Between 1760 and 1800 more than 1300 enclosure acts were passed and there were almost one thousand more to come. As fields were enclosed, woodlands and wastes or common lands disappeared, new hedges were planted and walls, fences and roads were built. But while farm profits were increased, the independence of many people who had previously felt themselves to be secure was threatened. These were the people who had small-holdings and relied on the common land which was vital to them for grazing. They had no capital to improve the yield from the little land they had, and they could not, like the big landowners and farmers, build barns, drains or fences to make what land they had more efficient. Those people who refused to move off enclosed land were evicted and they had no legal rights; there was nothing they could do. Some of them did get temporary work making and erecting fences and gates but later many were left to fend for themselves as paupers with no means of support.

The farmers who most favoured enclosure were of course the 'new men' of progressive knowledge and ideas and at first Arthur Young believed that enclosure encouraged enterprise; but as landlords came progressively under attack for oppressing the poor even Young eventually had to admit that the process of enclosure led to an unacceptable increase in human suffering. It turned what had been common land into private property and the farmer justices of the peace who administered the law and carried out the enclosures were regarded with great mistrust by the people which led in many villages to a breakdown of the hitherto stable relationship between the well off and the poor. Some villages were completely transformed by over-zealous enclosure - two-thirds of the population owned less than fifty acres and many of these small farmers disappeared - if they were fortunate they became rural labourers but all too often they were left paupers[9].

Soon the increasing rural poverty, which must have been felt even in relatively affluent Little Maplestead, made it necessary for a General Work-house Act to be passed which enabled parishes to build a work-house. By 1776 there were almost two thousand work-houses in England including one built in Little Maplestead.

Little Maplestead work-house was administered by the churchwardens and those appointed to be 'overseers of the poor'. Built to house and feed the out-of-work poor work-houses were often ill-administered. At first able-bodied paupers were allowed to enter the work-house but later as the numbers increased they were excluded to fend for themselves as best they could and only the sick and disabled were admitted.

The 1817 survey of the village shows that the work-house stood on the present site of Orchard House, Weavers and Saxby's.

By 1841 the Little Maplestead work-house had been pulled down. The care of the parish poor had been transferred to one of the newly-constituted Union Work-houses. On the site of Little Maplestead work-house, greatly enlarged by the enclosure of a large strip of land reclaimed from Hurrells Green, two groups of tenements were built between 1817 and 1841.

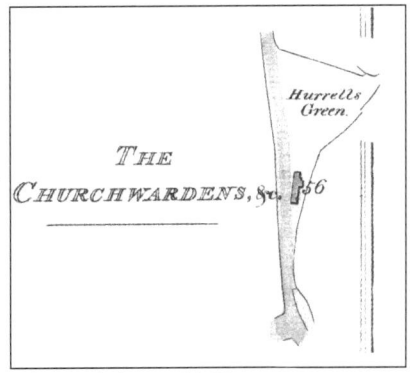

The Work-house 1817

SUNNYHOLT (NOW ORCHARD HOUSE), WEAVERS AND SAXBY'S, LAVENDER COTTAGE AND ATTADALE

THE SOUTHERNMOST of these new tenements was brick-built and divided into three; it later came to be known as Old Work-house Cottages or The Barracks. The northern group of tenements were the cottages now called Attadale and Lavender Cottage. Each small tenement was split into two and was occupied by farm workers from Maplestead Hall which owned the property.

It is difficult to distinguish between the different tenements from the census listings but at the 1841 tithe award the owner of the extended plot of land on which the tenements were built was James Brewster and it was occupied by William Bush. The 1841 census lists William Bush, 45, agricultural labourer, his wife Hannah and daughter Susan; James Byford, 34, agricultural labourer, and his wife Hannah; Rose Harrington, 70, a straw-plaiter, Hannah and Sarah Harrington, 18 and 12, also straw-plaiters. In 1851 we find Eliza Frost, 45, a pauper, daughters Sarah, 21, and Susan, 18, weavers, and sons John and William, 16 and 14, farm labourers; George Byford, 57, a farm labourer, his wife Sarah, their daughter Tabitha, a weaver, their son Thomas, 16, a farm labourer, and younger children Eliza, William and Frederick; possibly Tabitha Salmons, 75, widow and pauper; James Smith, 27, farm labourer, and his wife Sarah also lived in these tenements.

It is unclear who occupied the tenements in 1861 but in 1871 we find James Lavender, 71, shoemaker, and his wife Mary; John Frost, 30, agricultural labourer and his wife Mary-Ann, straw-plaiter; Samuel Bishop, 31, a farm servant, his wife Sarah and their children Benjamin and Esther; Martha Dixey, a widow of 75 and Charlotte, her unmarried daughter, both straw-plaiters, and Eliza, her widowed daughter, a crêpe weaver with two young sons George and Tim. Ten years later, in 1881, we find James and Mary Lavender; Samuel Bishop, now a farm labourer, his wife Sarah, a straw-plaiter, their son Benjamin, a farm labourer, and younger children Eliza and John; also listed are Charlotte Dixey, a straw-plaiter, her boarders George Bishop, a farm labourer, John Bishop, also a farm labourer, and young William Mayes.

Lavender Cottage and Attadale

At some date before 1880 the centre tenement burnt down and the remaining two became known as 1 and 2 The Barracks; each was still split into two. Later Number 1 came to be known as Saxby's and Number 2 as Weavers Cottage. Late in the nineteenth century, Number 2 and possibly Number 1 was used as a school for the teaching of straw-plaiting and also reading.

In the last census in 1891 the tenements were occupied by William Felton, 25, an agricultural labourer and Alice his wife, a silk weaver; Harry Plampin, 25, an agricultural labourer and his wife Sarah, also a silk weaver; Samuel Bishop, 49, a 'road char' and his wife Sarah; John Dixey, an agricultural labourer and his wife Charlotte, nephew George, an agricultural labourer, and niece Alice Bishop, a silk weaver, and Mary Lavender, their lodger.

In 1919 the occupant of Number 2 bought the property away from Maplestead Hall, renamed it Sunnyholt and developed it into a concentrated rabbit farm. In 1921 Mr E. G. Orchard bought it but very soon suffered grave losses forcing him to abandon the rabbit project. In 1923 he opened a shop in the front room of Sunnyholt which quickly proved to be a success. A few years later he seized the opportunity of buying the delivery rounds of Doubleday, Halstead's leading grocers. Soon the front of the house was coverted into a shop, a purpose-built post office was added, followed by extensive storerooms behind, including a private gas generated lighting plant. Soon after this he was employing seven assistants and supplying nine villages weekly.

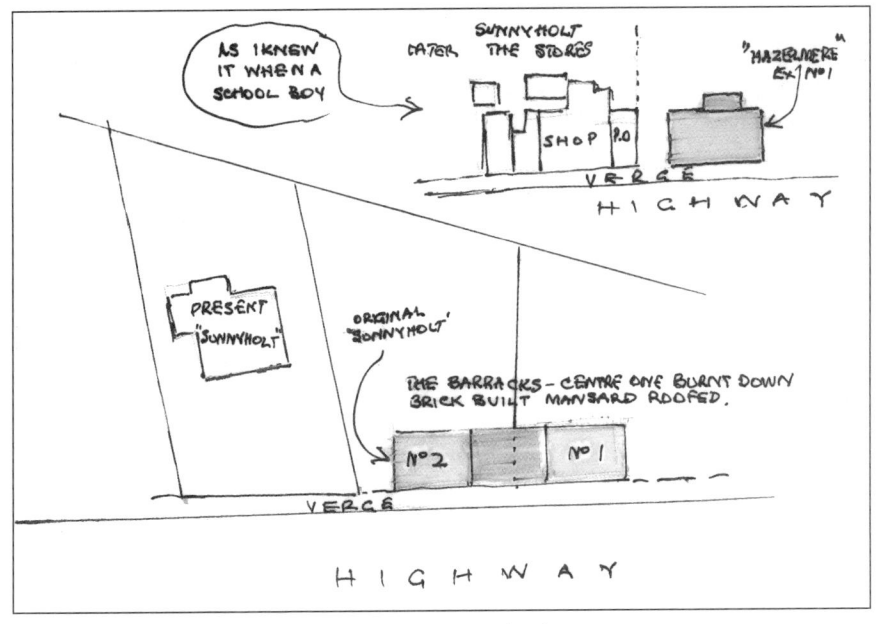

Plan drawn by Mr Raymond Orchard, Mr E.G. Orchard's son

In 1937 the present Sunnyholt was built, the name having been transferred, whilst Number 2 The Barracks became known as The Stores and was completely converted into store, clerical and serving areas, the post office already having moved back to Hall Corner. In 1947 The Stores rounds and business were sold to Mr Ted Charrington who after a number of years went bankrupt. The premises were then let to a Mrs Dent who re-opened them as a small village shop. In 1968 the property was sold to Mrs Dent and it was around this time that it was given the name Hall View and then Weavers Cottage. In the 1980s it was bought and demolished and the present Weavers built on the site - despite a preservation order having been placed on it. Number 1 The Barracks continued as a farm labourer's cottage and later was sold off privately changing its name to Hazelmere and then to Saxby's before it was demolished and the present-day Saxby's built on the site in 1989 (picture page 168).

Saxby's

STRAW-PLAITING

THE CENSUSES reveal that many of the women in Little Maplestead were straw-plaiters. By the late eighteenth century, the home wool industry had all but died out, causing increasing poverty in the countryside. To provide work, straw-plaiting was introduced in Gosfield by the first Marquis and Marchioness of Buckingham when they lived at Gosfield Hall around 1790. From Gosfield the industry spread to many other villages in the region including the Maplesteads. The straw plaits were sent to Luton for the making of straw hats and young women in the neighbourhood could make a good income from the craft. Straw-plaiting became a well-established and flourishing cottage industry in which practically all women, girls, boys and even some men were engaged. It proved a boon of the utmost value bringing to the homes of the poorer people a measure of comfort and prosperity. Straw-plait dealers bought the rolls of finished plait from the workers. The workers could earn as much as a guinea a week and the straw was usually given free to the workers by the farmers.

IVY COTTAGE

IVY COTTAGE, known earlier as Bennetts, was probably built about 1760. Originally part of the Maplestead Hall estate, early deeds show that in 1762 John French rented the property, followed by Richard French, possibly his son, in 1786. In the 1817 survey we find Richard French named as the proprietor of the cottage and garden.

Ivy Cottage

Other Maplestead Hall deeds reveal that in 1825 Richard French surrendered the copyhold property to James Chatters, a farmer and landowner, who converted it into four cottages. On 5 January 1830 'Bennetts, a cottage, tenement and orchard', was conditionally surrendered to William Hardy of Wickham St Pauls. At the 1841 tithe award Ivy Cottage is described as tenements, owned by James Chatters and occupied by Thomas Richer 'and another'. The 1841 census gives more detail; Thomas Richer, 50, was an agricultural labourer, who lived in the tenements with Eliza his wife, their daughter Sarah, and sons, Thomas, 13, an agricultural labourer, and baby Isaac. The 'another' was probably Joseph Cockerton, 50, an agricultural labourer and his wife Mary, Joseph's brother Samuel and their adult children Catherine and James.

Then in 1848 Bennetts was left to Mary Stuck, the niece of James Chatters, in Chatters' will.

In 1851 Thomas Richer, now a pensioner, and Eliza were still at Ivy Cottage with Isaac their son and grand-daughter Ellen French. So too was Joseph Cockerton, described now as a pauper, his wife, sister and great-grand-nephew who was working as an agricultural labourer. Ivy Cottage was also probably shared with Thomas Salmons, a tinker, his wife Mary, and their sons Thomas, a farm labourer, Samuel, and daughter Maria, a straw-plaiter, and a fourth family, the Howards, headed by James, a farm labourer.

Ivy Cottage 1817

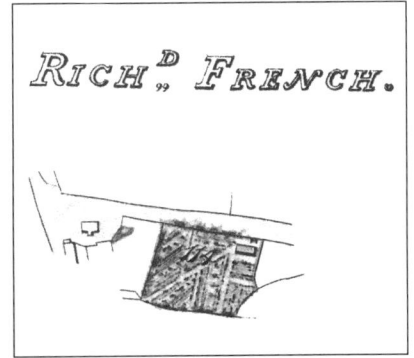

- 169 -

In 1853 the deeds record an absolute surrender of Bennetts by Mary Stuck to James Brewster, lord of the manor of Maplestead Hall. At this time the copyhold rent was threepence.

The census does not make clear who lived in Ivy Cottages in 1861, 1871 and 1881 but John Harward, vicar of Little Maplestead is shown to have been there by the 1891 census. We also know that by 1885 the copyhold messuage or tenement called Bennetts had been altered to two cottages.

THE REVEREND John Frederic Harward was appointed vicar of Little Maplestead in 1855 and came to live in the village, at first at The Grove. His living only amounted to £30 a year when he arrived, and there was no official vicarage or house provided. He raised £400 by collection for the building of a vicarage but the ecclesiastical commission added another £400 and invested it instead for the benefit of the incumbent, his income being about £1 a week.

Reverend Harward, whose name can be traced back to Hereward the Wake, was educated at Eton and St John's College, Cambridge and his family were the original founders of Harvard University in the United States. The Round Church in Little Maplestead was being restored when he arrived and he instigated archaeological investigations which convinced him that the original Saxon church had stood on the same site as the present church. He made the major discovery of what he described as a 'Saxon stone bowl' but which has more recently been described as early Norman. This is now the font and can be seen in the Round Church.

An interview with Harward was published in the local paper, the Essex County Chronicle, in 1909. He was described as the 'venerable vicar of Little Maplestead with his flowing white beard and shoulders bending under the weight of four score years and ten, in his little thatched cottage where he has lived alone for 28 years.

> *I have called my house Pink Cottage on account of the colour it is painted outside. Here I live alone paying £5 rent. Very humble circumstances but I am content with that. When I came to Little Maplestead first my wife played the organ and the church was filled to the porch. We had a surpliced choir then - very exceptional in the neighbourhood - Halstead people used to laugh at us for putting our men and boys in 'night-gowns'. Now they laugh at us again because we are too poor to have a choir at all.*
>
> *When I came to Maplestead the church was being restored on the site of the old foundations by archaeologists and clergy who had raised £1200 for the purpose. One of the first things I did after becoming vicar in 1855 was to discover, by a buttress, an old Saxon stone bowl which had evidently been used in the early times for a font. I was able to save it and also an old stone coffin which had been dug out of the body of the church and would*

> otherwise have been broken up and used to repair the roads. Both these pieces of ancient stone work are preserved in the church.
>
> When I took this cottage I had the garden, which was filled with gooseberry bushes and currant trees, transformed into a bowling green for the villagers to amuse themselves - but they won't come now - it's too slow for them. I also had some lawn skittles for their use but they don't want them - so I lent the skittles to the chapel meeting house for the young fellows there to use.

The Reverend Harward's wife died in 1881 and he died in 1912 aged 92. The present altar table in the Round Church was given by him in memory of his wife.

IN 1919 the 'double tenement cottage', Ivy Cottage, was conveyed from Charles Brewster to Alfred Blomfield and at this date was recorded as Ivy Cottages for the first time. Soon after this Mr Alfred Blomfield sold the property to Edward Percy from Deans Hall. He in turn then sold back by auction to Mr Joe Blomfield of Maplestead Hall for £150:

> the double tenement brick and tiled cottage, Ivy Cottages. One tenement is occupied and contains living room, 2 bedrooms, with brick and tiled detached kitchen at back and a timber built lean-to coal house with iron roof. Good and large garden, let to Miss Kett a quarterly tenant at the low rent of £4 per annum. The other tenement is used as a parish room and contains living room, kitchen, 2 bedrooms also copper and sink fixed. Estimated rental £10 per annum.

In 1926 Ivy Cottages were still referred to as the 'Old Vicarage'. Later, in the 1970s, the property was sold away as a private house from the Maplestead Hall estate.

EIGHTEENTH-CENTURY BARNS

BRAMBLE BARN

This barn, which once belonged to Hurrells Farm, is eighteenth century or perhaps even earlier and was converted into a dwelling house in the 1990s. It is marked on the 1817 survey as part of Hurrells Farm.

GRANARY BARN

Once belonging to School Farm, this barn was built in the eighteenth century and was converted to a dwelling house in the 1980s by the owners of School Farm. The barn can be seen on the 1817 survey of the village together with another large barn, also eighteenth century, that still belongs to School Farm.

WOODERTONS BARN, BRICKS BARN AND MOSSES BARN

These large barns were built in the eighteenth century and are living testimony to the flourishing agriculture of the time. Throughout this century it was the land and farming that drove the lives of the inhabitants of Little Maplestead. The cycle of the agricultural seasons still dictated the occupations of almost all of the villagers, as it had done since earliest times. But, even locally, there were signs that the industrial revolution was just around the corner. The Courtaulds built a mill at Halstead at the end of the eighteenth century to house and power the weaving looms in their new mechanized textile factory. Although these power looms finally spelt the end of the rural wool industry they also provided opportunities for women to work as silk or crêpe weavers in the new factory in Halstead. Nevertheless the lives of the villagers of Little Maplestead were still firmly rooted in the landscape, a landscape which was being recorded for posterity in the paintings of local artists John Constable and Thomas Gainsborough.

Notes to Chapter VIII

[1] Anon
[2] Statistics from Asa Briggs, *A Social History of England* (London, 1983)
[3] Adam Smith
[4] Document in ERO, Q/RSg p39
[5] Document in ERO, Q/RSg 3 p45
[6] Document in ERO, Q/RSg 4 p28
[7] Statistics from Asa Briggs, *A Social History of England*
[8] Halstead Hospital is now a beneficiary of the Henderson Trust, 1999
[9] Statistics from Asa Briggs, *A Social History of England*

EIGHTEENTH-CENTURY EVENTS

1700 Land values begin to increase as cultivation becomes more productive

1701 Jethro Tull invents the mechanized seed drill

1702 Anne becomes queen

1714 George I becomes king

1720 Sir Robert Walpole becomes prime minister

1727 George II becomes king

1742 Cotton factories established in Birmingham and Northampton

1752 Thomas Coke born, pioneer of scientific farming

1760 'Farmer' George III becomes king. First enclosure act

1770 Invention of the Spinning Jenny

1783 Britain recognizes American Independence

1789 George Washington first US President

CHAPTER IX

THE NINETEENTH CENTURY

So like the feelings of men in a higher sphere are those of the poor cottager, that if his habitation be warm, cheerful and comfortable, he will return to it with gladness and abide in it with pleasure.[1]

THE NINETEENTH CENTURY was the century of the triumph of the Industrial Revolution, a time of explosive economic development unparalleled anywhere else in the world, born of the scientific progress and spirit of investigation which had flourished in the eighteenth century. This and the fact that the Napoleonic Wars had ended in 1815 engendered a feeling of general optimism in the country and the expectation that the long awaited peace would now bring prosperity to all.

Far away from the rural village of Little Maplestead, in the black country of the Midlands, factories were springing up and coal production was increasing to support them; the manufacture of pig iron also increased as did imports of raw cotton necessary to feed the growing textile industry. Coal was the fuel of the Industrial Revolution and steam, first harnessed by James Watt, was its power. By 1848 the national output of iron was greater than anywhere else in the world, the amount of coal mined was two-thirds, and the production of cotton cloth one half of the total world output.

Good roads became essential to provide efficient routes for manufacturers to receive raw materials and to distribute their goods and consequently road building increased with the construction of many toll-charging turnpike roads; these were usually built by self-interested business trusts. One such turnpike road was the Sudbury to Halstead road which still runs through the eastern edge of Little Maplestead. According to legend this part of the road was frequented by highwaymen; however, horses as a means of travelling were soon to be superseded by steam trains and a rapidly increasing railway system would be under construction with a station in Halstead.

Although the villagers of Little Maplestead lived in rural East Anglia they did not escape the effect of the sudden growth of industry. By 1830 the factory system was well established in England and there began a general gradual shift from an agricultural society towards an industrial one. The inhabitants of Little Maplestead

LITTLE MAPLESTEAD in

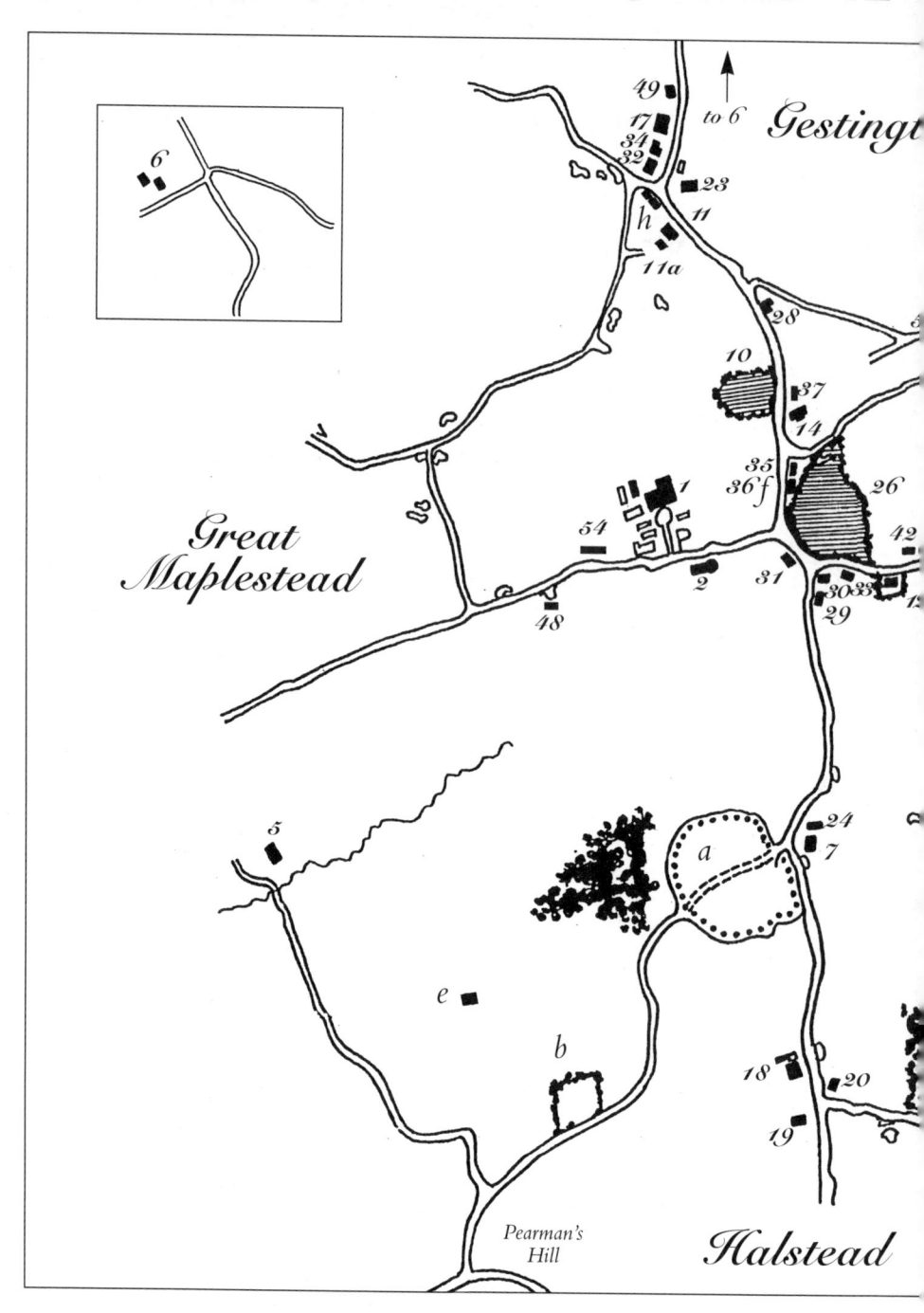

to 6 *Gestingt*

Great Maplestead

Pearman's Hill

Halstead

- 174 -

NINETEENTH CENTURY

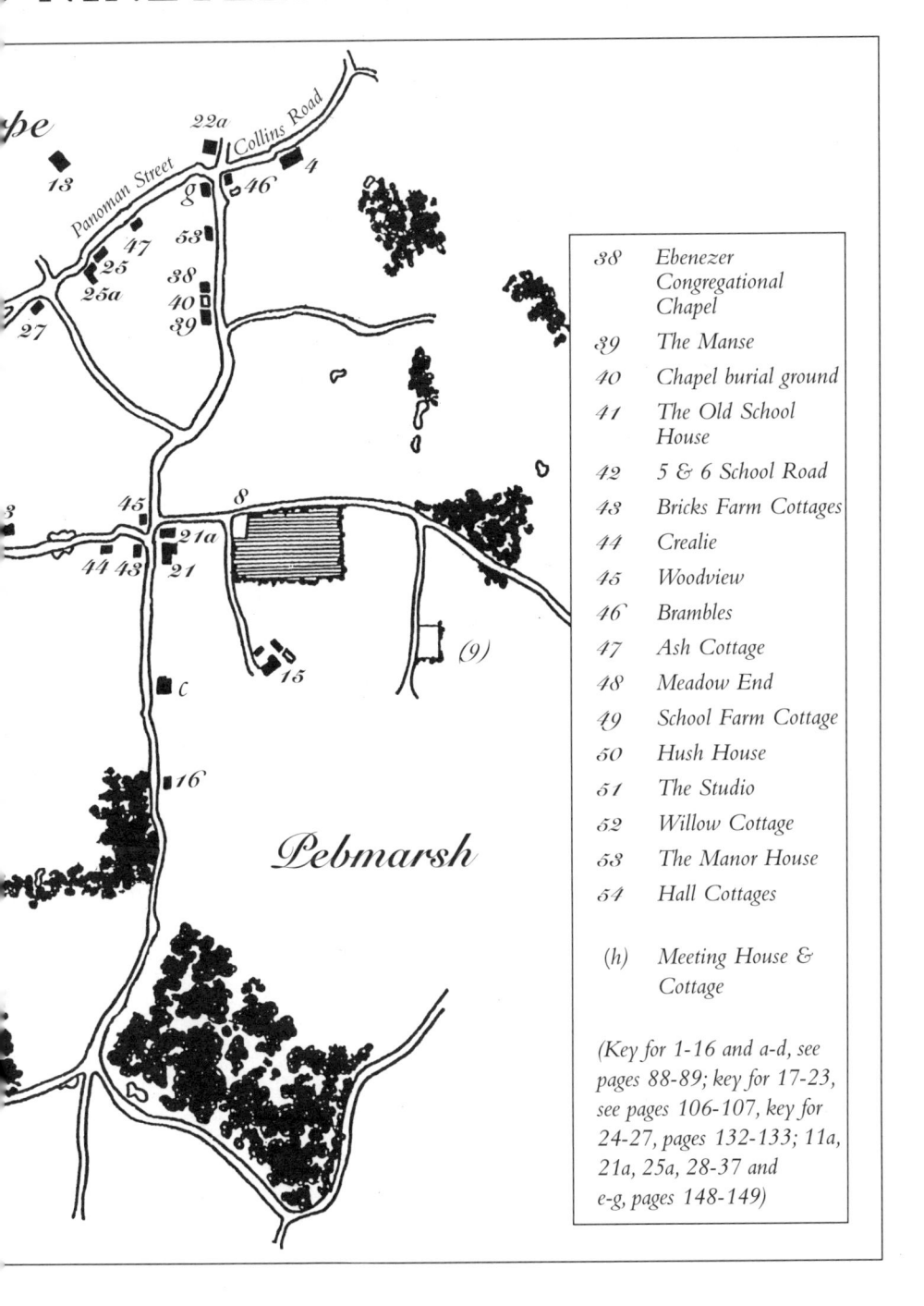

Pebmarsh

38	Ebenezer Congregational Chapel
39	The Manse
40	Chapel burial ground
41	The Old School House
42	5 & 6 School Road
43	Bricks Farm Cottages
44	Crealie
45	Woodview
46	Brambles
47	Ash Cottage
48	Meadow End
49	School Farm Cottage
50	Hush House
51	The Studio
52	Willow Cottage
53	The Manor House
54	Hall Cottages
(h)	Meeting House & Cottage

(Key for 1-16 and a-d, see pages 88-89; key for 17-23, see pages 106-107, key for 24-27, pages 132-133; 11a, 21a, 25a, 28-37 and e-g, pages 148-149)

had already suffered from the industrialization of the textile industry when power had come to the weaving looms in the mill which had been built by the Courtauld family in Halstead, depriving the home-workers of their employment. Countrywide, at the same time, farmers were experiencing a depression in agriculture which forced them to lay off men and wages fell amongst those farm labourers lucky enough to keep their jobs. However a breakdown of occupations in Little Maplestead in 1831 shows that although ten families now earned their living from handicrafts or trade, seventy-seven families still remained in farming[2].

From William White's *History, Gazetteer and Directory of the County of Essex* of 1848 we find amongst the traders and craftsmen such occupations as timber-carter, wheelwright and piano maker and repairer. But in the country as a whole there were still more domestic servants working for people in their houses (for example there were always at least three servants employed at Maplestead Hall) than there were factory workers in the entire cotton textile industry, and more men were still engaged in agriculture, horticulture and fishing than in the construction and mining industries put together[3].

Although most people in Little Maplestead still drew their incomes from the land, in general the proportion of people making a living in farming began to fall and conditions for the farm labourer deteriorated. Eventually, all over the country, protests against rural poverty escalated into sporadic rioting with demands for lower prices for bread; this eventually led, in 1846, to the repeal of the Corn Laws secured by Prime Minister Peel which allowed imports of foreign grain and so reduced the price of bread. But later the focus of unrest changed and the threshing machine was targeted because it was blamed for reducing employment, especially in the winter. Many of these machines were destroyed, particularly in East Anglia, and in some places the military had to be brought in to quell the protests. However, as in the past, Little Maplestead seemed to escape the worst consequences of the farming depression and there was probably little reason for serious discontent in the village. This was because during most of the nineteenth century the farm at Maplestead Hall was comparatively prosperous, perhaps due in part to the innovative John Sewell and the high moral principles of the trustees; this was reflected in the numbers of labourers' cottages built or improved at this time. That is not to say that there was no poverty in the village; the census reveals the presence of paupers but it is probably true to say that nowhere in the village were conditions as bad for the farm labourers of Little Maplestead as they were for those of other villages described in the *Essex Standard* of January 1850:

> Along the whole line of country from Castle Hedingham to Clavering there is an almost continuous succession of bad cottages. Among the worst of these might be mentioned those in the neighbourhood of Sible

Hedingham, Wethersfield, Bardfield, Wicken and Clavering. Great numbers of these cottages are situated in low and damp situations and their heavy and grass-covered thatches appear as if they had almost crushed the buildings down into the earth. Little or no light can ever find its way into the wretched, little windows many of which are more than half stopped up with rags and pieces of paper....

GENTRY AND TRADERS

KELLY'S AND Wright's trade directories began to be published in the nineteenth century[4] and these give us valuable information about the inhabitants of Little Maplestead. In 1845 we find a list of the gentry and traders in the village. The gentry were listed as James Brewster Esq, Little Maplestead Hall, Thomas Richbell Esq and Reverend Duncan Firman Vigers. Traders were listed as David Davis, day school; Henry Drane, blacksmith; Samuel Richbell 'Cock'; J. Stuck, beershop and shopkeeper; and Thomas Watkinson, beer retailer, shopkeeper and blacksmith.

The Reverend Vigers was the incumbent vicar and David Davis probably taught children in the straw-plaiting school basic educational skills such as reading and writing.

EBENEZER CONGREGATIONAL CHAPEL

EARLY NINETEENTH-CENTURY records of Little Maplestead show us that a Sunday school was established in the village by 1818; this was probably as a direct consequence of the strong nonconformist trusteeship of Maplestead Hall which was also reflected in the well-attended Congregational chapel existing in the village at the same time. At first this chapel was in the 'Meeting House' and the nonconformist Sunday school was probably held in the same place whilst the Round Church provided a place for religious education in the large west porch. By 1839 fifty children attended the Sunday school; there were probably more children in the village who were eligible to attend but farmers were often reluctant to release young boys from their employment which included such essential duties as sheep watching[5].

The meeting house and its cottage were recorded on the 1817 map of the village together with pieces of land, numbered plots 14, 15 and 16 on the survey. The tenant at this time was Joseph Watkinson who was the independent minister. In 1841, Joseph Watkinson, the independent minister, lived with his wife Rhoda, daughters Suzanna, 20, Sarah, 16, Rhoda, 10, and sons John (who worked in the grocer's shop), Samuel, 14, Joseph, 12, James, 8, and Charles, 6, in the cottage next to the meeting house. Ten years later, in 1851, Joseph Watkinson and his family had moved from the meeting

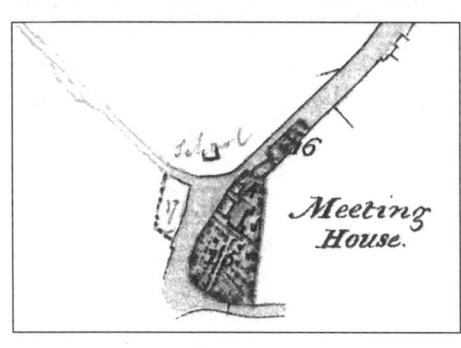

Meeting House 1817

house but it is not clear from the census where they lived.

At some time between 1841 and 1868 the meeting house was abandoned and a Congregational chapel was built on the Sudbury Road, about 200 yards from the Cock Inn. It was built of grey 'Chilton' bricks and was obviously very well-attended because in 1868 it had to be provided with new side galleries to prevent overcrowding. The minister at this time was Reverend Fairbank. By 1891 the village no longer had an incumbent independent minister but the Ebenezer chapel provided a place for nonconformist worship well into the twentieth century. It was described in the 1920s by Cecil Cook as a 'large building with a balcony upstairs'. He remembers that 'mothers' meetings' were held there once a week and the caretaker was Eliza Willsmore who lived in Bricks Farm cottages.

It was well known locally that the nonconformists from the Ebenezer chapel held their 'winkle teas' every Good Friday. This famous feast was eagerly looked forward to and Helen Blomfield from Hampers remembers that everyone was urged to take their own hat-pin to extract the winkles from the shells. After the tea, games were played amongst the villagers in the field opposite and often a special musical service was held which was called a 'sacred concert'.

Although the the Ebenezer chapel no longer had an incumbent minister after the 1890s the chapel continued to be used under the auspices of the Halstead congregational minister. But in the early 1930s the building was declared unsafe and was closed. The chapel was pulled down in the late 1930s and the village school, now Old School House, was then used as a nonconformist place of worship. But the chapel burial ground continued to be maintained and used until after the Second World War.

THE MANSE

THE LAND on which The Manse was built was bought from George de Horne Vaizey in 1871, after the attendance at the adjoining Ebenezer congregational chapel had proved worthy of a resident minister. There was already a house on the site called the Chapel House occupied in 1871 by Joseph Watkinson, 81 (by this time described as a minister without charge), his wife, Rhoda, and grand-daughter, Eliza, 14, who 'attended household duties', but this was not regarded as a suitable residence for the minister and was replaced. The new house, with its own well, stable and trap-

The Manse

shed was built in 1876 using local 'Chilton' bricks, matching the chapel. When, in the late nineteenth century, the congregation could no longer meet the expenses of a resident minister, the trustees of the chapel agreed to let The Manse. It was then used for many years as a small five-bedroomed guest house; amongst others the local school teachers lodged there and often the Sunday school treat for the children of the village used to be held in the orchard of The Manse[6].

In 1942 the Essex Incorporated Congregational Union sold The Manse and in 1950 Mr Orchard bought and occupied the premises; however, in 1954 a large piece of the front garden was compulsorily purchased to straighten and widen the Sudbury to Halstead road.

AT ABOUT THE same time as the Ebenezer chapel was being built, the Round Church underwent a major restoration latterly overseen by the vicar, Reverend John Frederic Harward. The work started in 1851 and took six years to complete. Some unfortunate decisions were made in the attempt to restore the church and many original features were destroyed during the 'improvements'. Sadly the restoration removed much of the atmosphere and spirit of the old church which was given new external wall facings, new window stonework and new roofing. Dormer ventilators were put in place in the roof and a new sexagonal wooden belfry was erected. A vestry was built but never completed and all the old fittings were removed from the church and the interior rearranged. A *piscina* and *sedilia* were uncovered in the south wall of the chancel and were most probably plastered over. The original large west porch was knocked down and a new smaller west porch built. In the past the old porch had been used as a simple school-room for the children of the village and had been heated by a stove.

OLD SCHOOL HOUSE[7]

THE 1817 survey of the village shows a cottage on the site of the school. This cottage and its land were owned by John Sewell, the tenant farmer at Maplestead Hall, and were sub-let to Samuel Johnson (see map page 158).

The Education Act of 1870 enabled the provision of a primary school in Little Maplestead and the school was opened in 1874. This gave the children of Little Maplestead, for the first time, the chance of a proper education. Except for the informal straw-plaiting school, where little may have been taught besides the plaiting technique, there had never been a regular school in the village. The primary school was a non-denominational board school which was run by a school board and financed by a school rate. The school board was elected in 1874 by the ratepayers and held its first meeting on 18 June. James Brewster was the chairman and Charles Brewster the clerk. Members were Reverend Fairbairn, the Congregational minister, Reverend Harward, the vicar, Mr Bentall and Mr Hearn. The school had cost £317 to build and provided accommodation for seventy-three children. It was supported by government grants as well as the school rates but the rates declined as government grants increased. Fees charged for each pupil also supported the school; these were four pence weekly, except for the children of farm labourers who paid only two pence for a first child and a penny for others. The fees were varied to accommodate tradesmen's children and those of small farmers but when parents could not pay James Brewster sometimes helped and so did the school board. The land on which the school was built belonged to James Brewster and so did the school house and the board paid rent for these. The first schoolmistress was a trained teacher and received forty pounds per annum together with the furnished house next to the school and free coal. The monitor, or the schoolmistress's assistant, got two pounds a year.

This first schoolmistress was Elizabeth Napier, aged twenty-one. When Elizabeth Napier opened the school she found her thirty-eight pupils very backward as they had never been to school before. Miss Napier taught arithmetic, letter-writing, working with copybooks, writing on slates, reading, poetry and singing and needlework for girls. Next term, grammar, geography and knitting were added. There was religious education every day and prayers were always said at opening and closing.

In 1880 Parliament had made school attendance compulsory and by 1881 almost every child in the country was attending school. By 1891 Little Maplestead school received a government grant of about forty-nine pounds and each child cost £2 6s 8d to educate.

Some of the schoolmistresses at the new primary school were Mercy Raven, 1881, Ellen Bogue, 1882, Jane Fairs, 1883, Mary Dawson, Henrietta Johns and, later, her husband Richard Goss who was monitor and in 1891 Elizabeth Johnson. Elizabeth Rayner was the schoolmistress in 1896. Born in Gestingthorpe in 1868, she lived in the 'little school house' and added musical drill and drawing to the curriculum. She also introduced kindergarten activities for infants such as threading beads and raffia mat weaving.

There were money prizes for regular attendance at school which varied due to the weather and illness. Early records show that the school was closed twice for influenza and once for fumigation after a case of scarlet fever. Holidays were always arranged around the harvest so that pupils could help their parents on the land but there were days off for treats and this included a trip to Sudbury when the famous tightrope walker, Blondin, came to the circus there. The school roll was also affected by the population of the community which was 302 in 1871 but had fallen to 193 by 1901; in 1902 there were only fifty-four children on the roll. The economic depression had meant that people, unable to find employment on the land, had moved away.

In 1903 the school board handed over its responsibilities to Essex County Council and Little Maplestead became a 'provided' school. By 1924 the school had two teachers - an infant teacher and a head mistress. Cecil Cook remembers that the infant teacher then was Miss Ives, and the head mistress was Miss Harfitt. There were forty children at the time and this dropped to thirty in 1930; all children over eleven years old had to go to school in Halstead. Eventually Little Maplestead Primary School closed in 1933 and the children went instead to the school at Great Maplestead. The school was used for a while as parish rooms and as a place of worship for the nonconformists after the chapel had closed.

FIVE AND SIX SCHOOL ROAD

THIS DOUBLE tenement cottage was originally known as School Cottages, and probably dates from around 1800. Six School Road, the tenement nearest the school, was the schoolmistress's cottage; Harriet Williams, who did a school project on this house when she lived there, discovered that the cottages were constructed of oak laths and wattle and daub and that some of the original walls still remained nearly 200 years later.

Five and Six School Road

In the 1817 survey of the village John Sewell of Maplestead Hall owned the double tenement and it was occupied by William Hurrell. It was described as a cottage and garden (see map page 158).

At the 1841 tithe award 6 School Road was owned by James French and occupied by James Turner but according to the census for 1841 it was occupied by John French, 40, jobber and his wife Elizabeth and daughter Hannah. Five School Road was occupied by John Stuck, 45, agricultural labourer, and his wife Elizabeth, daughter Elizabeth, 25, and sons John, 25, Thomas, 17, Joseph, 15, and James, 13, all agricultural labourers.

In 1851 6 School Road was still occupied by John French, 50, now described as a butcher, and he had married a younger wife, Sarah, 28, and had a baby, Susannah. The other tenement at 5 School Road was occupied by Thomas Firman, widower, 84, described as a pauper.

At the time of the 1881 census 6 School Road does not seem to have been used as the school house (the schoolmistress may have been lodging at The Manse), and the house appears to have been occupied by William Mayes, a farm labourer, his wife

Eliza, a factory hand, their son George, a farm labourer, and daughter, Agnes. Five School Road was occupied by George Warren, a farm labourer, Sarah his wife, a straw-plaiter, children Lucie, Arthur and Elizabeth, all scholars, and baby Harry.

In 1891 we find Mary Dawson, 24, the elementary teacher at the primary school, and Clara, her sister, aged 13, a scholar, living at 6 School Road, the school cottage. At 5 School Road, we find William Mayes, 60, a builder's labourer, Eliza his wife, William their son, 17, an agricultural labourer and Agnes, 13, their daughter, who had moved there from number 6.

In the 1919 auction catalogue the cottages were described as:

> A Double tenement cottage of plaster and slate construction known as School Cottages.
>
> No 2 cottage [6, School Road] contains a living room, a kitchen, 2 bedrooms, a scullery with sink, a coalhouse, a good garden. Let to Elizabeth Rayner, the school mistress, a yearly tenant at a rent of £5 per annum.
>
> No 1 Cottage [5 School Road] contains a living room, 2 bedrooms, a bakehouse with oven and copper fixed, a cellar with storeroom, a good garden. Let to Mr John Layzell on a quarterly tenancy at a rental of £5 per annum. The tenant claims the tortoise range in the kitchen.

The cottages were described as very convenient, very well built and in an excellent state of repair; they were bought by Alfred Blomfield who conveyed them to his daughter Kathleen in 1923. In 1953 Kathleen (now Titchmarsh) sold them to Mrs Row. From Mrs Row they passed to Mrs Vera Marsden, in 1959 from Mrs Marsden to Mrs Violet Warrick and in 1962 they were sold to Mr Norman Martin who still lives in Number 5.

IN 1851, at the time of the Great Exhibition, Britain was described as the workshop of the world. Large-scale industrialization had taken place and by this time farming too had been affected; economies of scale had made it profitable for large farms to come into being. A good example of this was the Maplestead Hall farm which by this time extended over 832 acres, employing forty-three men, twelve boys and five servants.

In 1855 Kelly's trade directory lists under 'gentry': James Brewster Esq, Magistrate, Little Maplestead Hall, Reverend Joseph Watkinson (Independent), Reverend Henry Whittington BA, curate. Traders included Thomas Callow, shop-keeper; Daniel Collar, carpenter; John Cooper, farmer; Henry Drane, blacksmith; William Hearn, senior, farmer; William Hearn, junior, pork butcher; William Howlett, farmer, Earls Farm [Hurrells]; Thomas Mayes, carrier; Robert Moss, baker; Thomas Oakley, wheelwright; Samuel Richbell, 'Cock'; Thomas Watkinson, blacksmith, and Edward Willsmore, farmer, Garlands [Gallants].

As the farms expanded and increased in acreage more accommodation was provided for the farm workers at Little Maplestead and it is at this time, in the first half of the nineteenth century, that many farm labourers' cottages were built for the workers at Maplestead Hall and Bricks farms. Bricks Farm Cottages and Crealie are examples of this trend.

BRICKS FARM COTTAGES AND CREALIE

BRICKS FARM COTTAGES and Crealie must be considered as part of a piece of land which extended from the site of Bricks Farm Cottages on the Sudbury Road down to the present pond at Crealie; this piece of land was called Hills, probably after a earlier occupant.

The earliest records available show that in 1769 Thomas Wood was admitted to Hills on the surrender of Edward Sewell, followed in 1791 by John Sewell. Bricks Farm Cottages do not appear on the 1817 survey map of the village but they were present at the 1841 tithe and were probably built about 1820 along with several other farm cottages and houses in the village. However, at the 1817 survey there was already one double cottage on the site of Crealie which was still owned by John Sewell and was occupied by John Waters and Thomas Chevill (see map page 158).

In 1836 John Allen was admitted to 'all those customary messuages or cottages with appurtenances called Hills with orchard and gardens' formerly in the occupation of John Gallant, Joseph Nott, John Kemp, John French and Thomas Tibbald and 'now in the occupation of Isaac Bocking and James Bishop'. This group of cottages must have

Bricks Farm Cottages

included Crealie plus another newly built labourer's cottage next to it and also the newly built double tenement now called Bricks Farm Cottages.

Crealie

By the 1841 tithe award, John Allen still owned the tenements now known as Crealie, together with the second cottage and Bricks Farm Cottages, all of which had been built on the site. The four dwellings were occupied by James Bishop 'plus others'.

It is not always easy to tell from the censuses who lived in the group of cottages which were known as Hills. In 1841 we know that the two cottages on School Road where Crealie is sited today were occupied by James Bishop, 64, an agricultural labourer, and his wife Rose, together with Thomas Watkinson, 28, blacksmith, his wife Ann and their children William and Sarah, together with a third family, James Lavender, 45, agricultural labourer, his wife Mary and a lodger, David Howard, also a farm labourer. It is probable that the occupants of Bricks Farm Cottages on the Sudbury Road were Eliza Wenden, 35, straw-plaiter and her daughters Ann, 7, and Hannah, 4, who lived in one tenement, while her older daughters Amelia, 17, and Rachel, 15, and Sarah French, 20, all straw-plaiters, and baby Benjamin, aged four months, lived in the other.

In 1850 the manorial court book for Little Maplestead records the surrender from John Allen to William Stebbing from Pebmarsh of Hills, described as:

> *two customary messuages or cottages and also two other messuages or double tenements, blacksmith's shop and other buildings erected (at the expense of John Allen) now in the occupation of Thomas Watkinson, John Waters, Aaron Lamprell and James Bishop, plus the waste land in*

front of cottages which lies parallel with the road leading from Bricks Farm to Maplestead Hall, in front of the garden of the said two cottages called Hills.

In the 1851 census for Bricks Farm Cottages we can only find Thomas Watkinson who is described as a beer-seller employing one boy, his wife Mary-Ann who was a dressmaker and their three daughters and one son. It is probable that the other tenements on the site were uninhabited at the time. In 1854 there is a record of John Allen of Pebmarsh, yeoman, owning:

> *the two customary cottages now or formerly called Hills and two double cottages or tenements erected on part of the premises also a piece of ground late waste now forming part of said premises with a Blacksmith's shop and beer house and other buildings.*

Later John Allen surrendered Hills to James Brewster and in 1885 it was occupied by John Frost and Joseph Dixey

In the 1891 census Arthur Harrington, 29, described as a dealer, Dorothy his wife, a tailoress, with their young son Stanley, labourer, occupied the tenement now called Crealie together with Joseph Lewis, 60, and his son Daniel, 18, both farm labourers. The adjacent cottage seems no longer to have existed by this date. Bricks Farm Cottages were occupied by Thomas Watkinson, 78, now described as a retired blacksmith, his wife Mary and lodger Charles Moore, 38, who was a groom and gardener, together with a second family, George Mayes, 32, farm labourer, his wife Betsy and young children Alice, George and Maud.

In the 1919 sale catalogue Crealie was described as a double tenement cottage built of plaster and part weather-boarded construction with a slate roof and let to A. Hasler and Thomas Wiseman, quarterly tenants at a rent of eight pounds per annum. It comprised:

> *the East End cottage with living room, kitchen with fixed copper, 2 bedrooms and a large garden:*

> *the West End cottage containing a living room, kitchen and 2 bedrooms, a detached brick and tiled wash house and bake house with copper fixed, large garden.*

In the same sale catalogue Bricks Farm Cottages were described as a 'cottage property' situated near Notts Corner, comprising:

> *a plaster and slate double tenement cottage each tenement containing a living room and 2 bedrooms. There is also a new brick and tiled kitchen with copper and sink fixed. These are let to Eliza Willsmore and John Bishop at a rental of £8 per annum.*

Like other village properties, the cottages were bought by Alfred Blomfield and became part of the Maplestead Hall estate. In a deed dated 1923 Bricks Farm Cottages, described as a double tenement or cottage, were occupied by Eliza Willsmore and John Bishop.

In 1984 Joseph Blomfield sold 2 Bricks Farm Cottages privately, followed in 1988 by 1 Bricks Farm Cottages together with the pump nearby.

WOODVIEW

THE FIRST COTTAGE on the site of Woodview was called Willow Cottage; it may have been occupied by George Nott when he first got married. However, this cottage burnt down and in the 1817 survey of the village we find the site of the cottage owned by George Nott (who farmed Bricks Farm) described as '109, piece formerly waste'. By 1841 the cottage had been rebuilt as two tenements; this is the cottage we see today called Woodview. It was owned by Suzanna and Adelina Nott and at the census one tenement was occupied by Daniel Roberts, 60, agricultural labourer, Elizabeth his wife, and sons Daniel, 21, and John, 14, also agricultural labourers. These tenants would probably have worked at Bricks Farm. The other tenement was occupied by Isaac Lewsey, 22, bricklayer, Mary his wife and their baby daughter.

At the 1851 census Daniel Roberts, the son, now aged 30 and head of the family, a farm labourer, with his wife Susan lived at Willow Cottage. The other half of the house was occupied by James Lavender, 51, described as farm labourer and 'church clerk' and his wife Mary who had moved there from what is now Crealie.

Willow Cottage (Woodview) 1817

In 1861 on census night only one part of the house was occupied, by James Lavender, parish clerk, and his wife Mary but ten years later, in 1871, we find Daniel Roberts and his wife are listed again at Willow Cottage this time with their nephew John, 19, a carpenter, and a lodger William Porter, 76, a farming bailiff.

By the 1891 census we find John Bogue, 25, a village baker, Ada, his wife, and Winifred, their baby daughter at Willow Cottage; once again they do not appear to be sharing the house with any other family.

In the early 1900s there was still a bakery at Woodview run by the Bogues; John Bogue was still the baker and the bake-house was on the premises. The Bogues also owned a small meadow just below Bricks Farm where they kept chickens. Today Mr and Mrs O'Connell live in Woodview where they run a nursery.

BRAMBLES

ACCORDING TO THE 1817 survey of the village Sir George Dennis, an absentee landlord, owned the land across from the Cock Inn on which Brambles now stands and at that time there were four tenements and a garden occupied by 'sundry tenants' on the site. These cottages had probably been built for agricultural workers around the turn of the century, as had adjacent tenements, Rose and Aster Cottages.

At the 1841 tithe award, the tenements were owned by Lady Pompel and were occupied by Thomas Mayes and others. The censuses reveal that the tenants held a fascinating variety of occupations.

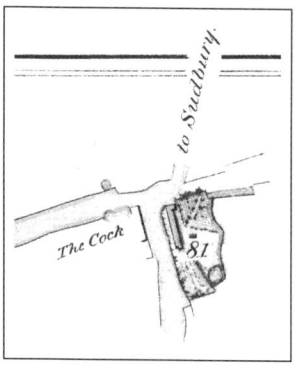

Brambles 1817

In 1851 the occupants were Thomas Mayes, 48, a carter, his wife Hannah, son William, 'employed at home', daughter Charlotte, and other sons Frederic, George and Samuel; William Carter, 63, farm bailiff, daughter Charlotte, 24, dressmaker; William Porter, 55, farm bailiff, and his wife Ann and grand-daughter Ann; William Firman, shoemaker, his wife Eliza, sons Thomas, 24, Frederic, 22, George, 19, and Stephen, 16, all farm labourers, and daughter Eliza; and probably Charles Partridge, 26, farm labourer, his wife Caroline and young children, Edward, Charles and Sarah.

- - 188 -

Brambles

At the 1861 census we find Alfred Johnson, 37, and Hepzibah, his wife, both agricultural labourers, Sarah Metser, 17, a boarder who was a silk weaver, daughter Selena Johnson, 12, a silk winder, sons Alfred and James, farm labourers, and younger children William, Harriet and John; Thomas Mayes, 60, a timber-carter employing one man, Hannah his wife, son Samuel who worked with his father, and young grandson, John; Ezekial Turp, 39, whiting maker, his wife Elizabeth, and young children William and Mary-Ann. It was young William who became 'Bill' Turp, the village tramp.

By 1871, the tenements were occupied by Henrietta Felton, a widow of 74, charwoman, with her grandson John; Benjamin Digby, 48, a gardener, Elizabeth, his wife and daughter Sarah, 17, both of whom did needlework for a living; James Walls, 23, an agricultural labourer, his wife Louisa, a straw-plaiter and young sons Albert and John; Alfred Johnson, 48, a gamekeeper, his wife Hepzibah who did housework, sons Alfred, James, William and John, all agricultural labourers, and young son Robert, daughters Selena, a silk weaver, Harriet, a straw-plaiter, and young daughter Emma, and baby grandson Arthur.

In 1881 we find the cottages at Brambles occupied by James Pamplin, a farm labourer, Eliza his wife, daughter Emma, a factory hand and sons John and Charles, both farm labourers; Edward Smith, a master horse-dealer; George Mayes, a farm labourer, Susannah his wife and Frances his daughter, a general servant, younger children Walter, Emma, Arthur and Charlotte; and William Finch, a farm labourer and Alice his wife.

By 1891 the tenants were William Finch, 70, now a farmer, with his wife; Robert Potter, 54, a pig dealer and his wife Jane and son Charles, 21, who worked with him, younger son William, 13, and daughter Emily, 4; Alfred Binks, 33, fish hawker, wife Matilda and sons Alfred, Charles, Frank, daughter Lily and their cousin Henry Howard, 19, a shepherd.

The cottages still existed in the 1920s and in one of the thatched cottages on the site lived a character called Hooky Cooky - according to Cecil Cook's *Memories:*

...he had no arms just hooks as he lost one in a reaping machine and the other in a chaff cutter. He rode a three wheeler bike with a loop of leather in each handle bar to put his hooks in and he had a back-pedal brake. When he had to get off on a hill, he put one of his hooks through the front wheel spokes and pulled his bike that way. He still managed to work - he could stack straw or feed the straw baler. His pitchfork had a leather loop so that he could hold it and work like any other man. He picked up a glass of beer in his teeth and drank it that way. Strangers used to buy him a pint to see him do it. I used to hold a bottle for him to drink, fill and light his pipe, cut him off tobacco to chew. Beer was 5d a pint, crisps 2p a packet, five Woodbines 2d and a large bottle of whisky was 12/6.

Hooky Cooky, by permission of Peter Cook

ASH COTTAGE

IN THE 1817 survey of the village there was a tenement on the site of Ash Cottage. Not present on the 1777 map, it must have been built between these two dates, probably around the turn of the century. The double cottage, owned by John Sewell and occupied by a Mr Finch, was a farm cottage.

By the 1841 tithe award the cottage was owned by George Nott of Bricks Farm and was occupied by George Byford and in the census we find George Byford, 40, an agricultural labourer, his wife Sarah and three sons, James (also an agricultural labourer), Thomas and Joseph, and daughters Elizabeth and Eliza and two others whose names are illegible. It is not clear if the cottage was occupied by another family at this date but by 1851 the cottage was occupied by George Byford, 47, a farm labourer, Sarah his wife, their daughter Tabitha, 19, a crêpe or silk weaver, sons Thomas, 16, and Joseph, 12, both farm labourers, and younger children Eliza, William and Frederic. The Byfords shared the cottage with Eliza Frost, widow, 45, a pauper, her unmarried daughters Sarah, 21, and Susan, 18, both crêpe and silk weavers, two smaller daughters Harriet, 8, and Eliza, 6, both straw-plaiters and sons John, 16, a farm labourer and William, 4.

Ash Cottage

Twenty years later, in 1871, the cottage was occupied by George Warren, 20, an agricultural labourer, and Sarah his wife who did 'household work'. Sharing the house was Sarah Tyler, a widow of 33, a tailoress, her daughter Clara, a straw-plaiter, and a young son William, 8, and probably also Joseph Partridge, 59, an agricultural labourer, Mary Ann his wife who did 'housework' and son John, 13, an agricultural worker.

In 1881 Abraham Bocking, a farm labourer, and his wife, Amelia, and daughter Emma, a factory hand, and sons Charles, Benjamin and John, farm labourers, and younger children Robert, Elizabeth and baby Sidney occupied what is now Ash Cottage. By 1891 the cottage was lived in by Samuel Turner, widower, 40, farmer, sons George, 17, and James, 14, both farm labourers, and younger sons John, Arthur and Frank, and by Samuel's sister, Charlotte, 40, his housekeeper.

It seems that sometime after this date, the tenement was pulled down and for a time there was an small ash grove on the site. However, in the 1960s, the owner of the Bulmer Brick and Tile Company built the present-day Ash Cottage on the cleared site using old bricks in a style which gives the impression that the house is older than it really is.

MEADOW END

THERE WAS A double cottage on the site of Meadow End at the 1841 tithe award, built since the 1817 survey of the village. It was a farm cottage built by James Brewster and occupied initially by John French, described as a jobber, with Elizabeth, his wife, and daughter Harriet. Later the two cottages were used as accommodation for the Maplestead Hall coachman and gardener. Eventually the cottages were pulled down and the site was used by the estate carpenters as a timber-yard. There was also a saw-pit which was covered over when the present-day bungalow was built in 1958 as a home for Laura Blomfield's father when he retired.

Meadow End

SCHOOL FARM COTTAGE

SCHOOL FARM COTTAGE, another example of a nineteenth century agricultural labourer's cottage, does not appear on the 1817 survey of village. However, in the manor court book for Little Maplestead in 1836 there is the following entry:

> *Whereas at a court held for the said manor on the 15 day of August 1831... George Firmin, a copyhold tenant of the said manor, had enclosed amongst other land or ground a piece or parcel of the waste of the said manor, abutting west onto a field called Home field, then the property of Doctor MacLachlan, east on the road leading from Little Maplestead to Gestingthorpe containing about ten rods and thereon erected a cottage without the lien or consent of the Lords and tenants of the said manor...*

This cottage was School Farm Cottage and, although George Firmin had to pay a fine for contravening the manorial law, the cottage was allowed to remain.

The 1841 tithe map shows the cottage and its enclosed land. It was owned by George Firmin and occupied by Joseph Partridge. In the 1841 census we find that Joseph Partridge was an agricultural labourer and that he lived with his sons Charles and Frederick. By 1861 the cottage was uninhabited but in 1869 it was described as a tenement erected by George Firmin and in the occupation of Henry Dixey and George Weybrew. At the 1871 census we find Thomas Dixey, stockman, his wife

Sarah, a charwoman, young daughters Charlotte and Ellen, Eliza, a crêpe weaver and son, William, an agricultural labourer, living at School Farm Cottage.

In 1881 the occupants were Henry Dixey, an agricultural labourer, his wife Esther, a shirt maker, and children Ellen, Harriet and Charles. Ten years later Henry Dixey and his wife and family were still living at School Farm Cottage; Charles, 14, was then an agricultural labourer and there was a young son, Ernest.

In the 1919 sale catalogue, School Farm Cottage was described as:

> *Tile and plaster construction, contains 3 bedrooms, living room, kitchen, pantry, washhouse (brick and tiled with cement floor) copper and fireplace fixed all in excellent order. Good garden. Let to Mr Harry King at the low rental of £4 per annum.*

THE SPATE OF building of so many farm labourers' cottages in Little Maplestead illustrates the fact that by 1860 England was the richest country in the world. All sections of society, including even the poorest agricultural workers, began at last to benefit from this prosperity. Farm profits were rising, as too were rents, farm incomes and prices but wages were increasing faster. All this meant that after the early agricultural depression the mid-Victorian years were seen as the golden age of high-profit farming. Even a tiny village like Little Maplestead began to support a wide range of trades.

Kelly's trade directory for Little Maplestead in 1866 lists under 'gentry': George Pinckard Esq, the tenant farmer at Maplestead Hall; Reverend John Harward MA (incumbent vicar); Reverend Joseph Watkinson (Independent minister). Traders included Ann Callow, shop-keeper; John Cooper, farmer; Robert Hearn, farmer, School Farm; Isaac Lewsey, bricklayer and farmer; Thomas Mayes, carrier; Robert Moss, baker; Samuel Richbell, 'Cock Inn'; William Taswell, beer retailer and shop-keeper; Thomas Watkinson, blacksmith and Mrs Mary Willsmore, farmer, Gallants Farm.

HUSH HOUSE, THE STUDIO AND WILLOW COTTAGE

HUSH HOUSE was built in the village during the years of relative prosperity. It dates from 1856 according to the year written on the back of the staircase. Originally called Bethel Villa, it stood on a small holding and orchard, which included the land now occupied by all the houses along the north side of Cock Road towards the church; in 1817 this was Watts Field, owned by Mary Cornell, whose tenant farmer was Lot Borrows. Mary Cornell also owned the field called Aldricks adjoining Woodertons and it was Joseph Baynes of Woodertons who probably sold off the land in 1841. The Studio and Willow Cottage were once outbuildings belonging to Hush House.

Hush House

There is no clear record in the earlier censuses of the occupants of the house but in 1891 Bethel Villa was occupied by John Alford, a gardener, 54, his wife Hannah, son Frank, 25, a baker, and daughter Louisa, 22, a silk weaver. The house was sold in 1893 by Lewis Downs to John Richbell the builder. In 1926 Cecil Cook described it as the first house in Cock Road, lived in by Mr and Mrs Richbell. Later on Arthur and Alfred Richbell sold Hush House to George Britton, a tractor driver, in 1940 for £640. He lived there until 1963 when the land was sold off and the house was sold to Ray Coates for £3300. It was named Hush House by Mr Coates' daughter as Mr Coates had a throat problem and could only talk in a whisper and it is still so called today.

Both The Studio and Willow Cottage are conversions from a hay barn, once the property of the small farm next door, now Hush House. The conversions were made in 1980.

THE MANOR HOUSE

THE MANOR HOUSE is probably the house originally called Cock Field House, built on a corner of land which had belonged to The Cock Inn. Built like many other of the village properties around 1820, Cock Field House is first recorded at the tithe award of 1841 when it was owned by George Firmin and occupied by John Porter, 55, an agricultural labourer, Mary his wife, sons John, 15, William, 12, George, 8, (all farm labourers), Robert, 6, and daughter Charlotte. In

1871 Cock Field House was occupied by widower Charles Watkinson, 36, a coach-smith labourer and his daughter Rhoda, aged 14, who looked after all the other younger children - Alice, Martha, Emily, Joseph and baby Ebenezer. By 1881 Samuel Simmons, described as a farmer, lived in Cock Field House with his wife Harriet and daughter Sarah and grand-daughter.

BY THE END of the 1870s the golden age of farming in Little Maplestead was fast fading as the village felt the repercussions of the deep depression that was affecting British agriculture as a result of the importation of cheap American wheat. Once again farmers were forced to economize by employing less labour. Farm workers in Little Maplestead had declined in number from seventy-seven in 1861 to forty-eight in 1881 and in the eighteen months between 1872 and 1874 at least seventy people were reported as having left the village. Most moved northwards to find work in the industrial Midlands but others emigrated to Canada or Australia. Many farm workers present in the village in 1870 were no longer there in 1881. The population had fallen in forty years from 407 to 261 and it continued to fall, reaching 193 in 1901[8]. Many cottages were left empty and were eventually demolished. Although there were still fifteen straw-plaiters at this date the industry was about to disappear from the village. However, this led to one positive development; the disappearance of work involving children, such as straw-plaiting for girls and farm jobs for boys, gave parents a good reason to keep their children at school[9].

In Kelly's Directory for Little Maplestead in 1878, the gentry listed were: C. E. Brewster of Maplestead Hall; Reverend F. Fairbank (Congregational minister); Reverend J. Harward, MA, Vicar. Under the heading of 'commercial': Charles Bentall, farmer, Gages Farm; Ann Callow, beer retailer and shop-keeper; Walter Callow, pig dealer; Henry Carpenter, carpenter; James Downes, farmer; F. Fairbank, farmer, Gallants Farm; James Felton, 'Cock Inn'; William Gatward, butcher and farmer; George Hearn, farmer, School Farm; Isaac Lewsey, bricklayer; Ezra Moss, baker and shop-keeper; Henry Shave, farmer; Mrs Sarah Shave, farmer, Lyes Farm [Leys] and Thomas Watkinson, blacksmith.

From 1881 the local economy of Little Maplestead began to change. The depression in agriculture had drastically reduced the number of farm workers who with their families had previously constituted the majority of the village population. Together with the decline in agricultural workers, there was an increase in numbers both of artisans and building workers. In the trade directory for Little Maplestead in 1888, the gentry listed C. E. Brewster, Maplestead Hall; Reverend Cornah, The Grove; Reverend F. Fairbank. Under the 'commercial' heading we find: J. Bogue, baker and shop-keeper; W. Callow, beer retailer; James Downes, farmer; William Gatward, butcher and farmer; J. Hammond, bricklayer; Thomas Richbell, 'Cock Inn'; H. Shave, farmer, Gages Farm; Mrs S. Shave, farmer, Lyes Farm and Thomas Watkinson, blacksmith.

The fortunes of farming, and therefore of the lives of the majority of the villagers of Little Maplestead, had fluctuated dramatically during the nineteenth century. Farming had flourished in the middle decades and the Maplestead Hall estate had grown to become a very large farm. But when there was a sudden and severe agricultural depression in the 1870s farmers and landlords suffered a marked drop in their incomes and this situation was reflected in a change in the appearance of the countryside as farmers switched 'from corn to horn' in an attempt to survive; this meant that once again there was an increase in pasture and meadow land, fewer fields of wheat and more market-gardens and orchards. But, as it had always been throughout farming history, land still gave the greatest status; 'even the insolvent squire will get five times as much respect from the common peasantry as the newly-made rich man'[10]. However, it was still the old-established rich that still held most of the land and, in a survey carried out in 1873-1875 called the New Domesday Survey, the land in England was found to be owned by only 7000 individuals, peers most prominent amongst them.

Despite the increase in the size of farms the numbers of farm labourers had gradually been declining as farming systems were changing and more machinery was being introduced. But alongside this decline in the numbers of agricultural workers and the shift to other occupations came an improvement in the lot of the men who worked on the land. Although conditions on the whole had been better than elsewhere for those who worked on the land in Little Maplestead, because it had been their good fortune to have as their landlords honourable Christian men, there is no doubt that the lives of most of the villagers during the nineteenth century had been hard. William Cobbett, the political essayist, reflected on the simple lives of such men in the following extract:

> ...yet when all were poor, or at least the vast majority were poor, the conditions were accepted by rich and poor alike. During these hard times the poor found happiness in family life and the small achievement of a good fire and a full plate...

A romanticized view perhaps, but one which was more likely to have been true for the villagers of Little Maplestead than many other places.

The building of so many farm labourers' cottages during the nineteenth century meant that by 1900 there were more houses in the village of Little Maplestead than at any time in its history. Once again the village was on the brink of great changes, more fundamental than ever before. The earlier arrival of the railway, the invention of the motor car, the creation of wealthy industrialists and the culture of John Ruskin and the William Morris group all combined to fuel the idea of the desirability of a rural idyll and make possible its realization. In the twentieth century we shall see how this was accomplished, by whom and how it changed the village into the place we recognize today.

Notes to Chapter IX

[1] John Wood, *Series of Plans for Cottages or Habitations of the Labourer* (1781)
[2] *The Maplesteads*, WEA booklet (1986)
[3] Asa Briggs, *A Social History of England* (London, 1983)
[4] From a series of directories in Colchester library (local studies department)
[5] Asa Briggs, *A Social History of England*
[6] From information supplied by the nephew of Mr E. Orchard
[7] From information supplied by Mrs N. Scurr
[8] *The Maplesteads*, WEA booklet (1986)
[9] *The Maplesteads*, WEA booklet (1986)
[10] Asa Briggs, *A Social History of England*

NINETEENTH-CENTURY EVENTS

1805   Britain victorious under Nelson in Battle of Trafalgar

1814   George Stephenson constructs first steam locomotive

1815   Wellington victorious at Waterloo. Economic crisis leads to large-scale emigration to North America

1819   Peterloo massacre

1820   George IV becomes king

1825   First passenger steam train runs

1830   William IV becomes king

1832   Great Reform Bill

1837   Victoria becomes queen

1846   Repeal of the Corn Laws, allowing imported wheat

1851   Great Exhibition in London

1853   Crimean War

1898   Start of Boer War

POPULATION OF LITTLE MAPLESTEAD

1801	298	1861	325
1811	290	1871	302
1821	313	1881	261
1831	373	1891	217
1841	407	1901	193
1851	367		

CHAPTER X

THE TWENTIETH CENTURY

*This is the age of progress. Let us meet
The new progressives of the village street.*[1]

AS THE TWENTIETH CENTURY arrived, the wages of the farm labourers of Little Maplestead, and of most other places, had not increased very much beyond the mid-nineteenth-century level. Even by the beginning of the First World War in 1914 wages had only risen slightly and this had been responsible for an escalating flight from the land which had rapidly become a serious public issue. The number of farm labourers, which had reached a peak in the 1850s with a million and a half workers, had fallen to about one half that by 1911[2].

Wages, however, were not the only problem for agricultural labourers; poor housing was another factor which was causing the workers to leave the land. Although the Housing Act of 1890 and the Housing and Town Planning Act of 1909 had given the Local Government Board authority to encourage councils to build houses, not many had been begun because it was still thought that private landlords should provide for the housing needs of their workers. However, in 1913 the government announced firm plans to build state or council houses for agricultural workers, but the First World War intervened and little was achieved. But despite the complaints about low wages, poor conditions and lack of adequate farm labourers' housing in the country as a whole, workers in Little Maplestead were, it seems, comparatively well housed and secure in their tied cottages and their apparently low wages would probably have been supplemented by payment in kind.

But economic changes were leading to anxieties, particularly in the countryside. 'England is changing hands'[3] became a well known phrase after more than one million acres of land were sold. It seemed that the many of the small country landowners were doomed to disappear and indeed, 1919 did see the beginnings of the dispersal of Maplestead Hall estate. Strikes too were prevalent and by 1921 England was in the grip of a deep economic depression which was to last until the Second World War.

After the war the number of farm workers needed on the land continued to decline as their jobs were taken by rapidly improving farm machinery. Good new housing was badly needed as the old tenements deteriorated. At last councils began to build new houses and, as the use of bicycles and motor-cars became more common, there

LITTLE MAPLESTEAD in

The Round Church and Maplestead Hall, looking north

Looking up Oak Road towards Gestingthorpe Road, School Road in the foreground

THE TWENTIETH CENTURY

School Road from the northeast, looking southwest

Collins Road in the foreground, looking across Sudbury Road towards Cock Road

was no longer any necessity to build close to the farms. Such houses could now be built in the village centre; however, they were often designed with scant regard to the local architecture. In Little Maplestead there are three distinct groups of council houses.

SEVEN AND EIGHT SCHOOL ROAD

THESE HOUSES were built in 1939 on land bought by Halstead Rural District Council from the Vaizey estate. They were the first council houses to be built in the village and were those referred to by Cecil Cook 'which stood on School Meadow, next to the school, where the children used to play and which often flooded so that they could skate in the winter time'.

Seven and Eight School Road

Mrs Florence (Florrie) Vickers, aged 92 years, lives at 8 School Road. She told us:

> *I have lived in the village for forty-nine years, in this house [8 School Road] for thirty years and before that at Southview [Attadale] when it was a small cottage. Mr Vickers worked at Deans Hall Farm, at one time all the water for the farm came from the pump in the yard. I worked for most of my life at the egg-packing firm based at The Grove, later in a hired barn in Pebmarsh. I felt that the village died with the loss of the village hall and then the shop, both were places where people could meet. But still, I would not like to live anywhere else.*

ONE, TWO, THREE AND FOUR SCHOOL ROAD

THESE FOUR HOUSES were built by the council in 1946. They were so-called Airey houses which were quickly and cheaply constructed from prefabricated parts. The land on which all four houses were built had belonged to Mr Joe Blomfield of Maplestead Hall and had been part of Bakersfield. Two School Road was bought by the tenants in 1985, and 1 School Road in 1991. Three and 4 School Road were bought by Braintree District Council in 1983 and were then sold to the Guinness Trust which demolished them in order to build three new houses. The new 4 School Road was built in 1992; 3 and 3a were built in 1994/5. Three and 3a, built after the right-to-buy legislation of the 1980s, are managed by Blackwater Housing Association, Braintree, and are exempt from the legislation so that they will remain as reasonably priced rented houses in perpetuity. They are let on a 'need' basis but with weight given to prospective tenants who have expressed a preference for Little Maplestead.

NINE, TEN, ELEVEN, TWELVE AND THIRTEEN SCHOOL ROAD

THESE FIVE council-provided houses were built in 1953 on land bought by Halstead Rural District Council from Leppingwells Farm. Ten School Road was bought by the tenants in 1980. Thirteen School Road has been lived in by the same family from the time it was first built; it was bought by them in 1989.

ONE, TWO, THREE AND FOUR COCK ROAD

THESE COUNCIL-PROVIDED houses were built in 1951 on land bought by Halstead Rural District Council which was originally part of Cock Field owned by Charles George Stanley from Bulmer.

MANY FARM labourers were grateful to move into these new houses built by the council preferring them to the old tied cottages, and, as the twentieth century progressed and their wages began at last to increase and the price of foodstuffs began to fall, they found themselves better off and better housed than they had ever been before.

Improvements were also made to the existing rural housing during the second half of twentieth century, as mains water and electricity were laid on, sewage schemes were built and septic tanks replaced the old earth closets, but despite this, the new modern council houses were still favoured by the farm worker. The traditional rural cottages which they abandoned were then bought up by immigrants from towns and cities seeking a rural existence. These urban newcomers to the village who began to arrive in the 1970s were often comparatively well off and could afford to repair, improve and maintain the old cottages and, as a fortunate consequence of this, ensure their preservation when they might otherwise have been lost.

Some of the newcomers to Little Maplestead did not choose to buy traditional cottages but, still wishing to live in a rural environment, bought up land and built modern houses in the village. These twentieth-century houses can be divided up according to the decade in which they were built. However one of the earliest new buildings in the village was not a house, it was the village hall.

THE VILLAGE HALL

CONSTRUCTED AFTER the First World War on land given by Alfred Blomfield to the village so that people should have a place to meet, and built with the help of money raised by Mr K.Vaizey and Mr Percy of Deans Hall the village hall was opened on 28 April 1925. It stood in School Road near Hall Corner and at its grand opening concert Mr Percy organized a troop of chorus girls to perform on stage! It was, for a time, the heart of the village where dances, whist drives and other social events were held which drew villagers together. In 1935 at King George V and Queen Mary's Jubilee a party for the children was held in the hall and each child was presented with a 'jubilee mug'. The hall was an important centre for the village during the Second World War and at one time, when a large party of 'boy-helpers' came to clear thistles in order to increase the available productive land at Maplestead Hall farm, they all stayed in the hall and were looked after and given meals by the villagers. Sometimes an admission fee was levied at events such as beetle- and whist-drives and this paid for the annual church choir and Sunday school outings to Clacton in the summer.

The Village Hall, by permission of Peter Cook

The following extracts from letters written in 1944 by Mr Joe Blomfield to his sister, Helen, show the part that the village hall played in community events:

> *In May we had a fête at the Hall for 'Salute the Soldier Week'. One thousand people turned up with about 300 children. The garden looked beautiful all the trees being in bloom. Walter Mayes was showing people the vegetable garden which looked very well. Mrs Felton was a tower of strength serving up the tea. It was a very hot day, we soon ran out of lemonade and people were going to the pump for a drink. We had a large auction and people were generous with their gifts. Village social life was at its height then with whist drives and dances in the village hall every week and we have now paid for the new piano. Laura [Mrs Blomfield] danced with a yankee in the Paul Jones. He was overheard to ask her 'Say lady, are you the squire's wife?'!*

> *July 23, The Round Church, Little Maplestead*

> *We are now getting through the crisis [lack of farm hands at Maplestead Hall] of Eric [the cow-man] and Doris [a land girl] being married yesterday and George Felton on holiday. Fortunately the honeymoon is being spent at Hall Cottage so that, as Eric said 'We can just keep an eye on them [the cows!].' The wedding was a huge success, frantic preparations for days right up to the last moment when Laura was stitching something up at zero hour. The bride wore white satin. The two senior bridesmaids pale blue and the two smaller bridesmaids (Lily Cook and the small niece) wore pink. Mrs Moore made all the dresses. Everything was put forward an hour, from the morning milking onwards so as to get to church at 3.30. At 2 pm I was horrified to discover the bride, Hetty [the housekeeper] and a guest frantically mixing meal in the barn owing to some breakdown in the plan for the day. They left from the front door. The church seemed full of people and it was a nice service and playing of the Wedding March. Mrs Cook was on the organ which was somewhat overwhelming. The reception at the village hall was a fine affair lasting from 4 pm to 11 pm but we did not stay all the time.*

The white satin that the bride wore - a real luxury in war time - had been specially imported for her from America by servicemen from the base at nearby Wethersfield.

Winnie Mayes, who sadly died soon after she spoke of her memories of the village, also remembered the village hall:

> I used to live at Tanglewood. I remember picking stones off the fields working all day for a few pence. In the summer I remember helping with the farm work, hay-making was fun and we rode on top of the hay carts; we used to take tea out to the farm workers. During the war I worked at Crittalls ammunition factory doing a man's heavy work. My family used to attend the Sudbury Road chapel and my sister and brother are buried there. I used to work for five shillings a week at 'housework' mostly at Maplestead Hall. I also worked at the wood factory making spills for the fire. My last job was at Courtaulds in Halstead, I used to walk there and back even during the very worst weather. My mother was a caretaker at the village hall for many years and she used to go and help keep it clean when she was a child. It was always spotless - everything scrubbed and polished. The village hall was badly missed when it was pulled down, I especially missed the village dances.

The village hall continued to be the centre of village life until the early 1970s when the life-styles of villagers began to change. Sadly the hall fell into disuse and was eventually pulled down. The land was sold by the parish council and two new houses, Maple Chalet and Baytrees, were built on the site soon afterwards.

'SALUTE THE SOLDIER' week was held to boost morale during some of the darkest days in the Second World War. As in other agricultural villages, both in the First and the Second World War, some of the young men from Little Maplestead could not enlist in the services but were required to stay at home to work on the land. They played a vital part in ensuring that food production did not falter. Some women, too, like Winnie Mayes, took on men's work to support the 'war effort'. However some villagers did get called up to the forces and found themselves in foreign lands fighting to defend their country - their village and their homes - and some lost their lives. A list of their names can be found in the Round Church.

Helen Blomfield remembers well the part she played during the war. She joined the War Agricultural Committee which involved mapping in detail all the farms in the Halstead Rural District, listing all the crops that were grown, which fields were arable and which were pasture. This was to ensure that all farms produced what the government decreed was necessary for the good of the country under threat of invasion. The work took one year to complete. Where changes in agriculture had to be made, it was up to the committee members to enforce them and this was not always easy. Mr Joe Blomfield, the secretary of the Halstead committee, had a shotgun pointed at him from a window by an elderly lady farmer who did not wish to plough up her pasture!

WELLAWAY

THIS UNUSUAL cottage, originally called Rosedene, is one of the earliest of the houses built in Little Maplestead in the twentieth century and dates from 1926, just after the building of the village hall. It started off as a simple shack-like building which was modernized and extended several times in the 1970s and 1980s; more land was also added to the garden.

SAMSON'S FACTORY

ABOUT 1926 Mr Percy, a London businessman, who lived at Deans Hall, opened a small factory called the Maplestead Woodworks in one of his barns. It made matches at first but then adapted to produce coloured spills and fruit baskets using willow and poplar wood. Many girls and men from the surrounding villages worked here and they had their own tree-felling gang.

Samson Furniture

Later the factory began to manufacture Christmas crackers and then, in the 1970s, it started to make good quality pine furniture and, changing ownership, became known as Samson Furniture.

THE COCK INN

The Old Cock Inn, by permission of Peter Cook

THE PRESENT Cock Inn was built in 1936. The original inn was much nearer the roadside and the present inn was built behind it; business was transferred from old to new when it was completed but the old and the new inns existed together for a short while before the old inn was demolished.

The Cock Inn

There are few records about the very early history of the Cock Inn but the 1600 map of the village marks a plot on the site at that early date which may have indicated the presence of a building. There was certainly a building there in 1777, most probably the old Cock Inn, situated on what would have been then a busy turnpike road.

In the 1817 survey of the village we find that the proprietor of the Cock public house and outbuildings at that time was the tenant farmer at Maplestead Hall, John Sewell, and that the tenant landlord was Timothy Fisher.

Using the census records and the trade directories we can build up a list of the landlords of the Cock Inn over the next hundred years or so. Unfortunately the 1841 tithe award is illegible but from 1845 to 1850 we have entries in the trade directories for Samuel Richbell who was landlord at the Cock Inn. In the 1851 census we find Samuel Richbell, widower, aged 60, described as a victualler living at the Cock Inn with Anne Basham, 26, his housekeeper, Jeffrey Salmons, 37, the ostler, and a lodger, James Ely, who was a tea dealer.

Trade directory entries for 1855 and 1859 continue to list Samuel Richbell and we find him once again in the 1861 census, now aged 70, listed as innkeeper and a farmer of ten acres employing two men although what land he farmed is not clear. Remarkably he had a wife, Sarah Scott, aged 26, and two young children, Thomas and Richard.

Trade directories between 1862 and 1870 continue to list Samuel Richbell as landlord of the Cock Inn and at the time of the 1871 census Samuel Richbell, now 84, publican and farmer of ten acres, was still there with his young wife Sarah and their four children, Thomas, John Scott, Mark and baby Sarah. There was one lodger at the inn, James Felton, a widower of 43, who was the horseman or ostler. Then, in 1874, a trade directory names James Felton as the innkeeper at the Cock Inn and in the 1881 census we find him again, surprisingly, married to Sarah Scott Richbell, now aged 47! They lived at the inn with Sarah's son, John Scott Richbell, 18, who was a bricklayer. In 1886 James Felton was still the landlord of the Cock Inn but by 1888 the inn had reverted to the Richbells and Thomas Richbell, the eldest son of Samuel and Sarah, now aged 30, was landlord.

At the 1891 census the landlord of the Cock Inn, described as a brewer and innkeeper, was still Thomas Richbell. He lived there with his wife Emily and young sons, Thomas and John. But the Richbell dynasty was soon to end; a trade directory for 1898 lists Samuel Whybrew as landlord of the Cock Inn; from 1900 to 1919 the landlord was John Layzell, in 1922 Charles Jeggo, in 1926 Frank Weston, in 1929 Albert Ponsford and in 1933 the landlord of the Cock was Frank Perry.

Cecil Cook gives us a description of the old Cock Inn from memory – his grandfather was the landlord, John Layzell.

On entering the door there was a passage - on the left there was a tap room - a room with a brick floor and a large fireplace at the far end with a beer warmer hanging near by so that you could warm your beer on a cold day. There were heavy tables and forms to sit on, and an old barrel organ in the corner. On the right as you entered there was the best room with seats built into the wall, a large bay window and carpets! This room was where the better-off people went! There were also two further rooms which could be turned into one - this was used just before Christmas when the 'slate club' [a savings club] broke up - Mrs Layzell used to cook large joints of meat and make Christmas puddings to share with all the customers until they were all gone. A few yards down the road stood an old barn where the horses used to stay when the stage coach stopped for the night. No car park was needed then, just a rail in front of the pub to lean your bicycle on or tie your horse to.

Cecil also quotes a fascinating fact - that the level of the doorstep at the Cock Inn is the same as the top of St Andrew's church tower in Halstead.

COVEHYTHE

THIS IS AN UNUSUAL cottage which was named after the place from which it originated. It began life as an ex-army billiard hall, brought to Little Maplestead from Covehythe on the Suffolk coast by a villager, Mr Tokeley, in about 1947-1948. It was made in wooden sections with a corrugated iron roof and transported to the village on a low-loader. It was rebuilt in the grounds of The Grove where it was used first as the gardener's house and then as a house for the foreman of the egg-packing company. Later Covehythe was lived in by Mr Tokeley's son and his family and Mrs Tokeley remembers how, in the autumn, they could hear a cacophony of acorns bouncing on to the tin roof from the tree above! Later, in the 1980s, Covehythe was modernized and today it would be difficult to guess at its highly unusual early history.

PARKS BUNGALOW

THIS PREFABRICATED bungalow was also built in 1947 by Mr Gosling from Parks Farm for one of his farm workers. It was sold in 1998 as a private house.

LITTLE ACRE

ONE OF THE FIRST new houses built privately in the village, this house dates from the early 1960s but there was a cottage, now lost, which was situated in what is now Little Acre's back garden next to the green lane. It is marked on the 1817 survey of the village as a double cottage and garden owned by Mary Cornell and occupied by David Felton and Mary Percival. This cottage had disappeared by the tithe award of 1841.

COPPICE

THIS HOUSE was also built in the early 1960s by Essex County Council as a police house. By the early 1980s, when Little Maplestead no longer had a permanent police presence, it was sold as a private house.

GRIFFINS

GRIFFINS WAS BUILT in the 1970s for Mr and Mrs R. Cook on a plot which was purchased from Little Acre. The name of Griffins comes from the family's brewing association with the Griffin Inn in Halstead.

OTHER HOUSES which date from the 1960 to 1970 spate of building include Aviemore, Daunsington, Greystones, Hawthorn House, Larchmont, Littlehame, Lyntree, Maplecroft, Olde Orchard, Rosanne, Shardleas, Springfield, St Aubin House, Sydenham Place, Willow End and Wyndhams.

CECIL COOK'S SON, Peter, spent his childhood in the village and remembers many of its houses and the people who lived in them. His memories of Little Maplestead in the 1950s and 1960s were written specially for this book:

'Mum and Dad moved from Hall Corner Cottage to Hampers Farm during the summer of 1952. Dad had lived as a boy at Leppingwells Farm and Mum at Brook Cottage, Great Maplestead. During the 1950s I can recall going to Mr Argent's house down Hampers Lane. This lovely old gamekeeper's house was later completely demolished. It stood on a wonderful hill-top site. The house was surrounded by trees and shrubs and even as a young boy I felt sad to see it pulled down [This was the cottage at Pearman's Hill].

'Most of my memories centre around Hampers Farm, where I lived until 1973. During the 1950s and 60s it was still a working farm with stables and lots of sheds and barns that have been swept away. The stack yard had a large Dutch barn alongside the road, then a long row of thatched cart sheds containing old farm machinery. I can remember Jim Wiseman living in a caravan in the corner by the pond and Mr Hardy the local bee-keeper who lived at Woodertons kept some hives there for honey. The barn itself was a wonderful place for a child. If it was raining Mum would say "Go and play in the barn". There were still links to the old ways of farming; a threshing machine stood outside and inside there were numerous bits and pieces and lots of dusty corners for a child to explore. I can remember climbing around on the thatched roof and walking along the ridge, nobody seemed to mind!

'The barn was used every autumn for riddling the potato crop; village women would work in the barn for several weeks and I, as a pre-school child, would help out. From an early age I would always carry a stout stick to kill any rats I came across in the barn. At this time there were numerous wild cats living around the stack yard and as a child I was scratched many times. Bagged corn was stacked in the barn and we had great fun having sack and barrow races through the different parts of the barn.

"Our" side of Hampers, that nearest to Hampers Barn, has not altered much since the 1950s. The present kitchen had an old range for heating water and the present bathroom was our kitchen and bathroom combined. The bath had a removable top which served as a draining board and work surface. Our living room was smaller as we had an extra room between it and the front room. This was always referred to as the "dark room" as it had no windows. It was as long as the living room and about six feet wide, it had old whitewashed walls and lots of bits and pieces were kept in there - a great place to hide and play.

'The gardens were all very productive. Dad had the whole of the back garden down to vegetable plots with a good sized chicken run, plus some tame rabbits and his ferrets. I used to go out with Dad to get rabbits and to shoot game - in those days we still used snares to kill rabbits.

'The woodworks was a bustling place during this time, employing about thirty men and women, with gangs of wood-men going out and felling trees. I remember them felling a lovely tree down Hampers Lane with just axes and wedges. At this time there was a small house at the end of the woodworks where Mr and Mrs Gladwell lived - this has also been demolished.

'The house now called Tanglewood was three cottages when I can first recall them.

They had fallen into a bad state of repair. I can remember going inside with Dad when the water had got in and brought the ceiling down, the water had then frozen solid in all the downstairs rooms. Mr Bevan-Smith purchased the left-hand side and slowly renovated it and when Mr and Mrs Mayes moved from the right-hand side he did the same there and created a first-class cottage. He also purchased some land from Mr Blomfield to extend his garden. For many years the hedge leading towards the Great Maplestead junction bore the shape of the American jet that skimmed low over the village, before crashing next to the church in 1958.

'The bungalow past the church, Meadow End, was built during the 1950s for Laura Blomfield's father, Frank Nott. I can remember talking to him many times, he lived to over one hundred years old. But I cannot recall many changes at the farm cottages opposite; Alan Wiseman has been there since I can remember and I can recall lots of different people next door, prior to Fred Jeggo moving in.

'Maplestead Hall itself was always such an active place, always lots of men coming and going. I used to go and knock at the door and ask for any casual work when I was only nine years old. I don't think Joe Blomfield ever said "No". I can remember burning straw on Church Field with about five village boys, the total sum to be split between us was one shilling and sixpence but this was around 1962. I cannot recall the Hall having changed much but the barns and buildings around it have. I now realize how lucky I was to have complete freedom to wander around the farmyard, to talk to the men and help out where I could. Everybody was so friendly and patient.

'My great-grandfather used to live in Hazeldene [now gone, the site of Saxby's]. Next to him the main village shop, now a house, belonged to Mr Orchard, I can recall the closing-down sale with "lots" all over the road. Mr and Mrs Hunt then ran the shop for several years, then they moved to Australia and the shop closed down for good. The post office was in the council house in School Road run by Joan Jelly and there was another small shop on the main Sudbury to Halstead road, there was also the pub and Maplestead Café filling station, so at this time the village was well served by small businesses.

'Gestingthorpe Road has changed very little. I gardened at the Red House and at The Grove. Cock Road really did change during the 1960s with several houses and bungalows being built. Again I gardened for a Mr Payne in the second bungalow and Mr Hodgkinson in the first house past the council houses.

'My family used to run The Cock in the 1900s and my father could recall the fire that destroyed the old pub. The present pub was built further back from the road in the 1930s. I used to call in for soft drinks and sweets, it had a public bar, saloon and off-sales.

'I worked at the café and filling station while it was being built and several years after, I can recall working all day on the petrol pumps - ten hours for one pound and five shillings. Doug and Betty Moles ran the business for several years.

'The egg-packing station was still in full swing, we used to supply several trays of eggs each week, it was a big employer during the sixties. The bungalows up the Twinstead Road [Collins Road] were built close to the site of two old cottages that were pulled down where Hooky-Cooky used to live. During this time The Manse was let to American servicemen who were very friendly to the village children and we were allowed to treat the garden as an extended playing field. For a few years they put on a bonfire and fireworks on 5 November.

'One of my strongest memories of childhood in Little Maplestead was the freedom we had to go anywhere. We knew all the tracks and footpaths but the farmers did not seem to mind us wandering around the fields watching birds or walking our dogs. We had, I suppose, a "right to roam". I do not get the same feeling when I visit Maplestead these days. Mr and Mrs O'Connell's house looks the same as it did when I was a child, but Bricks Farm has changed so much. It was a really bustling place where all the grain from Maplestead Hall was stored, and the house was divided into two.

'Just up School Road was a lovely orchard next to Mr Britton's house [Crealie] and the pond alongside was *the* place to fish! Leppingwells was empty and unused for many years, the doors fell off their hinges and windows were broken, the barn was in a poor state of repair and the garden was non-existent. It is interesting to look at Leppingwells now and see one of the best houses and gardens in the village!

'I have many happy memories of the village hall, with its music, games and its library and the old barn alongside [Barn Cottage], where Dad used to leave his lorry and I used to leave my bicycle when I went to school. The playing field was our meeting place and was extended during the 1960s so we could play football.'

THE PLANE CRASH that Peter Cook referred to was reported in *The Times* on 20 October 1958 under the heading 'Pilot's Escape in Crash Landing'. A dramatic account of the same incident in which the village of Little Maplestead had a lucky escape was given in the tabloid newspaper, *Weekend*. Written by the pilot the article was entitled 'My Life - or a Wrecked Village'. Here the pilot told how his plane had suffered a 'flame-out' and that he had virtually lost all control. He was losing height rapidly as he approached Little Maplestead but somehow he managed to guide his disabled plane away from the houses and by flying over one set of telephone wires and then under the next, narrowly missing the cottages now called Tanglewood, he succeeded in landing the plane safely in the field not far from the church. Mr Joe Blomfield rescued the pilot, pulling him out of the wreckage to safety. Mercifully there had been no explosion. The article ended with the following moving paragraph:

> ...the farmer, in whose field I had landed, looked towards that lovely, centuries-old church and the surrounding cottages of Little Maplestead, then he turned to me, 'Today we really do have something to thank the Lord for' he said with quiet sincerity.

I, THE AUTHOR of this history, came to Little Maplestead in 1976 with my husband and our four youngest children. We arrived on a hot day in June, delighted that we were now able to live in the countryside and to bring up our children in a healthy and natural environment. During the last twenty-three years I have seen the village continue to evolve and change. Even during this relatively short time some of the old houses have disappeared; the farm labourers' cottages which stood on the site of the present day Saxby's and Weavers have been pulled down, and some new houses have been built. But essentially the village is still the same Little Maplestead we came to live in all those years ago. There is more traffic, of course, and the village is perhaps not quite so neighbourly now that so many people are out at work all day, but the view from our windows at Hall Corner Cottage over the fields and towards Maplestead Hall and the Round Church has not changed one bit. And as I look at this view I am aware that generations of inhabitants of Hall Corner Cottage have looked out at almost exactly the same vista from the time it was built at the end of the eighteenth century. But, even earlier than this, as far back as the thirteenth century, my view would have still been the same - the same gentle curves and slopes in the landscape, the same colours in the vegetation, the same hedgerows, ditches, tracks and ponds. The fields would have been smaller, cultivation would have been in strips, the hedgerows would have been more numerous and the road would have been no more than a narrow rutted track, but I would still have seen the little church nestling amongst its trees, its colours of flinty grey and brown blending in with the earthy colours around it so that even then, as it does today, it would seem to be a natural part of an ancient landscape.

And as one walks down the village lanes, across the footpaths and bridleways, it is not difficult to set one's imagination free, to see in one's mind's eye Mill Farm with its water-wheel turning in the stream, to see L'Hospital on the site of Maplestead Hall with crusading knights coming and going, to imagine the rebuilding of the church with William Joy admiring his new round nave, to walk up Pearman's Hill and imagine Shakespeare riding by, or perhaps Ralph Josselin coming to preach, to look at the fields and imagine John Sewell growing his crops of hops and teazels. So much history has passed. And down through the centuries, one can imagine the ordinary villagers of Little Maplestead going about their day-to-day business, their lives becoming progressively easier as time rolls by, the Round Church constant at the heart of the village, until today we must all surely acknowledge our great good fortune to live here.

I will leave the final word on Little Maplestead with my daughter, Lucy:

'Looking back on my childhood spent in Little Maplestead during the 1970s, I realize now how simple, straightforward and wonderful my life really was. All I needed was my hardy little pony and my bicycle. I often wonder whether today's computer-age child would be so content and as easily pleased as I was. Little Maplestead certainly did not offer much entertainment for young people but there used to be occasional "discos" in the village hall at Great Maplestead. However, I don't really remember the discos too well, for my life was spent almost entirely on horseback! I remember getting up at 5am and cycling to Gages Farm where my pony was stabled for some years. I had to negotiate a rather muddy, bumpy and quiet lane and often had punctures which made my journey rather uncomfortable. I shudder now thinking about the possible dangers of such a venture but life then was simple and being unsafe or vulnerable didn't even enter my mind and there didn't seem to be nearly so much traffic in those days. I loved Gages Farm, it offered wonderful grazing, cosy little stables, barns and sheds to explore and many fields to gallop my pony in.

'I was later offered grazing at Maplestead Hall by Joe Blomfield who was always very kind to me. I remember he once made me a wonderful hunting crop out of holly wood. He had decorated it with brass studs and personalized it by burning my initials into the end. My bike ride to Maplestead Hall took me less time than going to Gages Farm and I could have walked there but I always chose to cycle despite my bike being in need of repair. I remember once riding down the hill with two punctures, a missing chain and no brakes (it was still faster than walking)!

'I used to enjoy my early mornings "mucking out" in the barns at Maplestead Hall. I had to get everything done before school and used to arrive there at about 6am. Bill Simmonds, the cow-man, used to feed the cattle in the pens at that time and so the lights were always on when I arrived which made me feel that I was not the only person up at such an early hour. I remember the smell of the pens so clearly, sugar beet pulp and fresh hay and the barns always seemed so very welcoming. Bill and I used to have interesting talks and he would reminisce about the old days.

'Maplestead Hall was a very important place in my eyes; all of the special village functions were held there and I remember clearly the Queen's Silver Jubilee. There were stalls selling royal memorabilia and fairground-type attractions, only on rather a smaller scale. We were all given a copper coin depicting the Round Church in a little plastic envelope. I still have mine today.

'I knew all the bridle paths round Little Maplestead like the back of my hand. My favourite ride was Hampers Lane, veering off up Pearman's Hill and through the little copse where we would make jumps. I had two good 'pony' friends and we used to visit places I am sure we were not allowed. We were braver when riding in a group; alone, I would have stuck very much to the actual bridlepaths round Little Lodge Farm and Parks Farm, but I do remember my pony bolting with me through a field of rape seed! Afterwards, on the way home, I hoped that my yellow-stained pony with yellow flowers stuck in his bridle would not draw attention from the farmer!

'Looking back, I think that Little Maplestead was *the* place to grow up and I wouldn't have changed it for the world. It was a super village, we knew most people then and everyone was friendly. I lived in Hall Corner Cottage, which I loved, and one of my friends lived opposite in Tanglewood. Her garden there was quite large and very good for camping out in! There was always something going on in the village and lots to talk about with my friends. I always felt safe and had a freedom that it's difficult to envisage today. I could go wherever I wanted within reason and often used to spend all day - from early morning until supper time - out and about in the village, riding my pony or my bike or just playing with my friends and exploring. I was rarely at home! I was always happy and I hope so much that one day our daughter is lucky enough to have such a privileged childhood. When I left home I missed Little Maplestead a lot and was delighted to have been able to return to get married in the Round Church which, with the rest of the village, will always have a very special place in my memory.'

Notes to Chapter X

[1] John Betjeman, *The Dear Old Village, Collected Poems* (London, 1958)
[2] R. J. Brown, *The English Country Cottage* (London 1979)
[3] 5th Marquess of Lansdowne, 1845-1927 (London, 1983)

SOME TWENTIETH-CENTURY EVENTS

1901	Death of Queen Victoria, Edward VII becomes king
1910	George V becomes king
1914	Beginning of First World War (1914-1918)
1930	First BBC television broadcasts
1936	George V dies, Edward VIII abdicates, George VI becomes king
1939	Beginning of Second World War (1939-1945)
1945	Dropping of atomic bombs on Hiroshima and Nagasaki
1950	Beginning of Korean war (1950-1953)
1953	Coronation of Queen Elizabeth II; Hillary and Tensing conquer Everest
1961	Yuri Gagarin is first man into space
1963	Assassination of President J. F. Kennedy
1965	Beginning of Vietnam war (1965-1975); death of Sir Winston Churchill
1967	First UK colour television transmissions; successful first heart transplant
1968	American astronauts land on the moon
1973	Britain joins E.E.C.
1982	The Falklands War
1989-90	Dismantling of the Berlin Wall, unification of East and West Germany

1841 TITHE MAP

PLAN of the PARISH of MAPLESTEAD, ESSEX.

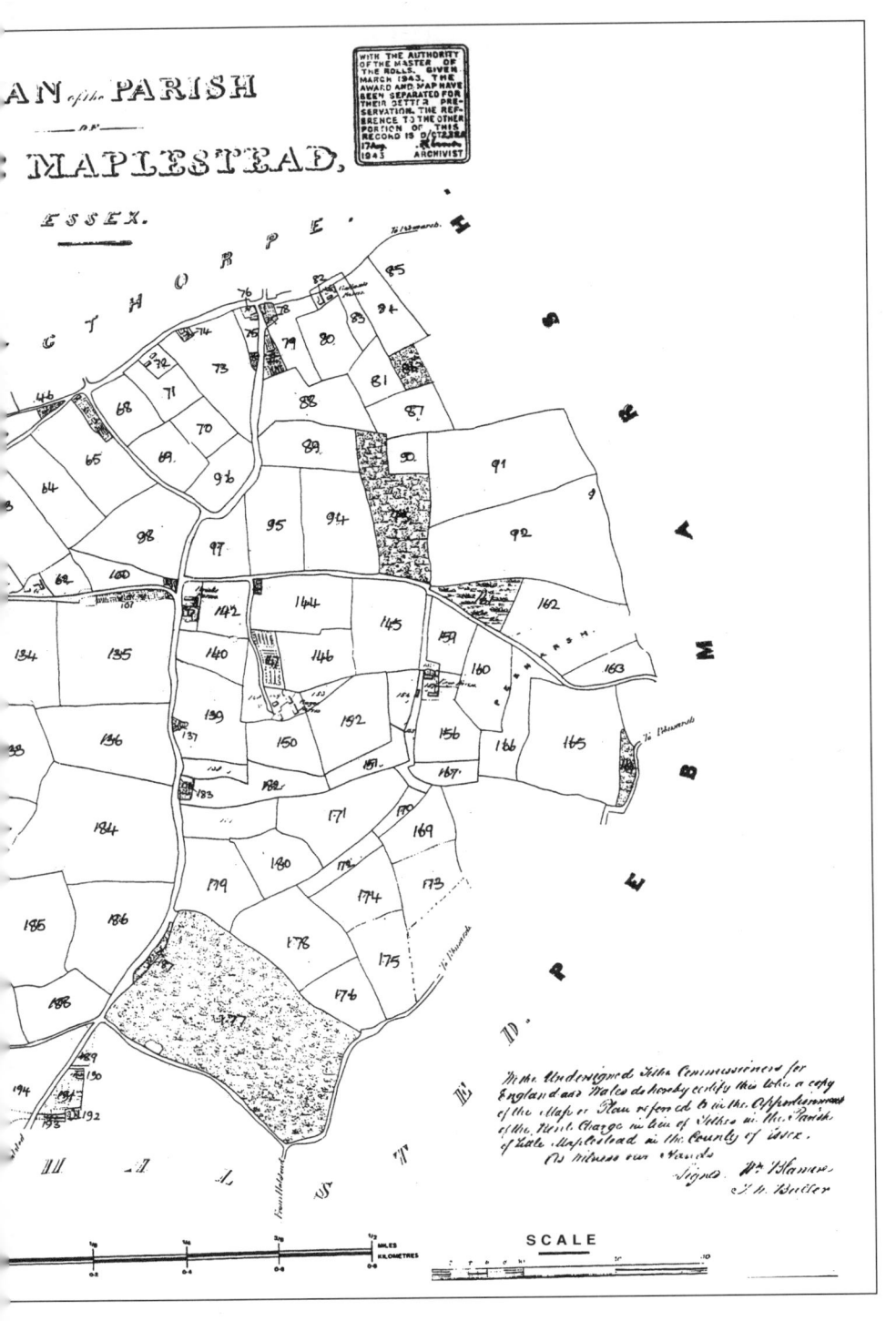

GLOSSARY

Advowson	English ecclesiastical law meaning the right of presentation to a vacant benefice
Cartulary	The register book of a monastery
Chancery	A court of public records
Copyhold	A tenure, less than freehold, of land in England evidenced by a copy of the court roll
Court of augmentation	Court established in the reign of Henry VIII to settle the disposal of the property of the monasteries upon dissolution
Free alms	Land grant where the only requirement was regular prayers for the souls of the donor and his family
Gersum	Sum paid or pledged to a landlord by a tenant on receipt of renewal of a lease
Hide	Land sufficient for the maintenance of one family, about 90-120 acres
Jetty	The upper floor of a building projecting beyond the lower floor
Messuage	Dwelling-huse with the ground around it, plus outbuildings
Peppercorn rent	Rent that is very low or nominal
Perpetual curate	Clergyman in charge of a new church or appointed at the request of a lay rector to execute the spiritual duties of a benefice
Pightle	Small irregularly shaped piece of arable land
Piscina	Church receptacle containing holy water
Preceptory	Subordinate community of knights templars or hospitallers
Quatrefoil	Carved ornament having four leaves arranged about a common centre
Rental	Amount paid by a tenant as rent/income derived from rents received
Sedilia	Seat in the chancel wall of a church
Sokeman	Form of feudal tenant in East Anglia who held land in return for money rent but was not required to give knight's service

Tenement	Originally a holding of land and buildings in manorial terms
Thegnhood	Holding of land by a member of the aristocracy in Anglo Saxon England from the king or another nobleman in return for certain services
Trefoil	Ornament in the form of three leaves arranged in a circle
Villein	Peasant personally bound to his lord, to whom he paid dues and services in return for land (strips to till plus grazing)

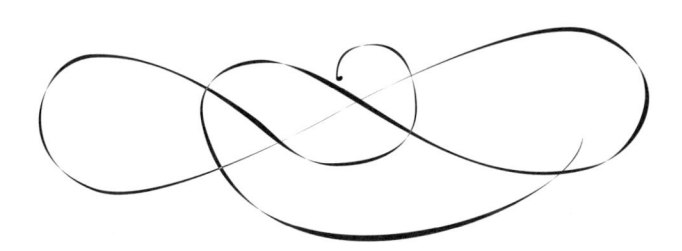

THE FIELD NAMES OF LITTLE MAPLESTEAD

Ancient field names from Cartulary linked with those of 1841 tithe map

Tithe Map
Reedons, Hurrells
The Ley, Maplestead Hall
Panamas, Starch-house
Spit Croft, Leppingwells
Popes Mead, Maplestead Hall
Baysland Field, Maplestead Hall
Byham Hall
Little Oxley, Maplestead Hall
Harlow Hill, Bennetts/Starch-house
Joyes, School Farm

Collins

Cartulary
Riedpihitell
le legh
Panymer, Panimere etc
Spitelcroft
Popismedewe (Great Maplestead)
Bayslandfield, Basilia's land [of Byham]
Byham [Beytha]
Hoxeneheye, Hokholt
Robert de Harlow
Joyespithill [see also Impnells and Napsted]
John Colyn

Deeds
Churley Meadow (Maplestead Hall 1627)
Little Pasture (Maplestead Hall 1747)
Asseesfield (Leppingwells 1652)
Hilliards Grove (Leppingwells 1629)

Charleyehead
Littlemeadow
Asciesfield
Richard Hildehard [Byham Hall]

UNIDENTIFIED 13TH-CENTURY FIELDS IN CARTULARY:

Alfledesfield
Gosemere (perhaps Gooseberry field, Hampers)
Grimsley (Grim's Ley)
Helles
Kuckelawe
Middlefield
Pilhundresland
Sagescroft
Sichieneland
Storiesfield
Wallcroft
Wodphittel

INDEX

A
All Saints Church 14, 32, 61
Ash Cottage 190-192
Ashford Lodge 46
Aster Cottage 188
Attadale 98, 165-167
Audelin, Lady Juliana & William 30-31
Aviemore 211

B
Bakersfield 142, 143, 203
Barn Cottage 157-161, 214
Barns 124, 171-172
Bays & Says 121, 131
Baytrees 206
Bentalls Farm 23
Blomfield, Alfred 47, 160, 171, 183, 187, 204
Blomfield, Helen 48, 178, 205, 206
Blomfield, Joseph 47-48, 125, 160, 161, 171, 187, 203, 205, 206, 213, 214, 216
Blomfield, Laura 47-48, 192, 205, 213
Bramble Barn 171
Brambles 188-190
Brewster, Charles 46, 112, 118, 128, 160, 171, 180, 196
Brewster, James 41-46, 116-118, 122, 165, 170, 177, 180, 183
Bricks Farm (Thistledown Cottage) 36, 120, 122-124, 187, 188, 214
Bricks Farm Cottages 178, 184-187
Broomhill Cottage 144-146
Byham Hall 20, 35, 54, 79, 112, 113, 120

C
Cade, Jack 87
Castle Hedingham 10, 15, 16, 25
Charles I 135, 138-139
Charles II 140
Chaucer, Geoffrey 79
Civil War 138
Cock Field House 195-196
Cock Inn 35, 76, 103, 141, 144, 178, 188, 194, 195, 196, 208-210, 213
Collins Road 62, 214
Colne Priory 20
Cook, Cecil 23, 47, 48, 69, 102, 124, 126, 128, 161, 178, 181, 190, 195, 202, 209
Cook, Peter 211, 214
Coppice 211
Corn Laws 176
Cornah, Joseph 128, 196
Cottage, The 23, 124-126, 134
Council Houses
  1-4 School Road 203
  7 & 8 School Road 202
  9-13 School Road 203
  1-4 Cock Road 203
Courtaulds Mill 176, 206
Covehythe 210-211

Crealie 184-187, 214
Cromwell, Oliver 138-140
Crouchers Cross 80, 109
Crusades 14, 28-29, 31-32, 51, 90

D
Danelaw 10
Daunsington 211
Davis, Joseph 36, 46, 140, 150
Davis Charity estate 36, 40, 42, 46, 140, 150
Deans Cottage 116-119, 120, 122
Deans Hall 21, 44, 57, 114-119, 120, 171, 202, 207
De Vere family, Earls of Oxford 15, 16, 17, 25, 28, 31, 51, 52, 54, 85, 87, 90, 131
Devereux, Robert, Earl of Essex 34
De Warenne, William 11, 12
Dissolution of monasteries 105, 110, 113
Domesday Book 11, 16, 17, 19, 25, 31
Dynes Hall 31, 114, 131

E
Earls Colne 85
Ebenezer Congregational Chapel 177-178
Edward II 76
Edward IV 90
Edward VI 121
Egg-packing station 128, 210, 214
Elizabeth I 34, 120, 131
Empire Cottage 119
Ethel's Cottage 155

F
Fairbank, Rev F. 19, 177, 178, 180, 196
Forge Cottages 102, 103

G
Gages Farm 21, 23, 96, 99-101, 102, 103, 120, 141, 196, 216
Gallants Farm 17, 20, 23, 120, 183, 194, 196
George III 155
Goldmillers (Strongmillers) 150, 158
Granary Barn 171
Greystones 211
Griffins 211
Grove, The 110, 126-128, 159, 163, 170, 196, 202, 210

H
Hale, Henry 108, 109
Hall Corner Cottage 157-161, 211, 215
Hall Cottages 46

Halstead 7, 14, 21, 36, 37, 48, 92, 96, 121, 128, 131, 137, 151, 157, 161, 167, 172, 173, 176, 181, 213
Hampers 16, 63, 64, 118, 120, 211, 212
Hampers Barn 134, 212
Harper, George 34, 108, 113
Harward, Rev J. F. 127-128, 170-171, 179, 180, 194, 196
Hawthorn House 211
Hazelden, Hazelmere see Saxby's
Henry II 25, 30, 31
Henry III 54
Henry V 87
Henry VI 90
Henry VII 103
Henry VIII 34, 105, 108
Hinckford Hundred 10, 20
Honour of Clare 21, 102
Hooky Cooky 190, 214
L'Hospital 31-33, 51, 54, 58-61, 73, 76, 78, 79, 85, 90, 91, 108-109, 114, 131, 215
Hundred Years' War 76, 87
Hurrells Farm 59, 84, 96, 97, 98, 99, 120, 141, 171
Hush House 194-195

I
Impnells 53, 63, 141
Industrial Revolution 173
Ivy Cottage 168-171

J
James I 131
John, King of England 51, 52, 54
Josselin, Ralph 139, 215
Joy, William 31, 55, 60, 61, 79, 215

K
Kett, Robert 121
Kistum Cottage 126
Knights Hospitallers 20, 31, 33, 34, 51, 54, 56, 73, 79, 90, 92, 103

L
Langland, William 79
Larchmont 211
Lavender Cottage 98, 165-167
Leppingwells 19, 35, 95, 120, 138, 141, 203, 211, 214
Leys, The 66, 101, 196
Little Acre 211
Littlehame 211
Little Maplestead post office 160-161
Little Maplestead school 180-181
Little Maplestead shop 167, 213
Lodge Farm 150, 216
Lyntree 211

- 223 -

M

Magna Carta 51, 54, 60, 69, 85
Manor House, The 195
Manse, The 178-179, 182, 214
Maple Chalet 206
Maplecroft 211
Maplestead Hall 14, 31-33, 36-37, 40-42, 45-48, 57, 99, 105, 108, 112, 113, 114, 120, 122, 124, 125, 131, 135, 141, 147, 150, 155, 157, 158, 159, 160, 161, 162, 165, 167, 168, 169, 170, 171, 176, 177, 180, 182, 183, 184, 186, 187, 192, 196, 197, 199, 203, 206, 213, 214, 215, 216
Maplestead Services 213
Meadow End 192
Meeting House, The 82, 177
Mercia 10
Mill Farm 12-13, 215
Morley, John 21, 151
Mosses Farm 135-138
Mot, William 83, 84
Motts Garden 83-84, 111

N

Napsted 10, 16, 63, 64
Norman Conquest 7, 10, 11, 14, 15, 24
Norwich 25, 28, 146
Nott family 48
Nott, George 122, 187, 188, 190

O

Odewells 31, 56, 77, 79
Old Bell Cottages 96
Old School House 178, 180-181
Olde Orchard 211
Orchard, Mr E. 167, 179
Orchard House, see Sunnyholt
Order of St John of Jerusalem 30, 31, 90, 105, 108, 113

P

Panoman Street 76
Parks Bungalow 35, 62, 211
Parks Farm 92-96, 120, 141, 216
Pearman's Hill 103, 128, 151, 154, 212, 215
Peasants' Revolt 84
Percy, Mr 119, 171, 204
Plague 73, 77-78, 79, 85
Plum House, see Woodcocks
(Old) Post Office Cottages 160-161
Potash Office 158

R

Red House, The 155-156
Reedons 59, 98
Richard II 84, 85
Richard III 103
Rosanne 211

Rose Cottage 188
Rosedene, see Wellaway
Round Church 14, 61, 77, 113, 128, 150, 170-171, 177, 179, 205, 206, 215, 216
Rows Hill 116

S

St Aubin House 211
St John the Baptist Church see Round Church
Samson Furniture (Maplestead Woodworks) 207
Saxbys 165-168, 215
School Cottages (5 & 6 School Road) 182-183
School Farm 57, 80, 109, 110-113, 120, 162-163, 171, 194, 196
School Farm Cottage 193-194
Sewell, John 21, 36, 40, 62, 83, 145, 150-151, 157, 158, 161, 176, 180, 182, 190, 192, 215
Shakespeare, William 103, 128-129, 215
Shardleas 211
Spoons Hall 19, 20
Springfield 211
Starch-house Farm 63, 76, 141, 151-154
Straw-plaiting 19, 168, 196
Studio, The 194-195
Sudbury 14, 21, 48, 92, 157, 161, 181
Sudbury, Archbishop 84, 109
Sudbury College/Grammar School 35, 109, 110, 112, 142
Sunnyholt (now Orchard House) 165-167
Syday, John 33, 90-92, 105, 113
Sydenham Place 211

T

Tanglewood 161-162, 206, 212, 216
Thistledown Cottage, see Bricks Farm
Toldishall 12, 44
Turp, Bill 23, 126, 189
Tyler, Wat 84, 134

U

Ulwine 15, 16

V

Vaizey family 21-23, 62, 69, 99, 101, 102, 137, 138, 146, 178, 202, 204
Village hall 204-206, 214

W

Wars of the Roses 90, 103, 139

Watkinson, Rev J. 177, 178, 183, 194
Watts Lane 81
Weavers 165-167, 215
Wellaway 207
Wessex 10
Whitecote 162-164
William I, the Conqueror 11, 15, 16
Willow Cottage, Cock Road 194-195
Willow Cottage, see Woodview
Willow End 211
Wiseman, Edmund, 34, 131
Wiseman, John 108, 113, 131
Wiseman, William 131, 135, 138-139
Woodcocks (Plum House) 61
Woodertons 48, 80-83, 120, 194, 212
Woodview 187-188
Wool trade 62
Workhouse 164-165
Wyndhams 211

X, Y, Z

Young, Arthur 36, 155, 157, 164

- 224 -